THE RISE OF BIG DATA POLICING

The Rise of Big Data Policing

Surveillance, Race, and the
Future of Law Enforcement

Andrew Guthrie Ferguson

NEW YORK UNIVERSITY PRESS
New York

NEW YORK UNIVERSITY PRESS
New York
www.nyupress.org

First published in paperback in 2020

Library of Congress Cataloging-in-Publication Data
Names: Ferguson, Andrew G., author.
Title: The rise of big data policing : surveillance, race, and the future of law enforcement / Andrew Guthrie Ferguson.
Description: New York : New York University Press, [2017] |
Includes bibliographical references and index.
Identifiers: LCCN 2017012924| ISBN 9781479892822 (cl ; alk. paper) |
ISBN 1479892823 (cl ; alk. paper)
ISBN 978-1-4798-6997-8 (pb ; alk. paper)
Subjects: LCSH: Law enforcement—United States—Data processing. | Police—United States—Data processing. | Big data—United States. | Data mining in law enforcement—United States. | Electronic surveillance—United States. | Criminal statistics—United States. | Discrimination in law enforcement—United States. | Racial profiling in law enforcement—United States.
Classification: LCC HV8141 .F47 2017 | DDC 363.2/32028557—dc23
LC record available at https://lccn.loc.gov/2017012924

New York University Press books are printed on acid-free paper, and their binding materials are chosen for strength and durability. We strive to use environmentally responsible suppliers and materials to the greatest extent possible in publishing our books.

Manufactured in the United States of America

10 9 8 7 6 5 4 3 2 1

Also available as an ebook

To the police, citizens, and advocates interested in improving policing, thank you for engaging these ideas.

To my colleagues at the UDC David A. Clarke School of Law, thank you for encouraging my scholarship.

To Alissa, Cole, Alexa, Mom and Dad, thank you for everything.

CONTENTS

Introduction

Big Data Policing

A towering wall of computer screens blinks alive with crisis. A digital map of Los Angeles alerts to 911 calls. Television screens track breaking news stories. Surveillance cameras monitor the streets. Rows of networked computers link analysts and police officers to a wealth of law enforcement intelligence. Real-time crime data comes in. Real-time police deployments go out. This high-tech command center in downtown Los Angeles forecasts the future of policing in America.[1]

Welcome to the Los Angeles Police Department's Real-Time Analysis Critical Response (RACR) Division. The RACR Division, in partnership with Palantir—a private technology company that began developing social network software to track terrorists—has jumped head first into the big data age of policing.[2]

Just as in the hunt for international terror networks, Palantir's software system integrates, analyzes, and shares otherwise-hidden clues from a multitude of ordinary law enforcement data sources. A detective investigating a robbery suspect types a first name and a physical description into the computer—two fragmented clues that would have remained paper scraps of unusable data in an earlier era.[3] The database searches for possible suspects. Age, description, address, tattoos, gang affiliations, vehicle ownership instantly pop up in sortable fields. By matching known attributes, the computer narrows the search to a few choices. A photograph of a possible suspect's car is identified from an automated license-plate reader scouring the city for data about the location of every vehicle. Detectives follow up with a witness to identify the car used in the robbery. A match leads to an arrest and a closed case.[4]

A 911 call. A possible gang fight in progress. RACR Command directs patrol units to the scene all the while monitoring their real-time progress. Data about the fight is pushed to officers on their mobile phones.[5]

Alerts about past shootings and gang tensions warn officers of unseen dangers.[6] Neighborhood histories get mapped for insight. Officers scroll through photographs to visualize the physical geography before they arrive. All of the data is instantaneously sent to officers, allowing them to see the risks before they need to act.[7]

Roll call. Monday morning. Patrol officers receive digital maps of today's "crime forecast."[8] Small red boxes signify areas of predicted crime. These boxes represent algorithmic forecasts of heightened criminal activity: years of accumulated crime data crunched by powerful computers to target precise city blocks. Informed by the data, "predictive policing" patrols will give additional attention to these "hot" areas during the shift.[9] Every day, police wait in the predicted locations looking for the forecast crime. The theory: put police in the box at the right time and stop a crime. The goal: to deter the criminal actors from victimizing that location.

Soon, real-time facial-recognition software will link existing video surveillance cameras and massive biometric databases to automatically identify people with open warrants.[10] Soon, social media feeds will alert police to imminent violence from rival gangs.[11] Soon, data-matching technologies will find suspicious activity from billions of otherwise-anonymous consumer transactions and personal communications.[12] By digitizing faces, communications, and patterns, police will instantly and accurately be able to investigate billions of all-too-human clues.

This is the future. This is the present. This is the beginning of big data policing.[13]

Big data technologies and predictive analytics will revolutionize policing.[14] Predictive policing, intelligence-driven prosecution, "heat lists" of targets, social media scraping, data mining, and a data-driven surveillance state provide the first clues to how the future of law enforcement will evolve.

At the center of policing's future is data: crime data, personal data, gang data, associational data, locational data, environmental data, and a growing web of sensor and surveillance sources. This big data arises from the expanded ability to collect, store, sort, and analyze digital clues about crime.[15] Crime statistics are mined for patterns, and victims of violence are mapped in social networks. While video cameras watch our movements, private consumer data brokers map our interests and sell that information to law enforcement.[16] Phone numbers, emails, and finances can all be studied for suspicious links. Government agencies collect health, educational, and criminal records.[17] Detectives monitor public Facebook, YouTube, and Twitter feeds.[18] Aggregating data centers sort and study the accumulated information in local and federally funded fusion centers.[19] This is the big data world of law enforcement—still largely in its infancy but offering vastly more incriminating bits of data to use and study.

Behind the data is technology: algorithms, network analysis, data mining, machine learning, and a host of computer technologies being refined and improved every day. Police can identify the street corner most likely to see the next car theft[20] or the people most likely to be shot.[21] Prosecutors can target the crime networks most likely to destabilize communities,[22] while analysts can link suspicious behaviors for further investigation.[23] The decisional work of identifying criminal actors, networks, and patterns now starts with powerful computers crunching large data sets almost instantaneously. Math provides the muscle to prevent and prosecute crime.

Underneath the data and technology are people—individuals living their lives. Some of these people engage in crime, some not. Some live in poverty, some not. But all now find themselves encircled by big data's reach. The math behind big data policing targets crime, but in many cities, crime suppression targets communities of color. Data-driven policing means aggressive police presence, surveillance, and perceived harassment in those communities. Each data point translates to real human experience, and many times those experiences remain fraught with all-too-human bias, fear, distrust, and racial tension. For those communities, especially poor communities of color, these data-collection efforts cast a dark shadow on the future.

This book shines light on the "black data" arising from big data policing:[24] "black" as in opaque, because the data exists largely hidden within complex algorithms; "black" as in racially coded, because the data directly impacts communities of color; "black" as in the next new thing, given legitimacy and prominence due to the perception that data-driven anything is cool, techno-friendly, and futuristic; and, finally, "black" as distorting, creating legal shadows and constitutional gaps where the law used to see clearly. Black data matters because it has real-world impacts.

Black data marks human "threats" with permanent digital suspicion and targets poor communities of color. Black data leads to aggressive use of police force, including deadly force, and new forms of invasive surveillance. Big data policing, and these new forms of surveillance and social control, must confront this black data problem.

This book examines how big data policing impacts the "who," "where," "when," and "how" of policing. New technologies threaten to impact all aspects of policing, and studying the resulting distortions provides a framework to evaluate all future surveillance technologies. A race is on to transform policing. New developments in consumer data collection have merged with law enforcement's desire to embrace "smart policing" principles in an effort to increase efficiency amid decreasing budgets. Data-driven technology offers a double win—do more with less resources, and do so in a seemingly objective and neutral manner.

This book arises out of the intersection of two cultural shifts in policing. First, predictive analytics, social network theory, and data-mining technology have all developed to a point of sophistication such that big data policing is no longer a futuristic idea. Although police have long collected information about suspects, now this data can be stored in usable and sharable databases, allowing for greater surveillance potential. Whereas in an earlier era a police officer might see a suspicious man on the street and have no context about his past or future danger, soon digitized facial-recognition technologies will identify him, crime data will detail his criminal history, algorithms will rate his risk level, and a host of citywide surveillance images will provide context in the form of video surveillance for his actions over the past few hours. Big data will illuminate the darkness of suspicion. But it also will expand the lens of who can be watched.

The second cultural shift in policing involves the need to respond to outrage arising from police killings of unarmed African Americans in Ferguson, Missouri; Staten Island, New York; Baltimore, Maryland; Cleveland, Ohio; Charleston, South Carolina; Baton Rouge, Louisiana; Falcon Heights, Minnesota; and other cities. This sustained national protest against police—and the birth of the Movement for Black Lives—brought to the surface decades of frustration about racially discriminatory law enforcement practices.[25] Cities exploded in rage over unaccountable police actions. In response, data-driven policing began to be sold as one answer to racially discriminatory policing, offering a seemingly race-neutral, "objective" justification for police targeting of poor communities.[26] Despite the charge that police data remains tainted by systemic bias,[27] police administrators can justify continued aggressive police practices using data-driven metrics. Predictive policing systems offer a way seemingly to turn the page on past abuses, while still legitimizing existing practices.

For that reason, my aim in this book is to look at the dangers of black data arising at this moment in history. Only by understanding why the current big data policing systems were created and how traditional policing practices fit within those systems can society evaluate the promise of this new approach to data-driven law enforcement. Black data must be illuminated to see how it might be abused. The promise of "smarter" law enforcement is unquestionably real, but so is the fear of totalizing surveillance. Growing "law and order" rhetoric can lead to surveillance overreach. Police administrators, advocates, communities, and governments must confront those concerns before—not after—the technology's implementation. And society must confront those challenges informed by an understanding of how race has fractured and delegitimized the criminal justice system for many citizens. Black data, of course, is not just about African Americans, although the history of racially discriminatory policing runs deep in certain communities. But black data exposes how all marginalized communities face a growing threat from big data policing systems. People of color, immigrants, religious minorities, the poor, protesters, government critics, and many others who encounter aggressive police surveillance are at increased risk. But so is everyone, because every one of us produces a detailed data trail that exposes personal details. This data—suctioned up, sold, and surveilled—can be wrong. The algorithmic correlations can be wrong. And if police act on that inaccurate data, lives and liberty can be lost.

Big data is not all dystopian. The insights of big data policing need not be limited to targeting criminal activity. The power of predictive analytics can also be used to identify police misconduct or identify the underlying social and economic needs that lead to crime. In an era of heighted concern with police accountability, new surveillance technologies offer new avenues to watch, monitor, and even predict police misconduct. Systems of "blue data" can be created to help "police the police."

Similarly, big data technologies can be redirected to identify and target social, economic, or environmental risk factors. This is the promise of "bright data," in which the surveillance architecture developed to police criminal risk can be redirected to address environmental risks and social needs. After all, just because big data policing identifies the risk, this does not mean that law enforcement must provide the remedy.

The big data policing revolution has arrived. The singular insight of this innovation is that data-driven predictive technologies can identify and forecast risk for the future. Risk identification is also the goal of this book—to forecast the potential problems of big data policing as it reshapes law enforcement. Long-standing tensions surrounding race, secrecy, privacy, power, and freedom are given new life in digital form with the advent of big data analytics. New technologies will open up new opportunities for investigation and surveillance. The technological environment is rich with possibility but also danger. This book seeks to initiate a conversation on the growth of these innovations, with the hope that by exposing and explaining the distorting effects of data-driven policing, society can plan for its big data future.

1

Big Data's Watchful Eye

The Rise of Data Surveillance

The world is full of obvious things which nobody by any
chance ever observes.
—Sherlock Holmes[1]

Data Trails

You are being watched. Surveilled. Tracked. Targeted. Every search on
the internet recorded.[2] Every purchase at the store documented.[3] Every
place you travel mapped.[4] They know how fast you drive, your preferred
cereal, your dress size. They know your financial situation, all of your
past jobs, your credit limit.[5] They know your health concerns, reading
preferences, and political voting patterns. They also know your secrets.
They have been watching for years.[6] In truth, you live in a surveillance
state. The watchers know you because of the data you leave behind.

But it is not just you. These watchers also know about your family,
friends, neighbors, colleagues, clubs, and associates. They see the circles
you contact, the friends you ignore, and the political issues you embrace.
They see you as part of a group, but they also see all the other parts of
the group.[7] Links expand outward, so that all of your contacts can be
visualized as a web of interrelated, interconnected groups.

Welcome to the world of big data, where one's data trail reveals the
mosaic of lived experience and has become the currency of a new econ-
omy.[8] "They" are companies, companies that enable a digital world by
offering convenience, information, and services all in return for one
thing: data. Your personal data and interests—all of those points of
commercial interaction, consumer choice, "likes," links, and loves—
have been vacuumed up, processed, and sold to others wanting to get to
know you. Currently, this widespread surveillance remains in the hands
of for-profit companies, for the purpose of offering consumers conve-

nience and choice. But law enforcement is interested too.[9] And most of this information is a subpoena (or warrant) away from being part of a criminal case. The investigative lure of big data technologies is just too powerful to ignore.

What Is Big Data?

To understand the potential of big data policing, the scope of big data must be explored. So what is big data? In general, "big data" is a shorthand term for the collection and analysis of large data sets with the goal to reveal hidden patterns or insights.[10] A report from the Executive Office of the President summarized: "There are many definitions of 'big data' which may differ depending on whether you are a computer scientist, a financial analyst, or an entrepreneur pitching an idea to a venture capitalist. Most definitions reflect the growing technological ability to capture, aggregate, and process an ever-greater volume, velocity, and variety of data."[11] In simple terms, large collections of data can be sorted by powerful computers to visualize unexpected connections or correlations.[12] Machine-learning tools and predictive analytics allow educated guesses about what the correlations mean.[13]

A simple example of how big data works can be seen at Amazon.com. Beneath each item for sale is a recommendation section that displays information about what "customers who bought this item also bought" and items that are "frequently bought together." Amazon generates these suggestions from the purchasing patterns of its 300 million customers who bought related items. Correlating the historical data of billions of transactions leads to an insight into which goods customers usually purchase together. Amazon, of course, also knows everything you have ever bought from the company. But Amazon can sort the purchasing data of any particular product to show the consumer patterns of all past customers. Amazon can use that large data set to predict what items you might actually want in the future.[14] After all, if you bought a coffee maker today, you may need coffee tomorrow.

A more unusual example involves the correlation between Pop-Tarts and hurricanes. Walmart—a company that collects more than two and half petabytes of data every hour from customers[15] (equivalent to 50 million four-drawer filing cabinets filled with text)—discovered that just before a hurricane, people buy an unusual amount of Strawberry Pop-Tarts.[16] Why? No one really knows. Perhaps the reason for the uptick is because Pop-Tarts are nonperishable comfort food, and sometimes sugary comfort is just what you need after a big storm. Or perhaps not. Big data demonstrates the correlation, not the cause. It offers insight without explanation—a reality that is both useful and unsettling.

Obviously, big companies like Amazon and Walmart collect personal data, but what is the extent of big data collection across our daily lives? More than can be comprehended. As Julia Angwin termed it, "We are living in a Dragnet Nation—a world of indiscriminate tracking where institutions are stockpiling data about individuals at an unprecedented pace."[17] The World Privacy Forum—a watchdog group on personal privacy—estimates that there are 4,000 different databases collecting information on us.[18] Every time we interact with computers, sensors, smartphones, credit cards, electronics, and much, much more, we leave a digital trail that is revealing of ourselves and valuable to others.[19] These are the breadcrumbs of the big data maze. Follow them and they lead right back to you.

Where Does Big Data Come From?

Big data comes from you. You provide the building blocks of big data's power in small digital bits.

Think of the normal patterns of your life. You probably live in a house or an apartment. Even if you do not live in a wired "smart home" that comes equipped with a "smart fridge" to order milk when you run out, or a Nest "smart thermostat" to turn down the heat when you leave, your home does reveal basic data about your lifestyle.[20] You have an address. The address reveals general information about your income (as implied by the cost of the home) and your family size (number of bedrooms). Your zip code provides clues about demographics, wealth, and political sentiment.

You probably get mail at that address. First to note, the United States Postal System runs the Mail Isolation Control and Tracking program, which photographs the exterior of every single piece of mail processed in the United States.[21] So data about your address is tracked along with the 150 billion letters mailed each year.[22] But more obviously, your mail

ngs about you. Magazine subscriptions reveal your po-
ral interests, and catalogues reveal your hobbies and
ences. Mail reveals your friends and associates, just as
your styles, interests, and lifestyle choices. Even junk
something about what marketers think you want.

You likely also use the internet. Some of those packages came from
online shopping. Those online retail companies track your purchases
and even those things you looked at but did not purchase.[23] Inferences
from those purchases are also valuable. If you bought infant diapers for
the first time, you might also need age-appropriate children's toys for
the next holiday season (and for the next 18 years). If you bought a "how
to quit smoking book," you might not be the best candidate for a new
cigar magazine. But you don't even have to shop to give up your data.
Google records every internet search, really every click of the mouse.[24]
That means every health query, travel question, childrearing tip, news
article, and entertainment site. Google and other search engines provide
little windows into your thinking (if not your soul). Your internet pro-
tocol (IP) provides your exact location,[25] and while your IP addresses
might change as you switch from your home computer to your iPhone
to your work computer, Hotmail knows where you are at all times. Amazon knows the page you stopped reading on your Kindle ebook reader.[26]
Your cable provider (which may also be your cellphone and wireless provider) knows what TV shows you watch late at night. Netflix and other
streaming entertainment services rely on personalized predictive formu-
las based on past viewing data.

Social media expands the web of data from yourself to your friends
and associates.[27] On Facebook, you literally display your "likes" of certain
things. Professional sites like LinkedIn add more information about what
you do, who you know, and what accolades you have received. Personal
and social updates broadcast life changes, and charity or community service activities get promoted. Photos provide data about where you have
been and who you were with. Geotagging of information from those
photos and other services reveal the time, location, and date of the picture.[28] Facial recognition links people together, so that your photos (and
thus your identity) can be tracked over different social media platforms.
And sometimes you might simply tell people on Twitter what you are
doing or upload photos of your dinner entrée on Instagram or Snapchat.

You might leave your home in a car—a car registered to your address with a name, gender, birthdate, and identification number. The car can be tracked through a city via surveillance cameras, electronic toll collectors, or automated license-plate scanners.[29] Your type of car (hybrid or Hummer) might reveal a lifestyle preference or environmental worldview. The car itself might have Global Positioning System (GPS) tracking through something like a GM OnStar program to allow for instant help in an accident or emergency.[30] But that helpful service requires constant locational tracking. Or maybe you have an insurance provider that monitors real-time driving data of your habits in return for lower car-insurance rates.[31] You drive carefully, you save money.

But, no matter, if you possess a smartphone with locational services turned on, the speed, location, and direction of your car is being monitored in real time.[32] Your iPhone knows a wealth of locational information about where you go, which health clinic you stopped at, and the Alcoholics Anonymous meeting you just attended. Locational data from Google Maps tracks your church attendance, political protests, and friends. Other mobile apps leech data to companies in return for targeted advertisements or travel tips.[33] Games, services, geotracking ads, emergency calls—all depend on location. Everything that little pocket computer does can be tracked and recorded in granular detail. That means that every YouTube video, every photograph, and every check of the weather is collected, to reveal the things you do on a daily basis, as well as where you were when you did them.[34]

Maybe you took that car to work. Your employment history has been harvested by credit agencies.[35] Your job, finances, professional history, and even your education are recorded.[36] Maybe you went shopping. That customer-loyalty card offering in-store discounts also tracks each purchase you make.[37] Stores know not only everything you have purchased going back years but also your physical location when you made the purchase. Maybe you went to the bank. All of your financial information, account balances, late fees, investments, credit history—all are recorded.[38] Your credit card statement is a little reminder of everything you did and where you did it for the past month. Maybe you took the car to have fun. The Google search of local restaurant reviews followed by a map search of a particular restaurant and an Open Table reservation provide a pretty good prediction of your Saturday-night plans.[39]

If you add in "smart devices" connected through the Internet of Things (Fitbits, smart bandages, smart cups) or sensors built into our transportation infrastructure, clothing, and bodies, you have a very revealing web of data about our activities.[40] Researchers predict that there will be over 50 billion smart things connected among the "Internet of Everything" by 2020.[41] These "smart devices" are scarily aware of you. If your television responds to your voice or your electronic personal assistant answers your questions, it means these smart devices are always listening and always on.

Finally, public records filled with census data, property records, licenses, Department of Motor Vehicle information, bankruptcies, criminal convictions, and civil judgments can be purchased by companies seeking to understand us.[42] This official, bureaucratic record of life, linked as it is to governmental data systems, has become the foundation for many credit histories and personalized data dossiers on individuals.[43]

This is how big data becomes big. This is why big data can be such a threat to privacy, associational freedom, and autonomy. Your self-surveillance provides the currency for commercial profit but also the building blocks for an intrusive police state. Every digital clue—with the appropriate legal process—can be demanded by police and prosecutors. Whereas in an earlier era, only your family might know what you did, what you ate, how you dressed, or what you thought about, now the digital clues of life online can be collected, reassembled, and mapped to mirror this same knowledge. In fact, your digital clues may reveal secrets you have kept hidden from your spouse, family, or best friends.

Who Owns the Data?

Private data brokers collect, buy, and sell personal data to companies interested in selling products, determining financial credit risk, or conducting employment background investigations.[44] Data brokers sell your data to others—including law enforcement—for investigative purposes.[45]

Data brokers challenge conventional assumptions about individual privacy. Aggregated private transactions are repurposed and repackaged into a composite targeted profile of you as a consumer.[46] The United States Senate Commerce Committee detailed how big data companies like Acxiom claim to have information on over 700 million consumers worldwide with over 3,000 data segments for nearly every U.S. consumer.[47] Another company, Datalogix, claims to have data on almost every U.S. household.[48] Much of this information is demographic, such as name, address, telephone number, email, gender, age, marital status, children, educational level, and political affiliation. Some of the information is available through consumer transactions, detailing where one bought something, and some of the information focuses on health problems and medical data. The Senate report detailed how "one company collects data on whether consumers suffer from particular ailments, including Attention Deficit Hyperactivity Disorder, anxiety, depression, diabetes, high blood pressure, insomnia, and osteoporosis, among others; another keeps data on the weights of individuals in a household."[49] And "an additional company offers for sale lists of consumers under 44 different categories of health conditions, including obesity, Parkinson's disease, Multiple Sclerosis, Alzheimer's disease, and cancer, among others."[50]

The level of detail can be remarkably creepy.[51] Here are two excerpts from the Senate Commerce Committee's report:

> Equifax maintains approximately 75,000 individual data elements for its use in creating marketing products, including information as specific as whether a consumer purchased a particular soft drink or shampoo product in the last six months, uses laxatives or yeast infection products, OB/GYN doctor visits within the last 12 months, miles traveled in the last 4 weeks, and the number of whiskey drinks consumed in the past 30 days.[52]

> Some companies offer "data dictionaries" that include more than one thousand potential data elements, including whether the individual or household is a pet owner, smokes, has a propensity to purchase prescriptions through the mail, donates to charitable causes, is active military or a veteran, holds certain insurance products including burial insurance or juvenile life insurance, enjoys reading romance novels, or is a hunter.[53]

The companies know if you have allergies, if you smoke or wear contacts, if your elderly parents live with you, if you speak Spanish, the type of roof on your house, and if you have more than 250 Twitter followers.[54] The creepiness crosses into almost comedic stereotypes as large groups of people become lumped together on the basis of shared demographics or income. Data brokers segment out certain groups. Single men and women over age 66 with "low educational attainment and low net worths" are targeted as "Rural Everlasting."[55] Other singles in the same age group but with more disposable income are known as "Thrifty Elders." Certain low-income minority groups composed of African Americans and Latinos are labeled as "Urban Scramble" or "Mobile Mixers."[56] Private data companies regularly sell and repackage this information about consumer activity to other data brokers, further expanding the webs of shared data.

If you think about what big data companies do in the consumer space, you will see the allure for law enforcement. Data brokers collect personal information to monitor individuals' interests and inclinations. They investigate connections among groups of like-minded people and uncover patterns in the data to reveal hidden insights. This is also what law enforcement investigators do with criminal suspects and gangs. Police monitor, investigate, uncover, and target. Police look for suspicious patterns. Police watch. The tools of big data are the tools of surveillance, and law enforcement relies on surveillance to solve and prevent crime. Unsurprisingly, police have shown great interest in the possibilities of big data policing.

A Permanent Digital Record

The first step in solving any crime is analyzing the clues. Knowing who might be the likely suspect has been part of policing since the mid-1700s, when courts first recorded those who were thought to have been involved in a fraud or felony.[57] Unsurprisingly, as policing developed in sophistication, so did data collection and use. The modern "police blotter" now sits on a cloud server accessible to officers across the jurisdiction or the country.[58]

Federal databases like the National Crime Information Center (NCIC) contain 13 million active records, all searchable by police officers on the street or in their patrol cars. In a routine traffic stop, if a police officer "runs your name" through the system, NCIC will provide personal details about any arrests, warrants, gang affiliations, terrorism ties, supervised release, or fugitive status, as well as information about property including gun ownership, car and boat licenses, and even if you have been the victim of identity theft.[59] This massive database filled with state, local, and federal information is reportedly accessed 12 million times *a day* by authorities.[60] The federal government also maintains watch lists focused on terrorism, including 700,000 names in the Terrorist Screening Database (TSD), a million names in the Terrorist Identities Datamart Environment (TIDE), and 50,000 names on the "No-Fly List."[61]

States also collect and generate data sets to monitor citizens. Eleven states maintain extensive electronic gang databases on suspected gang members.[62] Over 800,000 men and women are listed in federal and state sex-offender registries for convicted sex offenders.[63] Individuals convicted of gun crimes in some states have been required to register.[64] Details about where these offenders live, work, and go to school; what cars they drive; and even their appearance (tattoos, facial hair, scars) are updated constantly in digital archives.[65]

After the terrorist attacks of September 11, 2001, federal and state officials joined forces to establish a national intelligence strategy to improve criminal justice data collection and information sharing.[66] A vast array of law enforcement organizations now share personal data about suspects, crimes, and crime patterns. These organizations include state, local, tribal, and territorial agencies, the Department of Justice (DOJ), the Department of Homeland Security (DHS), the Federal Bureau of Investigation (FBI), the Drug Enforcement Administration (DEA), and the Bureau of Alcohol, Tobacco, and Firearms (ATF). A network of fusion centers seeks to share threat-related information across federal and state lines.[67] Regional Information Sharing Systems (RISS) Centers coordinate incoming data, while Crime Analysis Centers (CACs) analyze collected data. These new data-sharing entities also coordinate with the 17 different agencies that make up the United States intelligence community, including outward, international-facing data-collection agencies like the National Security Agency (NSA) and the Central Intelligence Agency (CIA).

Data projects like the National Data Exchange Program (N-DEx) have been set up "as a giant data warehouse" to pull together otherwise-incompatible police databases.[68] As described in N-DEx's "Privacy Impact Assessment,"

> N-DEx provides a national investigative information sharing system available through a secure Internet site that allows criminal justice agencies to search and analyze data representing the entire criminal justice cycle, including crime incident and investigation records; arrest, booking, and incarceration records; and probation and parole records. As a repository of information from local, state, regional, tribal, and federal criminal justice entities, N-DEx provides these agencies with the capability to make linkages between crime incidents, criminal investigations, and related events to help solve, deter, and prevent crimes. . . . N-DEx contains the personally identifiable information (PII) of suspects, perpetrators, witnesses and victims, and anyone else who may be identified in a law enforcement report concerning a crime incident or criminal investigation.[69]

As of 2014, N-DEx had over 107,000 users and over 170 million searchable records.[70] Start-up companies have been building similar private data-management systems to assist law enforcement in organizing the ever-growing stores of data.

Beyond investigative records, law enforcement now collects biological data. Biometric collection regularly includes DNA, fingerprints, photographs, and iris and retina scans—all secured in searchable databases to investigate crimes.[71] The Combined DNA Index System (CODIS) includes 12 million searchable DNA profiles.[72] The FBI's Next Generation Identification (NGI) system integrates fingerprints, palm prints, facial recognition, and iris scans in one larger searchable database. The FBI has over 23 million searchable photographs and the largest collection of fingerprints in the world.[73] All of this data pushes police investigation into the future, and all of it opens the opportunity for new big data tools to sort, search, and discover otherwise hidden connections between crime and criminals.

Data has also revolutionized how certain police run their day-to-day operations. Many large police departments follow the crime numbers to guide strategy.[74] Some bigger police departments like the New York Police Department (NYPD) have gone so far as to hire a director of analytics to assist in crunching the numbers.[75] Other police departments have partnered with private data-analytics companies or consultants to sort and study the collected data. Professional crime analysts routinely participate in strategy sessions in big police departments.[76] While relying on data differently, most have accepted the underlying principle that the big data technologies created for the private sector can assist police administrators working to improve public safety. In fact, in 2009, Los Angeles Police Department (LAPD) chief Charlie Beck wrote a seminal article, titled "Predictive Policing: What Can We Learn from Wal-Mart and Amazon about Fighting Crime in a Recession?," which explicitly advocated adopting data-driven business principles to improve policing.[77] "Analytics," "risk-based deployment," "prediction," "data mining," and "cost-effectiveness" all emerged as new values and goals for the modern police professional.

Currently, consumer big data technologies and law enforcement data systems operate on separate tracks. What Google knows is not what the FBI knows. The NCIC system is not available to private data brokers. A patchwork of federal privacy laws theoretically restricts the direct governmental collection of personal identifiable information. These statutes include the Privacy Act of 1974,[78] Electronic Communications Privacy Act of 1986 (ECPA),[79] and Stored Communications Act (SCA),[80] Foreign Intelligence Surveillance Act (FISA),[81] E-Government Act of 2002,[82] Financial Privacy Act,[83] Communications Act, Gramm-Leach-Bliley Act,[84] Bank Secrecy Act,[85] Right To Financial Privacy Act,[86] Fair Credit Reporting Act,[87] Health Insurance Portability and Accountability Act of 1996 (HIPAA),[88] Genetic Information Non-discrimination Act (GINA),[89] Children's Online Privacy Protection Act (COPPA),[90] Family Educational Rights and Privacy Act,[91] Telephone Records and Privacy Protection Act of 2006,[92] and Video Protection Privacy Act.[93] In addition to being dated (since some were drafted decades before the big data era), these laws do not prevent law enforcement access. As Erin Murphy has written, "The United States Code currently contains over twenty separate statutes that restrict both the acquisition and release of covered information. . . . Yet across this remarkable diversity, there is one feature that all these statutes share in common: each contains a provision exempting law enforcement from its general terms."[94] Police can obtain certain data with a court order or subpoena.[95] With a valid warrant, police can obtain most anything big data companies have collected for consumer purposes. This patchwork of privacy law also does not stop law enforcement from purchasing the same big data information like any other customer.[96] Just like a private data broker, police can purchase your cellphone and internet information directly from the companies.[97]

A complete big data convergence between private consumer data collection and public law enforcement collection has not yet occurred. But the lines are blurry and growing fainter. Once data has been collected in one place, it becomes harder and harder not to aggregate the information. Private data becomes part of public records, and then public records become the building blocks of private and government databases. Data gets sold and repackaged such that the original collection point becomes obscured.[98] If police want to know about a suspect, and the data has been collected by private third parties, those private companies are hard-pressed to push back and protect the information from lawful government requests. A few powerful technology companies have on occasion rejected government requests for assistance in obtaining customer information or have designed encrypted systems to avoid being in a position to provide information to police investigators.[99] But other companies have been good corporate citizens and provided the information as requested.

Big Data Tools

What big data knows is one thing, but the technology used to manipulate and organize that data is the bigger thing.

The real promise of big data remains with the ability to sort, study, and target within large data sets.[100] Big data becomes intelligible because of algorithms and the large-scale computer-processing power now available. Algorithms are just mathematical processes established to solve a particular task. Using algorithms, pattern-matching tools can flag abnormal financial patterns; social network technologies can link groups via emails, addresses, or any common variable; and predictive analytics can take data-driven insights and forecast future events. Machine-learning algorithms powered by artificial intelligence models can sort vast streams of data in ways unimaginable in earlier eras. Collectively, these math tools allow data analysts to divine insight from an otherwise overwhelming amount of information.[101]

As an example of one such insight, the retail giant Target figured out a way to predict when women are pregnant.[102] By studying women who signed up for an in-store baby registry, Target noticed that these self-identified pregnant women shared a similar, repeating purchasing pattern. Pregnant women would purchase folic acid and vitamin supplements in the first trimester (to improve prenatal health), unscented lotion in the second trimester (due to heightened olfactory sensitivity), and hand sanitizer close to their due dates (to protect the newborn from germs). So now if any woman's purchases follow that pattern (even if she has not signed up for a baby registry), Target flags her as pregnant.[103] The correlation of three unrelated consumer purchases leads to a very personal future prediction.

Big data policing is no different. Law enforcement can identify drug dealers from patterns of supplies (purchasing tiny ziplock bags, rubber bands, digital scales), suspicious transactions (depositing cash, high-end all-cash purchases), and travel patterns (to and from a source city for drugs). The information does not need to be 100% accurate (just as sometimes you receive the wrong catalogue in the mail), but—the theory goes—better information allows police to prioritize and target the higher risks to a community. As Cathy O'Neil wrote in her book *Weapons of Math Destruction*, just as Amazon uses data to identify the "recidivist" shopper, police can use data to predict the future criminal.[104]

Big data tools create the potential for big data policing. The combination of new data sources, better algorithms, expanding systems of shared networks, and the possibility of proactively finding hidden insights and clues about crime has led to a new age of potential surveillance. Instead of consumer surveillance, the goal of big data policing is criminal surveillance.

Chapter 2 looks at why police administrators have been open to big data's embrace. Technology has not been the only force pushing innovation. Budget cuts after a national financial recession forced police to change.[105] In addition, long-standing fissures in police/community relations widened as complaints of racial bias and unconstitutional policing grew louder.[106] Protests challenged continued police violence. Communities demanded change from systemic practices of social control like aggressive stop-and-frisks. Out of this frustration, the seemingly objective metrics of data-driven policing became quite appealing. Turning the page on human bias or racial discrimination became an important spur in the adoption of big data policing. The next chapter explores the lure of these new technologies to solve age-old policing problems.

2

Data Is the New Black

The Lure of Data-Driven Policing

> Predictive policing used to be the future. Now it is the present.
> —Former New York Police Department commissioner William Bratton[1]

Policing Darkness

The night patrol. At night, you stay in the squad car. At night, you wait for the radio run. At night, good guys look like bad guys. In the dark, you wait.

For police chiefs, every day is a night patrol. For years, all police leaders could do was react, respond to the crime scene, and answer to the media. In the dark of criminal activity, police administrators could only wait. But what if police could see in the dark? Map the crime patterns? Illuminate the bad guys for who they are? Such is the lure of new big data technologies. Digital crime maps could turn pushpin maps into real-time alerts.[2] Hot-spot policing could predictively target specific blocks of trouble. Databases could catalogue and monitor the bad seeds that needed to be weeded out.

Another type of darkness. Budget cuts. Layoffs. The 2007 financial recession in the United States gutted police forces, adding to police administrators' woes.[3] State taxes dried up. County and municipal budgets shrunk.[4] Hiring froze. Specialized training stopped. Overtime ended, and services were reduced. From 2007 to 2013, local police agencies across the country had to do more with less—sometimes dramatically less.[5] Then the federal government began cutting.[6] Sequestration meant cuts to federal grants for gang task forces, drug task forces, community policing projects, crime-scene investigation, and juvenile diversion, among many other initiatives.[7] And at the same time, a fear grew that with more people out of work, crime rates would rise.

But what if there was an answer? What if you could equip police officers with better information? What if smart policing technology could allow you to do more with less? What if data provided an answer to mayors and communities demanding a comforting response to this fear of crime? The thinking of many police chiefs could be summed up with one question: "You mean there is a black-box computer that can predict crime?" And with one answer: "Sign me up."

A Boiling Pot

"Hands Up, Don't Shoot." A chant. A crowd. Open hands toward the sky. A man stares down a tactical police vehicle rolling through suburban Ferguson, Missouri.[8] The image of armed police officers pointing assault rifles at protesters lit a fire in Ferguson that ended up burning downtown Baltimore and sparking a nationwide protest movement to reform policing.

In 2014, a grand jury's failure to indict officer Darren Wilson for the shooting death of Michael Brown touched off a wave of protests and attention to the problem of police violence.[9] Following Ferguson, news story after news story covered instances of police officers killing unarmed African Americans. Eric Gardner in Staten Island, Tamir Rice in Cleveland, Walter Scott in Charleston, Freddie Gray in Baltimore, Alton Sterling in Baton Rouge, and Philando Castile in Falcon Hills, Minnesota.[10] These stories, and dozens more killings of citizens by police, changed the conversation of policing in America.

Race became a central point of debate. The Black Lives Matter movement rose up and rallied social media and communities of color to protest patterns of racism and brutality.[11] Streets filled with demonstrators and conflicts with police turned violent. Cable news broadcast the events live, and this pot of simmering anger seemed to boil over regularly.[12]

The truth, of course, is that the pot had always been boiling. Discriminatory police practices dating back to before slavery fueled racial tension.[13] Aggressive policing systems created resentment, distrust, and fear in many minority communities. As James Comey, the director of the Federal Bureau of Investigation (FBI), admitted in a speech after the

Ferguson protests, "All of us in law enforcement must be honest enough to acknowledge that much of our history is not pretty. At many points in American history, law enforcement enforced the status quo, a status quo that was often brutally unfair to disfavored groups. . . . It was unfair to too many people."[14] In this speech on "race and hard truths," one of the nation's most senior law enforcement officials recognized that police needed to move beyond this unjust past, because certain discriminatory and constitutionally unsound police practices had undermined trust in police.[15] A similar sentiment was echoed by police chief and then president of the International Association of Chiefs of Police Terrence Cunningham. Cunningham apologized for the role of police in contributing to citizens' mistrust:

> There have been times when law enforcement officers, because of the laws enacted by federal, state, and local governments, have been the face of oppression for far too many of our fellow citizens. In the past, the laws adopted by our society have required police officers to perform many unpalatable tasks, such as ensuring legalized discrimination or even denying the basic rights of citizenship to many of our fellow Americans. While this is no longer the case, this dark side of our shared history has created a multigenerational—almost inherited—mistrust between many communities of color and their law enforcement agencies.[16]

Ferguson, Missouri, exemplified the past and present problem of systemic racial discrimination. In Ferguson, the Civil Rights Division of the U.S. Department of Justice (DOJ) documented a systemic pattern of racially discriminatory policing primarily focused on generating revenue for the local municipal government.[17] These practices fueled the figurative and literal fires of protest. Ferguson police routinely stopped African Americans more than they did whites and for all the wrong reasons. As the DOJ Ferguson report summarized,

> Data collected by the Ferguson Police Department from 2012 to 2014 shows that African Americans account for 85% of vehicle stops, 90% of citations, and 93% of arrests made by FPD [Ferguson Police Department] officers, despite comprising only 67% of Ferguson's population. African Americans are more than twice as likely as white drivers to be searched

during vehicle stops even after controlling for non-race based variables such as the reason the vehicle stop was initiated, but are found in possession of contraband 26% less often than white drivers, suggesting officers are impermissibly considering race as a factor when determining whether to search.[18]

Nearly 90% of the use of force incidents targeted African Americans.[19] Almost 95% of "failure to comply" and 94% of "walking in the roadway" charges (misdemeanors usually associated with social-control measures) targeted African Americans.[20] Statistics demonstrating racial bias, personal stories showing racial animus, and smoking-gun racist emails all painted a dark picture that race had discolored local policing practices.[21]

Worse, many of these unpleasant and unconstitutional police contacts were undertaken to collect money for the municipality, not for crime control.[22] The most damning finding of the DOJ report revealed a financial perversion at the heart of the policing structure in Ferguson:

> The City's emphasis on revenue generation has a profound effect on FPD's approach to law enforcement. Patrol assignments and schedules are geared toward aggressive enforcement of Ferguson's municipal code, with insufficient thought given to whether enforcement strategies promote public safety or unnecessarily undermine community trust and cooperation. Officer evaluations and promotions depend to an inordinate degree on "productivity," meaning the number of citations issued. Partly as a consequence of City and FPD priorities, many officers appear to see some residents, especially those who live in Ferguson's predominantly African-American neighborhoods, less as constituents to be protected than as potential offenders and sources of revenue.[23]

Together, the practice of aggressive, revenue-focused policing and the subsequent financial consequences to poor citizens destroyed the community's trust in police.[24] The report describes one seemingly minor police interaction with devastating personal consequences.

> In the summer of 2012, a 32-year-old African-American man sat in his car cooling off after playing basketball in a Ferguson public park. An officer pulled up behind the man's car, blocking him in, and demanded the

man's Social Security number and identification. Without any cause, the officer accused the man of being a pedophile, referring to the presence of children in the park, and ordered the man out of his car for a pat-down, although the officer had no reason to believe the man was armed. The officer also asked to search the man's car. The man objected, citing his constitutional rights. In response, the officer arrested the man, reportedly at gunpoint, charging him with eight violations of Ferguson's municipal code. One charge, Making a False Declaration, was for initially providing the short form of his first name (e.g., "Mike" instead of "Michael"), and an address which, although legitimate, was different from the one on his driver's license. Another charge was for not wearing a seat belt, even though he was seated in a parked car. The officer also charged the man both with having an expired operator's license, and with having no operator's license in his possession. The man told [DOJ investigators] that, because of these charges, he lost his job as a contractor with the federal government that he had held for years.[25]

The DOJ Ferguson report documents dozens of similar stories. After reviewing tens of thousands of internal documents, officer emails, and transcripts of hundreds of interviews, the DOJ report concluded that a system of racially biased, petty harassment for citation dollars had replaced a policing system focused on public safety. Change was recommended, and community protestors demanded immediate action for a new type of policing.

A different systemic policing practice undermined community trust in New York City. As the largest police force in the United States, NYPD regularly draws scrutiny. But in a federal lawsuit over "stop and frisk" practices, revelations of racial discrimination and systemic harassment came to light.[26] In a 2013 decision, *Floyd et al. v. City of New York*, Judge Shira Scheindlin of the United States Court for the Southern District of New York held that the NYPD's stop-and-frisk practices violated the Constitution.[27] Judge Scheindlin observed that the NYPD's informal goal to target "the right people, the right time, the right location" became in practice discrimination against poor people of color.[28]

Judge Scheindlin's findings revealed a demonstrated racial imbalance to stop-and-frisk practices. Of the 4.4 million police stops conducted between January 2004 and June 2012, 52% involved African Americans, 31%

Latinos, and 10% whites, even though as of 2010, the resident population was only 23% African American, 29% Latino, and 33% white.[29] Of those stops, contraband was recovered in only 1.8% of stops of African Americans, 1.7% of Latinos, but 2.3% of whites.[30] Weapons were seized in only 1.0% of stops of African Americans, 1.1% of Latinos, but 1.4% of whites. Of all the stops, only 6% resulted in an arrest and 6% in a summons, with 88% of police contacts resulting in no further law enforcement action.[31] Police used force in those stops 23% of the time against African Americans, 24% against Latinos, and 17% against whites. At the height of the stop-and-frisk program in New York City, police conducted 686,000 stops a year, with the brunt of these stops being felt by young men of color.[32] Similar programs existed in other big cities like Chicago, where the Chicago Police Department stopped upward of 700,000 people in 2011.[33]

In addition to the federal lawsuit, this policing practice led to major protests in communities impacted by the stop-and-frisk strategy. It also drew attention to the physical and psychological fear that such aggressive policing had on communities of color. The Center for Constitutional Rights—a nonprofit organization that helped lead the *Floyd* litigation—documented the impact on citizens' trust of police.[34] Two quotes from interviews with community members show the personal and societal impact of aggressive stop-and-frisk practices:

> It makes you anxious about just being, walking around and doing your daily thing while having a bunch of police always there, always present and stopping people that look like me. They say if you're a young Black male, you're more likely to be stopped. So, it's always this fear that "okay, this cop might stop me," for no reason, while I'm just sitting there in my neighborhood.
> —Joey M., a 25-year-old black man living in Central Harlem[35]

> The sheer number of stops is actually ostracizing a huge number of people who live in these communities that are impacted by crime. It doesn't make sense that you're spending so many man hours, so much energy and resources, to stop so many innocent people and end up with very little output. The number of guns that they found from the stops is extremely small. So it just doesn't seem effective.
> —Manny W. (pseudonym), New York, New York[36]

These voices and hundreds like them changed the narrative of the stop-and-frisk practice from one of aggressive crime control to abusive social control. Calls for reform altered the 2013 mayor's race and ultimately led to a reduction in aggressive stop-and-frisk practices (with no resulting increase in crime).

Similar stories of systemic racial discrimination and individual abuse can be told in other jurisdictions. Prior to the Ferguson report, the Department of Justice had investigated and taken corrective action against unconstitutional police practices in more than a dozen cities. DOJ has launched 68 significant investigations into local policing practice over 20 years.[37] Allegations of excessive force, discriminatory practices, unlawful stops, and unlawful arrests have drawn federal attention and concern.[38] Major police departments in Seattle, Cleveland, New Orleans, Albuquerque, and Newark had demonstrated patterns and practices of unconstitutional policing.[39] Other police departments such as those in New York and Philadelphia fell under court-monitored consent decrees as a result of civil rights lawsuits.[40] After the protests over the death of Freddie Gray, DOJ investigated the Baltimore Police Department and found systemic unconstitutional practices involving stops, frisks, arrests, and the use of force.[41] The Baltimore DOJ report documents a pattern and practice of racially motived abuse of government authority.[42]

In the face of long-standing claims of discrimination, systemic problems, and rekindled rage, police leaders began looking for new strategies to reorient policing. The status quo had been exposed as racially biased and unfair, and a new paradigm was needed to replace it. In response to demonstrated human bias, it is not surprising that the lure of objective-seeming, data-driven policing might be tempting. In addition, police administrators were being pushed from the inside to change policing structures and provide line officers more tools to do their jobs. Officers expressed anger at a failure to train, support, or even acknowledge the difficult jobs police were expected to do every day. Just as communities demanded change, so did police officers who felt caught in a trap between community rage and bureaucratic neglect.

Blue Lives Suffer

The backlash to the Black Lives Matter movement refocused attention on policing and the danger of patrolling high-crime neighborhoods. Police officers voiced frustration at staffing levels, training, and unrealistic expectations when having to confront daily poverty, anger, and mental illness. Police felt that their lives and the risks they took had been unfairly devalued.[43] After the tragic murder of five police officers protecting a peaceful 2016 Black Lives Matters protest in Dallas, Texas, and then the murder of three additional officers in Baton Rouge, Louisiana, a week later, an equally powerful call was made to value police lives and the difficult job they are called on to do.[44]

Take, as an example, the daunting task to police Chicago, Illinois. The city has approximately 100,000 gang members, 700 rival gangs, a homicide rate in 2015 of 17 persons killed per 100,000 (the national average is 5 per 100,000), and certain districts with homicide rates triple the city average.[45] In August 2016, the city recorded 90 homicides with over 400 shootings.[46] Yet, since March 2013, over $190 million has been cut from the police budget.[47] This reduction meant training programs had to be cut, supervisory positions ended, and rookie officers asked to police the most violent areas with the least amount of training or support.[48] Dropped off to patrol neighborhoods they did not know and surrounded by residents who largely distrusted them, the rookies emphasized physical force and physical control to establish authority. Neither side could see the other as merely responding to the systemic failure to provide adequate resources for community-based policing. Such ineffective policing strategies also led to internal frustration with police administration. The lack of training and resources led officers to believe they were set up to fail.

In similar fashion, after the death of Freddie Gray, Baltimore saw a dramatic spike in homicides.[49] Police officers publicly complained about the impact of the protests on previously sanctioned aggressive tactics. Tasked to fight an increase in crime but concerned that officers might not only be disciplined but criminally prosecuted by their fellow law enforcement brethren, officers felt abandoned.[50] One Baltimore police lieutenant, Kenneth Butler, was quoted as saying, "In 29 years, I've gone through some bad times, but I've never seen it this bad. [Officers] feel as though the state's attorney will hang them out to dry. . . . I'm hearing it from guys who were go-getters, who would go out here and get the guns and the bad guys and drugs. They're hands-off now. . . . I've never seen so many dejected faces."[51] Nationally, police administrators sensed this growing frustration. The conflict between black lives mattering and blue lives mattering undermined established relationships and created calls for something new.

Despite these calls, the daily reality of policing did not change. Men and women put on a uniform, entered a community, and saw all of the horror humanity can offer. On an almost daily basis, police in urban areas witness death, violence, and neglect. Predators hurt children, husbands hurt wives, and children hurt each other. Blood. Bullets. Bruises. Rape. Anger. Fear. Frustration. Mental illness. Addiction. Poverty. Despair. Every single shift. As a professional class, police officers suffer this daily trauma without sufficient mental health or social support.[52] Police face frightening personal experiences with their own physical safety at risk. Some studies suggest that one-third to one-eighth of retired and active-duty police officers suffer from posttraumatic stress disorder (PTSD) as a result of their jobs.[53] This unaddressed trauma, fear, and daily stress burdens officers who are required to respond every shift to a new emergency.

And police administrators still had to fill those shifts. Police administrators needed to do more with fewer officers. Demands for new tools increased, as did the demand for "smarter policing." Technology, as it has in other areas of society, became the answer to growing officer complaints and financial constraints. Technology promised to make hard jobs easier, so administrators and line officers all bought in, hoping for the best. Big data and predictive tools offered the chance to change the reality on the ground, but more importantly, they offered some hope that change was possible.

Responding to Crisis with Innovation

Out of the tension of black lives' frustration with police officers and blue lives' frustration with police administration, the lure of technology to add objectivity to policing and to do more with less began to grow.

"Smart policing," "intelligence-led policing," and "data-driven policing" became catchphrases and solutions for the future.[54]

At the center of this change in policing philosophy was William Bratton. If you had to pick a single law enforcement visionary for the birth of big data policing, Bill Bratton would be top on your list. First, as commissioner of the NYPD in the 1990s, Bratton, along with Jack Maple, pioneered a very data-centered approach to police management.[55] Under CompStat (computer statistics), district commanders reported crime statistics every week, and police commanders evaluated benchmarks for crime reduction and arrest rates in every precinct. Accountability for crime reduction based on crime statistics became the primary focus of police management. Then, as chief of police in Los Angeles, Bratton brought CompStat to the West Coast, and he gave the green light to the first predictive policing experiments with the LAPD.[56] Finally, as police commissioner again in New York City in 2014, he embraced an even more robust data-driven system of surveillance with the NYPD.[57] As a national figure and promoter of the original CompStat system and the first generation of predictive policing, Bratton remains a singular figure of data-driven influence.

But notable and largely ignored in the Bratton mythology is the reality that each of the data-driven shifts grew out of crisis and a need to turn the page on scandals that revealed systemic problems with policing tactics. In the 1990s, New York City was facing high levels of crime and wide-ranging police scandals that resulted in the Mollen Commission's scathing report on corruption in the NYPD.[58] In 1993, the Mollen Commission determined that the NYPD had "a deep-rooted institutional reluctance to uncover corruption in the department" and concluded it had "abandoned its responsibility to insure integrity."[59] Bratton took over the NYPD in 1994 and instituted the CompStat program that same year.

When Bratton arrived in Los Angeles in 2002, the police department was reeling from what Bratton himself called "corruption control."[60] Placed under a federal consent decree in 2001, the LAPD had been rocked by the Rampart scandal, which included allegations of widespread fraud, corruption, and criminality among the LAPD gang unit.[61] The entire police department had been tarnished with legal and media scrutiny about "rogue cops." A concern about police corruption had resulted in a defensive and counterproductive police culture. As Chief Bratton himself reflected on his challenge,

> Crime was up and morale was down. The relationship with the community was deplorable and line officers felt as though their only mission was to answer assigned radio calls and to stay clear of trouble. It was like a dysfunctional family where everyone knows something is wrong, but they are powerless to change the situation. Crime had risen for the three years prior to my appointment as Chief. The officers appeared tired and burned out from what was described by many as a relentless, vindictive and unfair discipline system. The Department was also suffering from lowered and poorly defined goals and expectations.[62]

The solution to this malaise involved the creation of an LAPD data-driven system of police management that evolved into the building blocks of CompStat-West and then predictive policing.[63] Data about crime, patrols, and patterns began influencing police management. Data increased accountability and professionalism and also reduced crime.

A similar pivot occurred in New York City after Judge Scheindlin declared the NYPD's stop-and-frisk practices unconstitutional. Judge Scheindlin's ruling came in August 2013, and Bratton took over as head of the NYPD four months later. Appointed to oversee a police department buffeted by allegations of racial discrimination with stop-and-frisk practices, again Bratton doubled down on data-driven policing. Stop-and-frisk was out. Predictive policing was in. Bratton ordered tens of thousands of crime-mapping tablet computers for his officers.[64] He oversaw the launch of a cutting-edge, real-time crime command center in Manhattan. Data-based policing, he argued, did not involve hunches or suspicion, and while critics challenged the accuracy of these claims, "intelligence-led policing" was sold as an acceptable alternative to the all-too-human practice of stop-and-frisk policing.

The pattern of police scandal and technological response is repeating again. Because of scandal over police violence and growing community tension, the door to big data policing cracked open. Communities wanted change. Officers wanted change. The times demanded change.

And technology offered change. Just as there was a need to turn the page from the past, big data surveillance offered an answer. Data, and the lure of data-driven solutions, became the hope for a better and smarter policing future.

A Changing Mind-Set

If big data technology has been a wave of hype and innovation, tension between citizens and the police has been the undercurrent that allowed the wave to grow more powerful. Yet there have always been strong currents pushing new technologies forward.

From the early forms of data collection in the 1990s in New York City's CompStat program to modern predictive policing programs, three forces helped spur interest in the first generation of big data policing. These societal factors made it easier for jurisdictions across the country to embrace the promise of new technology. None of these changes can be directly linked to the unrest post-Ferguson (because all predate the tension), nor are they related to the rise of commercial big data in the conventional sense. But these changes in mind-set helped seed the field for greater acceptance of how data-driven technology can improve law enforcement and reduce the tension between police and the community.

First, police administrators partnered with academic researchers including criminologists, sociologists, and law professors to study patterns of crime.[65] Police chiefs opened themselves to learn from academics studying crime patterns.[66] Theories like environmental criminology, focused deterrence, and pattern matching developed from academic settings into operational practice.[67]

Formal partnerships in Chicago, Los Angeles, and New York to study violence and gang networks significantly changed police practice on the ground.[68] These partnerships included developing data-driven metrics to measure what works, building on a rich literature of proactive policing theories.[69] During the early 2000s, researchers promoted the idea that data could lead the way to a smarter and cheaper law enforcement footprint.[70] This move toward intelligence-led policing, in turn, produced interest in crime-mapping technologies and in "hot spot" policing. Geographically targeted interventions began shaping police strategy, and the interest in data-driven insights grew. The national interest in big data and predictive policing really began accelerating in 2009 with the first National Institute of Justice (NIJ) symposium on predictive policing,[71] and from that time—mirroring the growth of other data-driven technologies—adoption of predictive analytics has rapidly increased across the country.

Second, the federal government provided millions of dollars in technology grants to fund research and implementation of data-driven technologies.[72] From small grants to examine predictive policing to large grants to modernize data collection to experimental grants to examine body-worn cameras, violence reduction efforts, and sex-trafficking, the government, through the Department of Justice's Bureau of Justice Assistance (BJA) and the NIJ, has spurred innovation through grant making.[73] The federal money allowed local police departments to experiment without significant institutional cost to the bottom line. In an era of cost-cutting, federal grants provided cost-free technological advancement. This governmental largess also created incentives for private companies to develop technologies to support law enforcement, such that many big technology giants and several small start-up companies now compete in the policing space to offer technology and services.

Third, the technology improved in dramatic ways. As described in chapter 1, the potential of big data grows almost daily. Technology adapted from mapping terrorists can now map local gangs. Large-scale databases of DNA, iris scans, photos, and other biometrics can now capture exponentially more personal data.[74] All of these developing techniques encouraged interest in big data policing. Each change promised greater accuracy, better information, and more useful tools. While the underlying goal of collecting, cataloguing, and using data about criminal actors is as old as policing, the new technological tools offered to make the job easier and more efficient. This, in turn, makes police officers and administrators more interested in the possibilities, and this belief has spurred excitement, innovation, and faith in a data-driven future.

Each of these factors adds to the argument that data-driven policing can help turn the page on a moment of crisis in law enforcement. For police chiefs, big data policing offers an escape, a talking point to shift the conversation from the past to the future. For the community, big data offers a more objective way to solve the very human problem of biased policing. For the media, it offers endless buzz-worthy headlines about futuristic "Minority Report" policing.[75] And for technologists, it offers a new world of opportunity and innovation. The time for big data policing has arrived. The only question is what it might look like in the real world.

data / as opportunity in times of Law enforcement crisis.

Could big data actually fix biases in policing?

3

Whom We Police

Person-Based Predictive Targeting

> We could name our top 300 offenders. . . . So we will focus
> on those individuals, the persons responsible for the crimi-
> nal activity, regardless of who they are or where they live. . . .
> We're not just looking for crime. We're looking for people.
> —Police Chief Rodney Monroe, Charlotte-Mecklenburg,
> North Carolina[1]

The Violence Virus

A knock on an apartment door. A man gives the prognosis to a wor-
ried mother. Your son might die. He is at grave risk. Others he knows
have already succumbed. An algorithm has identified the most likely
to be stricken. He is one of a few thousand young men who may die.[2]
In Chicago, Illinois, this scene has played out hundreds of times at
hundreds of doors. The danger, however, is not some blood-borne
pathogen. This is not a doctor giving a cancer diagnosis but a police
detective giving a life diagnosis. Violence is contagious, and you are
exposed. As a young man in Chicago, due to your friends, associates,
and prior connection to violence, you have been predicted to be the
victim or perpetrator of a shooting. Your name is on the "Strategic
Suspects List," also known as the "heat list," and a detective is at your
door with a social worker and a community representative to tell you
the future is not only dark but deadly.[3] A vaccine exists, but it means
turning your life around now.

In Chicago, 1,400 young men have been identified through big data
techniques as targets for the heat list.[4] Software generates a rank-order
list of potential victims and subjects with the greatest risk of violence.[5]
In New Orleans, Palantir has partnered with the mayor's office to identify the 1% of violent crime drivers in the city.[6] In Rochester, New York,

and Los Angeles, similar techniques are being used to identify juveniles who might be involved in repeated delinquent activity.[7]

This is the promise of big data policing. What if big data techniques could predict who might be violent? What if a policing system could be redesigned to target those who are at-risk in a neighborhood before the shooting occurs? This is the theory behind "person-based targeted policing."

This chapter examines how big data policing alters *whom* we police. Person-based predictive policing involves the use of data to identify and investigate potential suspects or victims. Part public health approach to violence and part social network approach to risk assessment, big data can visualize how violence spreads like a virus among communities. The same data also can predict the most likely victims of violence. Police data is shaping who gets targeted and forecasting who gets shot.

While these predictive technologies are excitingly new, the concerns underlying them remain frustratingly old-fashioned. Fears of racial bias, a lack of transparency, data error, and the distortions of constitutional protections offer serious challenges to the development of workable person-based predictive strategies. Yet person-based policing systems are being used now, and people are being targeted.

Focused Deterrence

Only a tiny percentage of people commit violent crime.[8] Police tend to know the people who commit those crimes, but the difficulty has always been getting "the criminals" to know that the police know they are committing the crimes. Enter "focused deterrence"—a theory that seeks to understand and dismantle the networks of criminal actors that drive violent crime.[9] Focused deterrence involves a targeted and explicit message to a narrow slice of the population that police, prosecutors, and the community know who is engaged in violence and that the killings must end.

In 2012, Kansas City, Missouri, implemented a bold data-driven, focused-deterrence experiment.[10] After suffering from a homicide rate two to four times the national average, Kansas City decided to target the particular men causing the violence in the city. With funding from the Department of Justice's Bureau of Justice Assistance (BJA), the Kansas

City Police Department used advanced social network analysis to visualize the at-risk men responsible for the violence.[11] In Kansas City, the
focused-deterrence process had three steps: (1) identify criminal actors,
(2) give notice to those actors that police are aware of their activities and
offer social services, and (3) arrest, prosecute, and punish those individuals who were warned but ignored the warnings.[12]

In step one, police generated a target group of suspects believed to
be involved in murders, shootings, or other serious assaults. Police then
looked through police records to determine who had been arrested with
these men.[13] These "co-arrestees" (people arrested at the same time)
tended to be close associates, even if they had not been involved in the
original crime. Police then replicated the co-arrest analysis going out another level to see everyone the co-arrestee had been arrested with at any
time. The full social network of associates thus extended three levels out
with targets, co-arrestees, and then co-arrestees of the co-arrestees included. Information about gang association, prior criminal history, and
other data about the individuals filled out the creation of this citywide
social network data set.[14] Once identified from this police data, these
targets became the focus of law enforcement attention.

In 2014, Kansas City police selected 884 identified individuals for
focused-deterrence intervention.[15] Community "call-in" events hosted
by prosecutors, police, and community leaders welcomed targeted suspects to listen to a warning about continued violence.[16] Part threat, part
intervention, part "scared-straight" lecture, call-in events provided clear
notice—any further violence would result in a harsh penalty for everyone in the network. More than 16% of the targets attended these events.[17]
Almost two-thirds met face-to-face with a social-service provider.[18] The
targets had been warned and told they were the problem and that they
would be taken out of society if the violence continued.

Tyrone C. Brown was one of the targets.[19] As reported by the *New
York Times*, Brown accepted the invitation of his probation officer to at-
tend a call-in meeting.[20] In a large auditorium with other targeted men,
police confronted him with a blown-up mug shot of himself. The image
linked him to a local homicide with a none-too-subtle message that police suspected him of violence and would tolerate no more. The intervention continued the next week when police confronted Brown at a
meeting arranged by his social worker. The message became even more

pointed. Police warned that they knew Brown was a leader of his crew but also knew he could lead his associates away from a life of violence.[21] He could make the choice, but he had to make the choice immediately. If he made the wrong one, police and prosecutors would use all of their leverage to punish him.

Mario Glenn learned about punishment the hard way.[22] After attending a call-in and being warned, Glenn then found himself caught in a police sting. He robbed a confidential informant of a gun and was arrested. On the basis of his status as one of those who had been targeted by the focused-deterrence project, prosecutors sought the maximum prison sentence possible under the law.[23] Such is the high cost of the program. Swift deterrence in theory means harsh justice in practice.

Brown took the other path and steered away from crime. Others have followed. Compared to the previous three years, homicide rates fell 26.5% in Kansas City. By the end of 2014, the homicide rate had dropped to levels last seen in 1972.[24] Unfortunately, homicides spiked again in 2015, and shootings have been trending upward.[25]

The Heat List

A different algorithm selects the young men on Chicago's heat list.[26] Designed by Miles Wernick of the Illinois Institute of Technology (IIT), the heat list uses 11 variables to create risk scores from 1 to 500.[27] The higher the score means the greater the risk of being a victim or perpetrator of gun violence. Who gets shot? The algorithm knows. And the heat-list algorithm has been tragically accurate. On a violent Mother's Day weekend in 2016, 80% of the 51 people shot over two days had been correctly identified on Chicago's heat list.[28] On Memorial Day 2016, 78% of the 64 people shot were on the list.[29] Using the heat list, police have prioritized youth violence to intervene in the lives of the most at-risk men.

Because of the Chicago heat list's algorithmic approach to focused deterrence, it has become a leading example of big data policing. Although starting out focusing on co-arrests like in Kansas City, the heat list has grown in complexity and scale. The algorithm remains a police secret, but reportedly the factors include past criminal history, arrests, parole status, and whether the target has been identified as part of a gang.[30] Everyone in the early lists had some criminal involvement. As described by the Chicago Police Department, "The software is generated based on empirical data that lists attributes of a person's criminal record, including the record of violence among criminal associates, the degree to which his criminal activities are on the rise, and the types of intensity of criminal history."[31] The algorithm ranks these variables to come up with a predictive score of how "hot" individuals might be in terms of their risk of violence.

Selection to the heat list can be accompanied by a "custom notification visit."[32] As described at the beginning of this chapter, it involves a home visit, usually by a senior police officer, a social worker, and a member of the community (perhaps a football coach or pastor). During the visit, police hand deliver a "custom notification letter" detailing what the police know about the individual's criminal past, as well as a warning about the future.[33] As described in another police department document, "The Custom Notification Letter will be used to inform individuals of the arrest, prosecution, and sentencing consequences they may face if they choose to or continue to engage in public violence. The letter will be specific to the identified individual and incorporate those factors known about the individual inclusive of prior arrests, impact of known associates, and potential sentencing outcomes for future criminal acts."[34] These custom notification letters symbolize formal messages of deterrence written in black and white. Mess up and you will be prosecuted to the fullest extent of the law. The message is also quite personal. You—the person named in the letter—are known by police and are being watched.

Because of the heat list's prominence in the national discussion about predictive policing, a few of the problems with the practice have emerged. For example, the *Chicago Tribune* reported on the story of Robert McDaniel, a 22-year-old man who was visited by a police commander at his home.[35] Like others on the heat list, he was warned to avoid a criminal path. The only problem was that McDaniel was not a hardened criminal. He had one misdemeanor conviction but had been placed on the heat list anyway. When he inquired about why he ranked high enough to warrant a visit, he was informed that his inclusion stemmed from the shooting death of his best friend a year ago.[36] His personal loss increased his risk of violence, according to the algorithm.

Others find themselves on the list for more obvious reasons. The *New York Times* profiled the death of aspiring rapper Young Pappy, aka Shaquon Thomas, a young man of 19 who had been arrested numerous times, had been shot, and at the time of his death was involved in an ongoing gang feud.[37] Young Pappy's heat-list score was 500+ (the highest number), and the prediction proved tragically accurate.[38] He was shot just weeks before he was scheduled to receive a custom notification visit.

Chicago has been a laboratory for this person-based prediction model. As Chicago police commander Jonathan Lewis publicly stated, the heat-list algorithm "will become a national best practice. This will inform police departments around the country and around the world on how best to utilize predictive policing to solve problems. This is about saving lives."[39]

But the hard reality is that violence in Chicago has only increased. In fact, 2016 has seen a heartbreaking uptick in violent shootings, leading to public criticism of the model.[40] Questions remain about the program's effectiveness and in particular whether enough has been done to remedy the social and economic risks identified. For example, there exists the open question of whether the algorithm adequately distinguishes between targets who are "high risk" (those who might get shot) and those who are "high threat" (those who might shoot). Intensive surveillance and police intervention for those who might be victims may not be as important as targeting those who might engage in violence. But if the heat-list formula counts the risk and threat equally, police resources may be misdirected.

In 2016, the nonprofit RAND Corporation examined the initial iteration of the heat-list system involving just social network co-arrests.[41] RAND found that as applied, the heat list 1.0 showed little predictive accuracy.[42] The system predicted 426 "hot" names, but the forecast did not turn out to be accurate. Worse, police did not follow up with custom notification letters or other social services to assist these individuals. Instead, the list became a shorthand "most wanted list" to arrest suspects. As the RAND reported concluded, "The main result of this study is that at-risk individuals were not more or less likely to become victims of a homicide or shooting as a result of the SSL [Strategic Suspects List], and this is further supported by city-level analysis finding no effect on the city homicide trend. We do find, however, that SSL subjects were more likely to be arrested for a shooting."[43] In fact, as shootings escalated in 2016, Chicago police began rounding up people on the heat list.[44] In May 2016, after weekend after weekend of double-digit shootings, Chicago police arrested close to 200 people on the heat list.[45]

Stepping back, two important insights arise from the heat-list experiment. First, the public health approach of mapping social networks of violence may successfully identify those who might be involved in violence. While the RAND study showed that the heat list 1.0 did not appear to be successful, the predictive model has since evolved.[46] The Chicago Police Department reported that "so far [in 2016], more than 70 percent of the people who have been shot in Chicago were on the list, as were more than 80 percent of those arrested in connection with shootings."[47] If true, that is an impressively accurate prediction of who might be involved in violence.

Second, studying the data to forecast who might be engaged in violence does not automatically end the violence. Custom notifications, while well meaning, may not have the intended effect if not implemented with a focus on addressing underlying social needs. The second step of providing interventions, resources, and redirection must also accompany the risk identification. Without targeted (and funded) social-service interventions, the algorithm just became a targeting mechanism for police. Plainly stated, mapping the social network of violence may be easier than ending the violence. Data identifies the disease but offers no cure.

Math and Murder

An example of a more successful, holistic approach to reducing violence can be found in New Orleans, Louisiana, once the murder capital of the United States.[48] In 2013, the Big Easy averaged 1.46 shootings *a day*, and Mayor Mitch Landrieu turned to data to get a handle on the societal problems driving violence in the city.[49] The city's ambitious public health approach to violence relied on insights from Palantir technologies, which identified largely hidden relationships in already-existing city databases.[50]

Mayor Landrieu's project—NOLA for Life—began with data.[51] Because the data sources included large-scale city systems with continuously generating records, Palantir engineers had to carefully integrate existing police and public-safety data into the system. This data included police calls for service, electronic police reports, probation and parole records, sheriff's office arrest and booking records, gang databases, field information cards, ballistics, and the current case-management system.[52] The analysts also added community and infrastructure details, including the location of schools, hospitals, libraries, parks, police districts, liquor stores, and even streetlights.

Using crime-mapping software, particular violent hot spots were identified.[53] Using social network analysis, particular individuals were identified as being most likely to be victims of violent crime. Like Kansas City and Chicago, in New Orleans analysts could identify particular individuals at risk for violence. Analysts predicted they could identify between 35% and 50% of the likely shooting victims from a subpopulation of 3,900 high-risk individuals.[54] In addition, linkages between these individuals in terms of rivalries, retaliations, and relationships could explain why these men were in danger. Analysts using Palantir systems identified 2,916 individuals from the general New Orleans population of 378,750 (the 2013 city estimate) most likely to be the victim of homicide.[55]

The data insights, however, continued beyond people. On the basis of the Palantir analysis, the Fire Department increased its presence around particular schools, and the Department of Public Works repaired missing streetlights. The Health Department targeted high-risk schools for violence prevention, and police mapped gang territory to identify areas of tension.[56] Alcoholic-beverage enforcement targeted liquor-store violations, and neighborhoods were targeted for street cleanup. All of these localized interventions came from the same data set that mapped crime, governmental services, and public infrastructure.[57]

Building from the data, the city launched a holistic strategy to address violence reduction focused on those who were identified as being most at risk. Some focused-deterrence policies were implemented with call-ins, "stop the shooting meetings," and police targeting of suspected offenders. Since 2013, a multiagency gang unit has indicted 110 targeted gang members.[58] But a host of other, non-law-enforcement social-services programs also were enacted (and funded). These programs included violence-reduction measures involving mediators, violence interrupters, community first responders, and other individuals who worked to defuse conflict and thus prevent retaliatory shootings. City officials also improved social-services programs addressing family violence, mentoring, fatherhood classes, behavioral interventions, and other mental and physical health concerns for those who were at risk. Programs focused on redirecting tension in public school by addressing trauma and on building restorative justice principles into discipline systems. All told, New Orleans adopted 29 different programs focusing on family, school, job training, reentry, and community and economic development.[59] The goal of all of the changes was to target those individuals most at risk of committing violence and then to provide alternatives, support, and an opportunity to change.

From 2011 to 2014, New Orleans saw a 21.9% reduction in homicide, a better statistic than could be found in similar big cities such as Baltimore, St. Louis, Newark, or Detroit.[60] More impressively, the city saw a 55% reduction in group or gang-involved murders.[61]

Targeting Bad Apples

In downtown Manhattan, an experimental prosecution unit has begun rethinking how to reduce violent crime. Under the leadership of district attorney Cyrus Vance Jr., the Manhattan District Attorney's Office created the Crime Strategies Unit (CSU) to target the bad apples in communities and take them out by any means necessary.[62] Call it the "Al Capone" approach to crime, only the targets are young men suspected of violence, not national mob bosses. Dubbed "intelligence-driven prosecution," police, prosecutors, and analysts target individuals for incapacitation and thus removal from problem areas of the city.[63]

Analytical and aggressive, CSU prosecutors build cases against the primary crime drivers in a neighborhood. First, crime data allows prosecutors to isolate high-violence areas for scrutiny. By crunching police crime data and mapping neighborhoods, prosecutors identify particular hot spots of violence. These areas become known as "Bureau Based Projects" (BBP).[64] A small team of prosecutors oversees each BBP and coordinates intelligence gathering in the area. These prosecutors work closely with the main CSU staff and may or may not take the cases that result from NYPD making arrests in the hot-spot areas. A "violence timeline" is created for each area, highlighting the past pattern of violence between groups, gangs, and individuals.[65] The timeline lists details of each shooting with suspects, victims, and facts, along with time, location, and date.

Second, as in Kansas City and Chicago, particular individuals are identified for police attention. Each BBP selects ten or so "priority targets"—"people whose incapacitation by the criminal justice system would have a positive impact on the community's safety and/or quality of life."[66] Field intelligence officers, detectives, and patrol officers help identify the priority targets for removal.[67] These individuals have at least five criminal convictions and a history of violence. Some have been uncooperative victims of past shootings. Others are associated with gangs or criminal groups. A "target tracker" of each young man populates the data system with photos, prior criminal history, and other personal information.[68] These individuals become the targets. Like Al Capone, who eventually faced prosecution for tax-evasion charges rather than the more violent crimes he engaged in, these priority targets do not have outstanding arrest warrants and cannot be arrested based on existing evidence.

Prosecutors input the names of priority targets into an "arrest alert system."[69] This arrest alert system then allows prosecutors to know if a target has been arrested. Routine fingerprinting keyed to a person's criminal history (rap sheet) triggers the alert. Under the old system, if a target got arrested for scalping Broadway tickets or simple assault (or some other minor offense), line prosecutors would have no way of knowing the level of threat posed by the individual. Now, alerts (usually an email) inform prosecutors throughout the office that a wanted target has entered the criminal justice system. The arrest alert system triggers a process whereby all the power of the prosecutors' office can be used to incapacitate the individual.[70] Enhanced bail applications can be used to argue for pretrial detention. Additional charges can be added to ratchet up pressure to plead guilty. Harsher sentencing recommendations can be sought to increase punishment. Even after sentencing, prosecutors are alerted to a defendant's release, so that the Manhattan parole system can monitor reentry back into society.

Data sharing also allows a more comprehensive intelligence-gathering operation. A new data system allows over 400 prosecutors to prosecute

85,000 cases a year.[71] Information about cases, suspects, neighborhoods, witnesses, gangs, nicknames, rivalries, crimes, tips, and a host of other data is coordinated through shared searchable databases. Prosecutors debrief individuals in the arrest alert system, looking for more information about networks of violence.[72] Photos of criminal associates, social media postings, and other tips become part of the data-collection system. NYPD police commissioner William Bratton called it a "seamless web" of shared data between police and prosecutors and termed the partnership one of "extreme collaboration."[73] Inspired by the sabermetrics approach to baseball and finance, Cy Vance Jr. likened it to a "Moneyball" approach to crime fighting.[74]

On a few occasions, this person-based targeting has led to large-scale arrests and prosecutions. Utilizing the intelligence-driven prosecution platform, the Manhattan District Attorney's Office has prosecuted several violent gangs in New York City. In one case, the District Attorney's Office in collaboration with the NYPD studied violence patterns, gang activity, and even social media before indicting 103 members of local crews.[75] In 2014, the prosecution of these youth gangs for homicides and shootings in West Harlem stood as the largest gang conspiracy indictment in New York City history.[76]

New York City has seen record low crime levels both before and after implementation of the intelligence-driven prosecution methods. Violence rates remain low in the targeted microareas, and shootings have dramatically declined. As a result of the initial success in Manhattan, the concept of intelligence-driven prosecution is being replicated across the country. In Baltimore, San Francisco, Philadelphia, Richmond, and Baton Rouge, intelligence-driven prosecution is using data to target the bad apples for removal from society.[77]

Theories of Predictive Targeting

The preceding examples show how person-based predictive targeting can work. Person-based predictive targeting builds off two foundational insights. First, by digitally mapping social networks of individuals, police can identify those most at risk to be involved in violence. Second, within those networks, a subpopulation can be algorithmically identified as being at even higher risk. By targeting those highest risk individuals—using either a public health approach or a prosecution approach—future criminal activities can be reduced.

Social network theory claims a long lineage of sociological research to back up its claims. From early experiments in Boston, Massachusetts, with the Boston Ceasefire Project, to modern Chicago, the idea that small, identifiable groups of people pose greater risk for violence than others has been well established.[78] One homicide study in Chicago found that "more than 40 percent of all gun homicides in the study occurred within a network of 3,100 people, roughly 4 percent of the community's population. Simply being among the 4 percent increased a person's odds of being killed by a gun by 900 percent."[79] Reasons for this heightened risk came from living in gang areas, associating with gangs, and being involved in drug-related criminal activities. Almost all of the individuals at highest risk were men. In Chicago, almost all were men of color.

As Andrew V. Papachristos has theorized, the key to gang violence is to understand the interaction between "the corner and the crew."[80] The corner is the part of the neighborhood that gangs protect. The crew is the young men who tended to act to defend themselves, their pride, or their territory.[81] Knowing the geographic friction between gangs and knowing the patterns of retaliatory action can allow police to understand the larger patterns of seemingly senseless violence.[82] When crunched into numbers, this understanding can lead to predictions of subgroups most at risk of harm.

Person-based predictive targeting takes this insight to the next level of granularity, drilling down to focus on particular risky individuals. Sociologists recognized that a violence-reduction strategy based on gang data could target individuals at a very micro level.

From [a violence reduction strategy (VRS)] perspective, going to the city's disadvantaged and high-crime communities to look for street gangs was not a focused strategy. Rather, VRS sought to use the available data to determine which individuals and which groups were involved in current and ongoing shootings to provide precise and strategic points of interventions. Thus, knowing that "gangs in Englewood" were fighting was insufficient. VRS wanted to know whether a dispute between the Disciples on 67th Street and a "renegade" set of Disciples from 71st Street was responsible for the violence. The entire premise of changing the street dynamics behind gun violence in Chicago is first to use data to determine the actors and disputes of said violence and then to bring the VRS message directly to those involved groups.[83]

Intervening before the 67th Street Disciples retaliated for an assault by the 71st Street Disciples could reduce crime. Designing custom notification letters that recognized not only a young man's connection with the 67th Street Disciples but also individual criminal history, social factors, and risk score made the entire data-driven enterprise very personal.

Person-based predictive targeting takes these insights and operationalizes them for police. Big data systems can crunch the wealth of accumulated data about criminal activity and prioritize who gets targeted. Lists can be generated for intervention, surveillance, or prosecution. Personalized dossiers can be created to monitor the most violent and dangerous people in a city, so that in any given jurisdiction, police can visualize the people driving crime and develop targeted strategies to intervene and disrupt them. This is the great promise of predictive policing—data can inform strategies to reduce violence in a more targeted and cost-efficient manner.

The open question is how to use the data. The Chicago RAND study suggests that the initial heat list did not adopt a true public health model but instead devolved into a most-wanted list for arrests.[84] Police administrators were not provided resources or even instruction about what to do with the people on the lists, and social services did not follow. A precise identification of the problem areas and people did little to stop the shootings because no resources or training had been provided about what to do next. In contrast, the more holistic project in New Orleans did much more than identify the high-risk people in a community. By using public data to address factors that created an environment for crime, the New Orleans project looked to widen the lens of big data technologies. Funding public resources to respond to the underlying economic and social problems appeared to offer more long-term solutions. Big data alone cannot stop the shooting without resources to address the underlying causes of violence.

Who Gets Targeted?

The question of who ends up on the heat list raises difficult questions about racial justice. Burglaries and car thefts may occur across the city (including in wealthy neighborhoods), but shootings cluster in poor neighborhoods. In Chicago and New York City, where poverty correlates with communities of color, predictive policing and intelligence-driven prosecution results in a focus on minorities.

Some of the reason for this racially disparate result is that young men of color constitute the vast majority of victims of violence.[85] The shooting deaths in Chicago and New York involve African American and Latino men, gang members, and the innocent residents of the inner city, all of whom belong to poor communities of color. But another reason involves the disproportionate police contact that permeates life in major urban cities.[86] While race would never be included as part of the algorithm, many of the variables (police contacts, prior arrests, gang affiliations) directly correlate with racially discriminatory law enforcement practices. If the data is colored black, it means that the predictive policing systems (using that data) could generate biased results.

So the question arises about how to disentangle legacy police practices that have resulted in disproportionate numbers of African American men being arrested or involved in the criminal justice system. As civil liberties lawyer Hanni Fakhoury stated, the concern is that the data-collection process reifies bias:

> It ends up being a self-fulfilling prophecy. . . . The algorithm is telling you exactly what you programmed it to tell you. "Young black kids in the south side of Chicago are more likely to commit crimes," and the algorithm lets the police launder this belief. It's not racism, they can say. They are making the decision based on what the algorithm is, even though the algorithm is going to spit back what you put into it. And if the data is biased to begin with and based on human judgment, then the results the algorithm is going to spit out will reflect those biases.[87]

Again, if input data is infected with racial bias, how can the resulting algorithmic output be trusted?

Interconnected racial realities result in a criminal justice system that arrests, prosecutes, and incarcerates more people of color than a race-blind system should. One ACLU study showed that despite equivalent rates of marijuana use by all races, African Americans were 3.73 times more likely to be arrested for marijuana possession than whites were.[88] In some states, that figure went up to 8.34 times.[89] The same study reported that "92% of marijuana possession arrests in Baltimore City, MD, were of Blacks; 87% in Fulton, GA (includes Atlanta); 85% in Prince George's, MD; 83% in Shelby, TN (includes Memphis); and 82% in Philadelphia, PA."[90] Another study, conducted by the Vera Institute in New Orleans, showed that over a five-year period, African Americans accounted for 94% of the felony marijuana arrests and 85% of the overall marijuana arrests despite constituting only 58.5% of the population.[91]

Recent statistics from the Sentencing Project's 2016 report *The Color of Justice* demonstrate continued racial disparity in stark terms:

- African Americans are incarcerated in state prisons at a rate that is 5.1 times the imprisonment of whites. In five states (Iowa, Minnesota, New Jersey, Vermont, and Wisconsin), the disparity is more than 10 to 1.
- In twelve states, more than half of the prison population is black: Alabama, Delaware, Georgia, Illinois, Louisiana, Maryland, Michigan, Mississippi, New Jersey, North Carolina, South Carolina, and Virginia. Maryland, whose prison population is 72% African American, tops the nation.
- In eleven states, at least 1 in 20 adult black males is in prison. . . .
- Latinos are imprisoned at a rate that is 1.4 times the rate of whites.[92]

Such disproportionate minority contact with the criminal justice system seeds the algorithms that generate heat-list-inspired predictive models. If prior convictions count as objective factors for dangerousness, then these statistics matter not just for past crime but for future predictions.

The same is true for predictive systems reliant on arrests or police contacts. For decades, studies in states as diverse as West Virginia, Illinois, Minnesota, and Texas have demonstrated that racial bias impacts policing discretion.[93] Traffic stops, pedestrian stops, and police contacts all fall on communities of color harder than on whites.[94] This is true even though less contraband is found on persons of color than on whites. In one Minnesota study, the hit rate for whites who were stopped and searched by police was 23.53%, but the rate was only 11.17% for African Americans.[95] In West Virginia, African Americans and Latinos are 1.5 times more likely to be stopped and 2.5 times more likely to be searched than whites, despite being less likely to have contraband.[96] If criminal justice contacts count as inputs in the risk model, then the same disproportionate impact will be observed in output data. In fact, those discriminatory data patterns will train the algorithms for future predictions, further obscuring the underlying bias.

Race distorts judgment. Recent studies into implicit bias confirm that the result does not come from explicit racial animus but deepseeded, unconscious, implicit associations that cause people of color to be viewed more suspiciously than whites are.[97] Implicit-bias studies have demonstrated that all people, of all races and education levels, share implicit associations of groups and that these unconscious influences shape decision making and judgment calls.[98] Police officers—of all races—share these human frailties and, thus, largely unknowingly replicate racial inequities in policing. This implicit bias shapes the raw material entering predictive systems and, thus, determines who gets targeted.

The same type of misjudgment holds true for gang identification, another critical input for algorithmic police targeting. Going to school with a gang member or being the cousin of a gang member or being "an associate" of a gang member remains an easily permeable distinction. If that connection results in being labeled a gang member in a gang database, such an error can have negative impacts on otherwise-law-abiding citizens. In a news story about the heat list, one Chicago police lieutenant described his discomfort upon learning that his own son had been mistakenly labeled a gang member by the police.[99] The California state auditor found the CalGang database to be filled with errors including identifying 42 infants as gang members.[100] The state auditor found systemic failures in the way gangs and gang members were identified, as well as weaknesses in training, policies, accountability, and security of the data.[101]

Predictive targeting, thus, raises the fundamental question of whether such algorithmic risk assessments can avoid being racially discriminatory. Studies of other criminal justice risk-assessment models provide little comfort. Investigative reporters at ProPublica examined pretrial risk-assessment scores for arrestees in Florida to see whether racial bias infected the algorithms.[102] Risk-assessment scores have become a common tool to help judges determine who should or should not be released from custody pending trial. A high risk score makes it more likely that a judge will hold the defendant in jail without bond.[103] A low score makes it more likely that the defendant will be released. Like person-based predictive targeting, the inputs include socioeconomic factors that correlate with structural racism and poverty.

The ProPublica investigators reviewed more than 7,000 risk scores in Broward County, Florida, in 2013–14 and compared them with actual outcomes two years later.[104] The goal was to see if a predicted outcome (for example, high risk of recidivism) accurately predicted whether the person would reoffend (be rearrested within two years). The risk assessments largely failed. For violent crime, only 20% of the people deemed "high risk for reoffending" did so, although for nonviolent crime, the arrest rate rose to 61%.[105]

More troublingly, however, the algorithm falsely assessed African American defendants as high risk at almost twice the rate as whites.[106] Conversely, white defendants were also deemed low risk more than African Americans were. The reason for this racial discrepancy involves the raw data going into the model. In Broward County, a series of "criminogenic needs" were assessed. These needs involved judgments about criminal personality, substance abuse, social isolation, and stability, as well as questions about whether the subject had parents in jail or prison or friends who use drugs or whether the subject got into fights in school.[107] The questions—which made up the data points for risk—while explicitly designed not to focus on race, encompassed socioeconomic risk factors that correlated with structural poverty, unemployment, and instability. So, as the ProPublica article details, an unemployed 18-year-old African American woman with no prior record (but an unstable family situation) might rate as a higher risk than an older white man with a job, despite the fact that the older man had several prior criminal convictions.[108] In that case, and in others, the risk-assessment prediction got the outcome wrong.

Yet this criticism of risk assessments has itself been criticized.[109] One academic study showed that while the ProPublica article exposed anecdotal inequities, its larger conclusions resulted from methodological flaws.[110] Using the same data, these researchers showed that the risk-assessment mechanisms themselves did not show predictive bias by race. As a pure mathematical test, no evidence of bias was found in the algorithm itself.[111] White or black, people with the same risk factors received similar risk scores. Yet the difficulty is that the data going into the system reflected existing societal inequities and bias. As Anthony Flores, a criminologist and author of the critical study, stated, "Perhaps, what looks to be bias is not in the tool—it's in the system."[112] So, while the risk-assessment instrument might not itself be racially biased, the data going into the algorithm might still replicate existing societal racial inequities, creating a disparate outcome.

Sonja Starr has forcefully challenged the growing reliance on risk assessments used for sentencing, finding fault with any use of "demographic, socioeconomic, family, and neighborhood variables to determine whether and for how long a defendant is incarcerated."[113] As she wrote in an important law review article challenging what has come to be known as evidence-based sentencing,

> The technocratic framing of [evidence-based sentencing] should not obscure an inescapable truth: sentencing based on such instruments amounts to overt discrimination based on demographics and socioeconomic status. . . .
> . . . The use of these and other variables, such as family and neighborhood characteristics, is also troubling on policy grounds. Equal treatment of all persons is a central objective of the criminal justice system, and [evidence-based sentencing] as currently practiced may have serious social consequences. It can be expected to contribute to the concentration of the criminal justice system's punitive impact among those who already disproportionately bear its brunt, including people of color. And the expressive message of this approach to sentencing is, when stripped of the anodyne scientific language, toxic. Group-based generalizations about dangerousness have an insidious history in our culture, and the express embrace of additional punishment for the poor conveys the message that the system is rigged.[114]

Evidence-based or risk-based or data-based criminal justice systems all share the same underlying bias problem. Relying on socioeconomic variables in a jurisdiction where socioeconomic conditions correlate with race will lead to a racially discriminatory result, even without any discriminatory intent.

Big Data Blacklisting

The concern that person-based big data analytics might contribute to false-positive stops, investigations, and arrests has made many people wary of the technology. Accurate "black box" targeting is unsettling. Inaccurate "black box" targeting is terrifying. Police data remains rife with error, and adding predictive analytics to faulty data can only exacerbate the fear. Like Robert McDaniel or the Chicago police lieutenant's son, people will be placed on these target lists erroneously.

Any discussion of the impact of big data policing must confront data error.[115] Data-quality problems plague all data-driven systems, and police systems are no different.[116] In fact, because of the volume of data coming in, the complexity, and the lack of resources to cleanse or correct mistakes, these systems are more likely to contain mistakes. Even the FBI's arrest records, which are routinely used for background checks, contain hundreds of thousands of mistakes.[117] Supreme Court justice Ruth Bader Ginsburg warned of the danger arising from reliance on expanding police electronic databases:

> Electronic databases form the nervous system of contemporary criminal justice operations. In recent years, their breadth and influence have dramatically expanded. Police today can access databases that include not only the updated National Crime Information Center (NCIC), but also terrorist watchlists, the Federal Government's employee eligibility system, and various commercial databases. Moreover, States are actively expanding information sharing between jurisdictions. As a result, law enforcement has an increasing supply of information within its easy electronic reach.
>
> The risk of error stemming from these databases is not slim. Government reports describe, for example, flaws in NCIC databases, terrorist watchlist databases, and databases associated with the Federal Government's employment eligibility verification system.

Inaccuracies in expansive, interconnected collections of electronic information raise grave concerns for individual liberty. The offense to the dignity of the citizen who is arrested, handcuffed, and searched on a public street simply because some bureaucrat has failed to maintain an accurate computer data base is evocative of the use of general warrants that so outraged the authors of our Bill of Rights.[118]

Individuals targeted because of police error will find it difficult to challenge the mistake, because currently the law makes it extremely hard to correct negligent record-keeping errors.[119] Worse, because of the secrecy of police databases, no independent auditing system exists to challenge their accuracy. The lack of transparency directly hinders attempts at accountability.

Fairness matters. Government decision making without fairness or accountability strikes at the core of due process protections. If the government wishes to deprive us of life, liberty, or property, fair process is due.[120] And this process usually requires notice of the deprivation and an opportunity to challenge the deprivation. In the context of who gets placed on police lists, such notice and opportunity remains absent. Although the knock on the door will let you know you made the heat list, there is no prior announcement or ability to challenge the designation. In many jurisdictions, the process of being put on a target list is decidedly unadversarial and largely secret.

Secretive databases and watchlists impact daily life. In the national security context, with the growth of the "No Fly List" or the "Terrorist Watch List" for airplanes, Americans have grown rather immune to such designations.[121] Despite the stigma or practical frustration or demonstrated errors in these target lists, they keep expanding. Scholars such as Margaret Hu have termed the process "big data blacklisting" and written about the due process limitations of the current practice.[122] How do you get off a secret list you did not know you were on? How do you challenge a list when you cannot know the criteria? Who can challenge? Who will pay for the challenge? How do you ensure transparency and accountability with opaque data-driven systems? Currently the mechanisms to get off the lists range from onerous and expensive to nonexistent.[123] Yet, even in the face of these concerns, a data-driven policing world has emerged, and these lists have become more, not less, important.

Big Data Suspicion

Beyond bias and error, person-based predictive targeting also alters the legal system in which police operate. Big data technologies distort traditional Fourth Amendment rules that protect citizens against unreasonable searches and seizures by law enforcement.[124]

Police operate within an established constitutional system. In order to seize a person on the street, police need "reasonable suspicion" that the suspect is involved in a crime.[125] Reasonable suspicion has been defined as "specific and articulable facts that taken with rational inferences of those facts warrant the belief that criminal activity is afoot."[126] In other words, police need something more than a hunch to prove that an individual is currently engaged in criminal activity. In order to arrest a suspect, police need "probable cause."[127] This Fourth Amendment requirement demands a higher standard of proof that gives more certainty (a fair probability) that the individual did in fact commit a crime or is currently committing a crime.

For decades, police officers in large urban jurisdictions patrolled the streets looking for criminal activities. Did someone look suspicious? Did the officer see a drug deal? What did the officer see after the report of a crime? Police used observational skills coupled with practical experience to make judgments about a suspect. Because police did not know all of the people who lived on their beat, most policing focused on criminal acts, not the criminals themselves. This type of policing is quintessential "small data" policing.[128] The facts are limited to the observational data points of human senses and perception. Police know what they see but not much more. Suspicion arises from individual officers' intuition and experience about what they observed.

The Supreme Court case that created the reasonable suspicion standard provides an illustrative example of small data policing in action. *Terry v. Ohio* involved the observation of officer Martin McFadden, a 39-year veteran of the Cleveland Police Department.[129] McFadden specialized in stopping shoplifters and others who committed crimes in downtown Cleveland. One afternoon, McFadden observed three men outside a jewelry store. McFadden did not know the men and had no prior reason to suspect them. He watched as the men walked past the jewelry store. Two of the men broke off and made another pass. They circled back to the third man. The pattern repeated several more times. At that moment, McFadden had a dilemma. He thought the men were up to no good. McFadden believed the men were casing the jewelry store in order to rob it, but he did not have probable cause to arrest them. Probable cause of acting suspicious around a store is not good enough to make an arrest.[130]

The question of reasonable suspicion presented a closer question. There had been no report of a crime against the jewelry store, and there existed dozens of innocent explanations for the men's actions. But Officer McFadden, solely on the basis of his observational data, became suspicious. McFadden approached the men, immediately searched them, and recovered a handgun from a man named John Terry.[131] Terry was arrested and charged with possession of the gun but not charged with any attempted robbery. The question for the Supreme Court was whether McFadden had enough suspicious information to stop and frisk Terry and thus invade his Fourth Amendment rights.[132] After all, Terry was physically seized and searched and had his property taken. If McFadden did not have sufficient information, the court would find the Fourth Amendment violated, and evidence about the recovered gun would be excluded from the case. With no evidence of the existence of the gun, the prosecution would be unable to prosecute Terry on possession of the firearm.

The Supreme Court decided that McFadden had constitutionally sufficient information—based on his observations and experience—to seize and then frisk Terry for weapons.[133] The Supreme Court held that looking at the "totality of circumstances," McFadden had reasonable suspicion to stop and frisk Terry. But in a world of small data—of only observational data—one can see how difficult the judgment might be for police on a daily basis. What if McFadden had seen the men walk past the store only twice? What if Terry had a shopping bag? Or a tourist map? Almost every police patrol presents similar judgment calls about unknown suspects. Police do not know much about the person they are observing before they make the stop. And after *Terry v. Ohio*, tens of thousands of cases asked that same question of whether police had reasonable suspicion to stop a suspect.

But what if John Terry were on the heat list?[134] What if he had been previously identified by a big data algorithm as one of the top potential offenders in the city? What if he was a CSU priority target? Suddenly the justification to stop seems much easier. Now Officer McFadden has specific, individualized, and articulable facts to justify a stop of this potentially violent individual. If McFadden were pressed by a court to justify his actions, he could easily explain that statistically speaking, people on the heat list are more likely to be involved in violence. But note that factually (or observationally), Terry has not done anything more or less suspicious. Terry's actions—criminal or innocent—were exactly the same, but the information about him as a person has changed the suspicion calculus.

Or skip into the near future and imagine that police have access through facial-recognition software and a police database to inform them that John Terry has several prior arrests, a conviction, and a substance-abuse problem. Or take one more step and imagine that through social network analysis, Terry could be directly connected with one of the city's current mob bosses, who is known for violence and wanted for murder. These facts (all interestingly enough true of the real John Terry but unknown to Officer McFadden) make it that much easier for police to justify suspicion. With a quick computer search in a patrol car, modern McFaddens can develop additional information about suspects to justify their suspicion. Again, the individual on the street has done nothing different, but the big data information has changed his constitutional protections.

Police suspicion can, thus, be altered by big data. Computer algorithms targeting individuals for high risk of violence, in turn, can provide justification for a stop or frisk. As discussed, in Chicago, 1,400 individuals are on that target list. In New Orleans, it is double that number. When prosecutors become involved by creating target lists in a community, the ease of justifying stops for investigative purposes will only grow. While it is likely that a court would reject the argument that one's mere inclusion on a heat list alone could justify a stop, not much more is needed to develop reasonable suspicion.

The point is that doctrines like reasonable suspicion that came of age in a small data world become distorted by big data.[135] With enough personal information about a person, police can create all sorts of suspicious links. Take a predicted area of crime, add a friendship with someone in a gang, and include a few prior police contacts in a heavily policed community, and suddenly a very ordinary young man walking home could be subjected to a stop on the basis of the confluence that he was in a high-crime area, was a known associate with a gang member, and had prior run-ins with the police. All the young man did was walk home, but the information around him created the suspicion. This should not constitutionally be enough, but the Fourth Amendment protections fade in the darkness of the data.

Big data targeting can distort reasonable suspicion. Worse, it can lower the level of suspicion for reasons that are correlated with race and class.[136] Individuals who live in high-crime areas or who have repeated contacts with police may increasingly be linked with others who have been targeted for increased police attention. This may fuel distorting cycles of explicit or implicit bias, whereby police will associate linked people as criminal actors even though the correlation is weak or really the result of environmental factors like neighborhood, family, or friend group.

On the other hand, big data suspicion offers certain advantages that traditional, small data policing strategies lack. First, the individualized nature of the suspicion provides a level of accuracy that police do not normally possess.[137] If police can obtain information about a suspect's prior record before the stop, this might assist in distinguishing between dangerous and nondangerous people. It might also distinguish between guilty and innocent people. If, for example, Officer McFadden ran John Terry's name through the system and found he had no prior record and was employed in the area, this might reduce the suspicion. Instead of using rough proxies of race, age, gender, and clothing, police could figure out exactly who the person is before the stop.[138] While nonviolent, employed, conviction-less people can commit crimes just as much as violent, unemployed felons, the information would be helpful to sort through suspicion and perceived level of danger. In fact, many unpleasant face-to-face contacts could be avoided if police could know something about the person they are observing before initiating contact. In a future big data world, police even might be required to check for exculpatory information before making a suspicion-based stop.

Accuracy of information strengthens the legitimacy of the police stop. It also adds a measure of accountability because the big data information will be available for courts to check after the fact.[139] If Officer McFadden explains to a judge that he observed John Terry and conducted a big a search for further information, all of that information will be available to double check. A judge could see if the facts supported suspicion or were exculpatory in nature. Lawyers could assess the documented—data-driven—record for the suspicion that generated the stop.

Finally, there is the simple argument of efficiency. With dwindling resources and more responsibilities, police need to figure out how best to use their time. If big data can sort the riskier people from the less risky people, then a measure of efficiency is gained. While one can never forget the liberty interests behind the police investigation, the ability to prioritize whom to target in an intelligent manner makes a tempting technological tool for investigation.

How Big Data Impacts Whom We Police

The idea behind person-based targeting is both old and new. Police have always known the bad apples in a community. Prosecutors have regularly targeted them. Yet a policing philosophy that uses data and predictive analytics to prioritize the crime drivers in a society signifies a new approach. Four main changes emerge from these technologies—insights that will shape the future of who gets targeted.

First, proactively targeting violent social networks will change how local police respond to crime. Traditionally, local police might react to calls for service, rely on observations on patrol, or respond to community complaints. With person-based predictive targeting, police can instead target suspects for surveillance or deterrence before needing to respond to a call. For local prosecutors, this represents a significant change.[140] As the former head of the Manhattan Criminal Strategies Unit stated, "It used to be we only went where the cases took us. Now, we can build cases around specific crime problems that communities are grappling with."[141] Big data policing makes police more proactive. In many ways, intelligence-driven prosecution and policing at the local level are really just mirroring some of the approaches federal investigators and federal prosecutors have used for years. While the FBI and U.S. Attorneys regularly investigate completed crimes, they also focus on surveillance and investigation of criminal networks to prevent or disrupt future crime. For local police, the study of gang networks means a similar change from reactive policing to proactive policing.

Second, the idea of viewing violence as a public health problem, as opposed to a pure law enforcement problem, opens up new opportunities to rethink how best to identify and respond to criminal risk. The idea that violence is contagious suggests that violence can be prevented. If a good percentage of shootings are retaliatory, then one can design a cure to interrupt the cycles of violence.[142] Medical science has changed our understanding of the risks of smoking cigarettes, such that lung cancer is no longer thought of as an unfortunate or random occurrence but one that can be linked to particular environmental risks. Address the root causes by changing the environment (stop smoking), and you lower the risk of getting cancer. So too with violence: seeing the environmental factors of negative social pressures in certain communities suggests targeted remedies to remove those pressures. The violence-reduction strategies designed by those who studied shootings in New Orleans explicitly adopted social-services programs as part of the model. At the table of every heat-list "call-in" should be community social-services representatives actually ready to help. The idea is to offer opportunities for young men and women to change their environment and thus reduce the risk.

Third, moving from traditional policing to intelligence-led policing creates data-quality risks that need to be systemically addressed. Intelligence-driven systems work off many bits of local intelligence.[143] Tips, crime statistics, cooperating witnesses, nicknames, and detective notes can get aggregated into a large working data system. Yet the quality of the data is not uniform. Some tips are accurate, and some are not. Some biases will generate suspicion, and some informants will just be wrong. An intelligence-driven policing or prosecution system that does not account for the varying reliability and credibility of sources and just lumps them all together in the name of data collection will ultimately fail. Just as national security intelligence agencies have layers of intelligence analysts to examine incoming information, so police departments must develop similar structures to vet this intelligence-like data.[144] Blind data collection without information about sources, reliability, or testability will result in an error-filled database. Systems must be designed—before adopting data-driven technologies—to source, catalogue, and make the information useful for officers. Especially when these systems are used to target citizens for arrest or prosecution, the quality-control measures of black-box algorithms must be strong.

Other data-integrity concerns may arise when detectives, gang experts, or police intelligence officers control the target lists. While these professionals have close connections to the community and valuable knowledge of local gangs and potential targets, the ability for risk scores to be manipulated by police interested in prosecuting certain individuals opens up questions of the objectivity and fairness of the lists. If a gang detective can put someone on the list and there is no process to change or challenge the list, the system could be abused. If there is one thing that has been demonstrated regularly with the proliferation of gang databases, these lists are rife with errors. After all, without formal criteria to be a member of a gang, rumor, assumptions, or suspicion can be enough to be labeled part of a gang and thus result in an elevated risk score. Worse, there is usually no easy way to get off the list, despite the fact that circumstances change, time passes, and the data grows stale.

Finally, big data policing may distort traditional roles of prosecutors and police officers. Prosecutors seeking to incapacitate individuals on their "priority target" list can bump against ethical lines.[145] During a training on intelligence-driven prosecution, one supervising prosecutor spoke of a case involving a young man (a priority target) running toward a street fight holding a lock in a bandana. While the man was likely up to no good, holding a lock in a bandana is not necessarily a crime. But prosecutors chose to charge the man with carrying a dangerous weapon with the intent to use it (despite equivocal evidence of intent).[146] Such a serious criminal charge might not have been pursued if the suspect had not been on the priority target list and may not even be supported by the facts. But when incapacitation is the goal, the prosecutor's power to use charging, sentencing, and bail determinations aggressively can distort the traditional focus of the prosecutor. Such a distortion is not necessarily bad. If the prosecutor was correct and the priority target was a violent risk to the community, maybe such aggressive predictive prosecution makes good sense. But if this type of human targeting is inaccurate and if it is misused or even if it is unchecked, it can be damaging to the perception of fairness in the justice system.

Similar distortions occur when police officers are provided information about who is on the heat list. Such information offers premade suspicion to justify stops. Predictive information may influence officers to police the list rather than to police the community. In addition to lowering the constitutional bar to conduct stops, issues of racial bias and transparency arise from this practice. Under the current heat list, men, primarily men of color who have no ability to see or challenge the designation, will be impacted. This reality raises serious constitutional concerns and threatens to delegitimize the entire person-based predictive policing strategy. These concerns only grow when place-based predictive technologies are overlaid onto policing practices. This is the subject of the next chapter.

4

Where We Police

Place-Based Predictive Policing

This is not *Minority Report.* . . . *Minority Report* is about predicting who will commit a crime before they commit it. This
is about predicting where and when crime is most likely to
occur, not who will commit it.
—Jeffrey Brantingham[1]

Cloudy with a Chance of Murder

Small red boxes dot a computer-generated map. These little boxes represent an algorithmic forecast of future crime: years of criminal activity
catalogued and crunched to divine a pattern of how crime works. Each
red box is an elevated chance of burglary, car theft, or theft from an
automobile.[2]

Police commanders hand out printed maps at roll call. Squad-car
computers electronically direct police toward the hot spots. Every police
shift, the boxes recalibrate, and every day, new data displays new probabilities. Police officers drive through the predicted areas during lulls
in their routine patrols.[3] The goal: "to deter and protect"—to disrupt
the predicted crime by putting police at the right place before the crime
occurs. In big cities like New York, Los Angeles, Miami, Atlanta, and
Seattle and in dozens of smaller cities, this idea of "predictive policing"
is shaping patrol routes and police routines.[4]

What is place-based predictive policing? Predictive policing involves
a data-driven approach to identifying criminal patterns in specific geographic locations and deploying police resources to remedy those risks.
Did burglaries spike in one neighborhood? The computer algorithm will
crunch the numbers to forecast other likely burglaries nearby. In fact,
the computer will provide predicted areas of heightened crime throughout the city. Other factors can be layered into the computer model. Fri-

day means payday, which correlates with an elevated risk of robberies around check-cashing stores. Sunday hosts a football game, which might generate a risk of car thefts around the stadium but a lower robbery rate during the hours of the game. If it rains, cancel the crime risk: bad guys don't like getting wet.

While these crime patterns intuitively may be known by police officers, now with advanced data analytics, years' worth of crime patterns can be studied, mapped, and proactively deployed.[5] Volumes of crime data, logged every day, on every reported crime, in all parts of the city, get fed into algorithms that shape this data, carving out certain hot spots for additional scrutiny. Then, police officers patrol those blocks looking to prevent the predicted crime or catch the unsuspecting criminal in the act.

This chapter explores the promise and problems of place-based predictive policing. "Where we police" impacts issues of race, community relations, and constitutional law. Utilizing big data's forecasts may provide efficiencies and crime reduction, but it also may change how those areas are policed.

A Computer-Generated Hunch

St. Louis, Missouri, a year after the Michael Brown protests in Ferguson, Missouri: As a partial response, neighboring police districts adopt a predictive policing strategy to prioritize resources and professionalize patrols. In partnership with a small Philadelphia-based start-up company called Azavea, the Jennings Police Department, in Jennings, Missouri, began experimenting with a predictive policing program called "HunchLab."[6]

The HunchLab model inputs crime data, census data, and population density and adds in other variables like the location of schools, churches, bars, clubs, and transportation centers. The algorithm then crunches the collected crime data, resulting in a constantly updated risk map of the area.[7] Color coded by crime, statistically grounded, and visually striking, the model spits out percentages of likely criminal activity. An officer on patrol can see that he or she is transitioning from a high-gun-crime area to a high-residential-burglary area by following the colors on the screen.

As detailed in an investigation by the Marshall Project, these predictive patrols have direct impacts on the police and those who are being patrolled.[8] On a December day, officer Thomas Kenner begins a routine patrol with HunchLab as his partner. Familiar with the area and its crime problems, he recognizes the reason behind one of the shaded-green predicted larceny boxes. He drives past some discount stores in a poor neighborhood that, like many neighborhoods, has a shoplifting problem. Discount stores plus poverty equals an elevated theft risk. This is not rocket science, nor is it wrong. The data confirms what the officer already knows.[9]

Officer Kenner next drives near to a spot on the map with another color-coded box, this one shaded to signify a higher risk of aggravated assaults. A white Chevy Impala with dark-tinted windows drives toward the shaded area, and Officer Kenner pulls the car over to investigate. By law, the tinted windows are dark enough to justify a traffic ticket, but this stop is not about the tints. The driver, a young African American man, is questioned by the officer. The traffic-stop investigation leads to the smell of marijuana and the recovery of a handgun in the car. No actual drugs are found, though the man admits to having smoked pot in the recent past. The gun is legal, and because possession of a handgun is not a crime in Missouri, after a full search, the stopped driver is allowed to go.[10]

This is the reality of place-based predictive policing. Would Officer Kenner have stopped the car without the HunchLab prediction? He had the legal power, but would he have made the decision without the predictive tip? Was this an accurate predictive hit or a false stop? A justified search or a pretextual inconvenience? Is such machine-generated suspicion any better or worse than the petty indignities that led to the Ferguson protests and the DOJ investigation? And how did the fact that this box was predicted to be an area for aggravated assault actually impact the officer's thinking? All the officer initially observed was a tint violation near an area known for aggravated assaults. As Kenner explained to the Marshall Project's reporter Maurice Chammah, "He could have been going to shoot somebody. Or not."[11]

Such is the nature of prediction: It could be the future. Or not.

A Seismic Insight

In an academic office at the campus of the University of California–Los Angeles (UCLA), Jeff Brantingham studies hunter-gatherers using computer models. An anthropologist by training, he has written articles on a variety of subjects, with such titles as "Speculation on the Timing and Nature of Late Pleistocene Hunter-Gatherer Colonization of the Tibetan Plateau" and "Nonlinear Dynamics of Crime and Violence in Urban Settings."[12] The connecting thread of his work is the ability to map dynamic patterns of human action using mathematical models. Today's criminals are just different types of hunter-gatherers—instead of animals, they hunt victims.[13]

The son of two renowned environmental criminologists, Brantingham turned the insight that environments amplify criminal risk into a multimillion-dollar business venture. It is called PredPol (short for "predictive policing"), and it has become a national leader in place-based predictive policing technology.[14] With the help of George Mohler, Andrea Bertozzi, Martin Short, and George Tita, Brantingham began studying whether certain place-based crimes—primarily residential burglary, automobile theft, and theft from automobiles—might be predictable.[15] Using an algorithm originally developed to measure seismic aftershocks from earthquakes, the researchers discovered that crime followed similar patterns.[16] A burglary in one neighborhood might trigger a second or third burglary in that same area close in time. A car theft from one parking lot would trigger others. Crime, it seemed, could be visualized as having ripple-like effects, and once identified, this pattern could be mapped and forecast.

The insight that certain crimes have contagious qualities is not new and, in fact, has deep support in criminology theory. Studies have repeatedly shown that certain place-based crimes like burglary encourage other like-minded crimes.[17] The reason is not terribly sophisticated. Criminals are creatures of habit and tend to keep working where there are few police and fewer chances of getting caught. If a particular home was broken into, and homes in the neighborhood are all built the same, then why not keep going back until the risk of getting caught increases? As Shane Johnson explained, "Having targeted a particular home for the first time, a burglar acquires knowledge to inform future targeting decisions. This may concern the internal layout of a burgled property, the ease of access and escape, the products that may be found were the offender to return, the risks of identification, and so on. This knowledge is likely to reduce uncertainty about nearby homes."[18]

Over the years, criminologists have differed as to the underlying reason for this phenomenon, but the "near repeat" effect, as it is known, is generally accepted.[19] There is something about the initial successful crime that either flags the area for other criminals or boosts the chances of a similar crime happening close in time to the original crime.[20] In one international study, a statistically significant increase in burglaries could be observed in different countries under very different environmental and cultural circumstances.[21] In another study, researchers found that 76% of interviewed burglars tended to keep going back to the same area (sometimes the same house) until caught.[22]

Place-based policing strategies evolved from place-based criminology theory.[23] For decades, social science research has influenced the development of hot-spot policing, problem-oriented policing, and even broken-window policing, all targeting the physical places where crime has occurred. Building off these strategies and the already well-established techniques of using computers to map "hot spots" of crime, Brantingham and his colleagues used data collection of crime statistics to operationalize these theories. Crime patterns in any city could be mapped, visualized, and with the help of an aftershock algorithm, forecast on a daily basis.

This initial academic insight turned into a real-life pilot project with the Los Angeles Police Department (LAPD). With the encouragement of then-chief William Bratton and then-captain Sean Malinowski, the Foothill Division of the LAPD began testing whether predictive policing could work in the real world.[24] A project was designed to test whether Brantingham's algorithm could reduce property crime (again focused on burglary, automobile theft, and theft from automobiles). Targeted areas, usually limited to 500-by-500-square-foot boxes, were identified around the Foothill Division north of downtown Los Angeles.[25] Officers had instructions to patrol those areas when not responding to calls for service or handling other priorities. The expressed goal was to be a deterrent—a presence of police authority to discourage the "near repeat" temptation. An initial pilot project in 2011 showed a 25% reduction in burglaries,[26] and other targeted crimes also dropped. Suddenly, the idea that a computer algorithm could predict and prevent crime became a national phenomenon.

Almost overnight, predictive policing went from an idea to a reality and then to a for-profit company. *Time* magazine heralded predictive policing as one of the top-50 best inventions of the year.[27] The Department of Justice invested millions of dollars in grants to fund studies.[28] Smaller cities like Santa Cruz, California, promoted the technology,[29] and Norcross, Georgia, made headlines because on the very first day of rolling out PredPol, officers made a burglary arrest in a precisely predicted burglary box.[30] News stories in the *New York Times* and other major national and international publications drew increased media attention,[31] and PredPol began heavily marketing the idea that targeted, place-based crime technology was the "must have" resource for modern police departments.

Today, several dozen cities are using some form of predictive policing technology.[32] PredPol, which limits its data inputs to crime type, location, and time of offense, takes a minimalist approach to data variables.[33] PredPol also limits predictions to quite small geographical areas (500 by 500 square feet), which change daily depending on the data. Other companies have adopted more complex approaches with the same basic goal: map crime patterns using predictive data systems in an effort to reduce the risk of crime.

Risk Terrain Modeling

What makes an area vulnerable to crime? What drives up risk? Joel Caplan and Les Kennedy at Rutgers University have used data to identify environmental crime drivers. The method is called "risk terrain modeling" (RTM), and the key is to study the overlapping spatial dynamics of environmental risks (in other words, why certain areas attract crime).[34] In a recent national study, examining five diverse jurisdictions with very different crime problems, the RTM approach isolated environmental risk factors and then partnered with police to create specific solutions to remedy those risks.[35]

Colorado Springs, Colorado, has a car-theft problem. In certain areas of that city, the likelihood of having your car stolen is 48 times greater than in other places. But how do you identify those places? The risk terrain model identified six overlapping risk factors that could identify the area in which your car was most likely to be stolen. In Colorado Springs, the risk factors included (1) calls for service about disorder, (2) foreclosures, (3) multifamily housing units, (4) parks, (5) sit-down restaurants, and (6) commercial zoning. By mapping the location of risk factors and where the risk factors overlapped, RTM could isolate 4% of the geographic area as having the highest risk for car theft.[36] But why?

The answer lies in the physical, environmental reality of crime. In general, multifamily housing units have large parking lots, so that one's car is parked at a distance not visible to the apartment. On cold Colorado mornings, people would run unattended cars to warm them up. These "puffers," as the police called them, became tempting targets for car theft, especially near parks or foreclosed homes that allowed cover to wait for the right opportunity.[37] Sit-down restaurants (as opposed to fast-food restaurants) offer similar temptations of unattended cars at a distance from the owner. Limited visual surveillance of the parking lot plus a set time with the car unattended resulted in an uptick of theft. Once the predicted areas were identified, police targeted them with additional code enforcement for property inspections, proactive targeting of disorder crimes, traffic enforcement, and the deployment of license-plate-recognition technology to track stolen cars. Compared to the control area, the RTM target area utilizing risk-reduction strategies saw a 33% reduction of car thefts.[38]

Newark, New Jersey, has a gun problem. Young men are shooting and killing each other at disturbingly high rates. But the locations of the shootings are not evenly distributed, such that the highest risk areas have a 58 times greater likelihood of crime than some other locations.[39] And those areas are only 5% of the Newark area.[40] So how do you find out which areas are the most likely to be locations of future shootings? The risk terrain model isolated 11 factors: (1) narcotics arrests, (2) foreclosures, (3) restaurants, (4) gas stations, (5) convenience stores, (6) take-out restaurants, (7) bars, (8) abandoned properties, (9) schools, (10) liquor stores, and (11) certain kinds of housing.[41] As these risk factors were analytically laid atop each other on a risk terrain map, the risk grew that a shooting would occur. Why?

What most of these factors have in common is that they signify places in which one can hang out. For young men in Newark, hanging out without being stopped by police means hanging out near an acceptable open place of business. Some places, like sit-down and take-out restaurants and convenience stores, provided cover for hanging out. Other places like liquor stores and bars added a place to hang out plus a risk of alcohol consumption. The data showed that the most dangerous of those places were open businesses near otherwise-neglected infrastructure (abandoned properties, foreclosed buildings, etc.). The abandoned buildings could be used to sell drugs, use drugs, or hang out, and the proximate public space provided the targets for violent crimes (be it robbery or retaliation). Also, late at night after most other services were closed, 24-hour gas stations turned out to be the location of a disproportionate number of shootings. The response was to send police to frequent the businesses identified (gas stations, convenience stores, restaurants) and to target nearby neglected buildings that could be used as hangouts. After this response, violent shootings dropped 35% in the RTM target area compared to the control area during the study.[42] Interestingly, while these techniques achieved significant crime reduction, they resulted in no significant increases in arrests.

Similar experiments were conducted in Kansas City, Missouri; Glendale, Arizona; and Chicago, Illinois, with a similar risk-based analysis of environmental factors.[43] Earlier projects in New Jersey also successfully predicted high-risk areas for shootings.[44] By studying the spatial dynamics of crime in particular geographic environments, police could use data modeling to identify, predict, and potentially remedy the identified risk of violence.

Does Predictive Policing Work?

Place-based predictive policing—as a data-driven innovation—should have data to support it. But at least as currently understood, the data remains inconclusive as to its effectiveness. Rather than illuminating, the data remains dark. Crime rates have gone up and down in cities using PredPol. For example, in Los Angeles, the initial testing ground for PredPol, early successes were met with more sobering realities after overall crime rates rose. On the positive side, during a year period from January 2013 to January 2014, the Foothill Division of LAPD saw a 20% drop in predicted crime.[45] But then in 2015 and 2016, crime rose across the city.[46] Other cities have seen initial crime drops for property crimes.[47] And while many new jurisdictions have embraced the technology, a few have discontinued using PredPol or declined to start after initial interest.[48]

The only academic examination of PredPol's algorithm involves a single peer-reviewed research study authored by the founders of the company.[49] The article examines two real-world experiments comparing PredPol's computer-based predictions with police crime analysts' human predictions. In Los Angeles, California, and Kent, United Kingdom, the two methods of crime prediction were compared head to head.[50] In Los Angeles, the crime analysts predicted 2.1% of the crimes, and the algorithm predicted 4.7% of the crimes.[51] In Kent, the crime analysts predicted 6.8% of crimes, as opposed the algorithm's better average of 9.8%.[52] In Los Angeles, during the period of testing (117 days), the PredPol model demonstrated a predictive accuracy 2.2 times greater than the control.[53]

Such testing offers important, although limited, proof of the utility of place-based predictive policing. Big questions still remain. The first, most obvious question is whether being 2.2 times better than a crime analyst is a meaningful measure. To say X is better than Y is only really meaningful if you have a baseline understanding of the value of Y. Maybe both the algorithm and the analyst are terrible, so being better than terrible is not necessarily worth the investment. Currently, no scientific studies exist on the accuracy of crime analysts. But to be fair, predictive policing happens in the real world, and it is difficult to conduct scientific experiments in the real world. PredPol's study appears to beat hot-spot mapping and human analysts over the time studied, even if adequate empirical validation of the control groups does not exist. Perhaps most importantly, PredPol is ahead of some companies in being willing to test its program through the peer-review process. Most other companies do not have any peer-reviewed studies to support their crime-reduction claims.

To test the theory behind predictive policing, the National Institute of Justice funded a RAND pilot project in Shreveport, Louisiana.[54] The hope was to objectively evaluate the theory behind place-based predictive policing. In collaboration with the Shreveport Police Department, researchers conducted a 29-week study using an independent algorithm designed by Shreveport crime analysts and RAND analysts.[55] Similar to PredPol, the model focused on property crimes in known hot-spot areas. Similar to RTM, the analysts isolated particular geographic factors to input into their risk model. The Shreveport factors included (1) the presence of residents on probation or parole, (2) reports of tactical crime over the previous six months, (3) forecasts of tactical crime, (4) 911 calls for disorderly conduct, (5) vandalism, (6) juvenile arrests, and (7) weighted 14 days of tactical crime data.[56] Patrols targeted the spots with the highest risk-factor score. After reviewing the information and comparing the prediction with the control, RAND concluded that there "was no statistically significant impact of the program on crime overall, but it is unclear if that is because of a failure in the program model or a failure in the program implementation."[57] In short, the RAND study failed to support the efficacy or accuracy of predictive policing, but the analysts were unsure of exactly why the study failed.

Despite the uncertainty, the theory behind predictive policing should work. Place has always mattered in criminology. Violence tends to cluster in observable and predictable spaces. For example, in Boston, Massachusetts, over a six-year period, researchers found that shootings occurred in a limited area (5% of the larger geographic area).[58] To respond, police isolated 13 target areas and deployed special police units to patrol those hot spots. The result was that violent crimes dropped in those areas and across the city.[59] Targeting place meant targeting crime.

Gang violence presents another example of place-based prediction theory because gangs tend to be territorial. Gangs involved in the competitive business of drug dealing tend to guard gang territory with violence: if you try to deal drugs on my corner, you get shot. Gangs also respond to violence with violence, leading to retaliatory cycles of shootings.[60] But, while socially destructive, the combination of territoriality and predictability means that future gang violence can be forecast with some accuracy. A shooting will occur in response to another and along territorial boundaries. One study of Los Angeles gangs found that 83% of gang crimes occurred within three blocks of a known gang border.[61] Similar predictions have been made about particular clubs, bars, and other hangouts that combine alcohol, early-morning hours, and rival groups of people.

These examples show the promise of illuminating the darkness of criminal activity. Hints of success, theories that make sense, and the growing ability to test algorithms in the real world shed some positive light on the future of data-driven policing. But studying crime in the real world has always been complex. Disaggregating the cause and ef-

fect of crime drops is always contested, and the algorithms keep changing, making it difficult to evaluate their current accuracy. So the literal
million-dollar question remains unanswered. We do not yet know if predictive policing systems work, even as they populate the policing strategies in many major urban centers.

Data Problems

Big questions remain open about the data underlying place-based
predictive policing. The biggest might be, *what crime data should be
counted?* One of the reasons for the early focus on burglary, car theft,
and theft from automobiles is that that those crimes tend to be more
regularly reported to police. Because of insurance claims and the ability to prove the crime, we have a good sense of the frequency of those
property crimes. This is not so with many other crimes. Interfamily violence, sexual assault, gang violence, and many drug- and gun-possession
offenses never become the raw data for predictive policing. In fact, the
Department of Justice reports that 50% of violent crime goes unreported,[62] which means that systems dependent on crime statistics
necessarily will have a distorted outcome.

As predictive policing grows in scope, this focus on property crime
can create further distortions. In the hierarchy of community concern,
violence usually outweighs property crimes, and yet a system focused
on reported crime data would miss much of that violence. Many gang
shootings would remain under the radar, as would other victims who
might also be involved in unrelated criminal activities (for example, victims themselves involved in drug dealing, robbery, or gang activities). If
the goal of data-driven policing is to maximize accuracy using data, one
must be cautious of the limitations of data collection.

Another big question involves *how crime data is counted.* In New
York City, under the first data-driven revolution of CompStat, scandals
arose about how police were recording and categorizing arrests.[63] Supervisors wanted arrests to go up (demonstrating productivity) and crime
to go down (demonstrating safe communities), so serious crimes were
reduced to minor charges, but more arrests were encouraged.[64] Thus,
an arrest for a purse snatching would be counted but catalogued as a
misdemeanor theft, maintaining the number of arrests but decreasing

the number of felony robberies. Audits of the NYPD arrest system demonstrated recurring errors in categorizing types of crime, mistakes that happened to benefit the political story of crime reduction being told to the public.[65] Despite crime rates actually going down, systemic errors resulted from systemic pressures caused by a need for increased data collection. Similar issues arose in Memphis and Chicago, when documented, unflattering incidents of police data manipulations undermined the accuracy of data-driven systems.[66]

An even more basic problem involves inadvertent data error. Predictive policing strategies operate at a level of precision that targets particular blocks at particular times. But the collection process does not always reflect that precision. Imagine that police see a man they believe has just been involved in a drug deal. They chase him five blocks and stop him and find more narcotics. Did the crime happen in the first block or the second? The address that the officer memorializes in the report changes the profile of the block. What if the officer transposes the address? Or writes down the wrong crime code? Or estimates a block near enough to the arrest? Or forgets to input the data at all? None of these issues is necessarily critical to the criminal case involving suspected drug distribution, but they do negatively impact the accuracy of the future crime forecast. Again, this is why early predictive policing systems focused on burglary (with a fixed address) and theft of cars or theft from cars (at a fixed location). Add to the indeterminacy of crime the natural crush of business for police making multiple arrests each shift and the annoyance of paperwork, and mistakes will happen. Data error infects data systems, and as will be discussed later, these data errors can undermine the reliability of the system.

Is Predictive Policing Racially Discriminatory?

A deeper problem arises from the systemic bias in police crime data. If policing patterns like those in Ferguson or New York City generate racially skewed statistics, then what do we do with predictive policing algorithms based on that data? As Ezekiel Edwards, the director of the ACLU Criminal Law Reform Project, has criticized, "Chief among . . . concerns is that predictive policing as currently deployed will harm rather than help communities of color. If there is one reliable prediction about our criminal justice system, it is that unwarranted racial disparities infect every stage of the criminal law process. Time and again, analysis of stops, frisks, searches, arrests, pretrial detentions, convictions, and sentencing reveal differential treatment of people of color."[67] If predictive policing results in more targeted police presence, the system runs the risk of creating its own self-fulfilling prediction. Predict a hot spot. Send police to arrest people at the hot spot. Input the data memorializing that the area is hot. Use that data for your next prediction. Repeat. Kade Crockford, director of the ACLU's Technology for Liberty Project, terms this type of data analysis "tech-washing" of otherwise racially discriminatory police practices.[68]

Predictive policing advocates might respond to this charge by arguing, first, that some predictive systems use reported crimes, not arrest data, and second, that race has been explicitly removed from all predictive models. The first argument distinguishes between reported crimes (my car was stolen) and arrests (we arrested the suspect for suspicion of car theft). The report that "my car was stolen" involves an actual crime with a fixed place and time; the arrest involves only the suspicions of police. In direct response to the self-fulfilling prophecy argument, Sean Malinowski of the LAPD stated,

> We . . . stress that this is a place-based strategy that develops and plots forecasts based on a three year look at crime patterns and that arrests are not part of the equation. We felt this was important because we heard from some community members that they were concerned about the program creating a kind of self-fulfilling prophecy from under which a community could not recover. For instance, if the police deploy to an area due to a forecast based on crime AND arrests and do, in fact, make additional arrests that go back into the model, it could skew further forecasting. In our model, we would hope to deploy the officers based on *crime only* and then hopefully deny the criminal the opportunity to commit the crime in the first place. We don't want to necessarily be tied up taking a report or making an arrest if we could just as easily be in the right place at the right time and deter the criminal from carrying out their plans to commit a property crime.[69]

This argument minimizes the role of arrests or contacts in predicting areas of crime and thus also minimizes some potential police bias.

The difference between predictive policing systems that focus on *arrests* and those that focus on *reported crimes* deserves some unpacking because it is often confused in debates about predictive technologies. Predictive systems based primarily on arrests will mirror policing patterns more than predictive systems focused on reported crimes will. A burglary happens and is reported, so the police data arising from that incident is not police driven. A drug arrest also happens but can be influenced by where police happen to be stationed. The models that abide by those reported crime-only limitations avoid some of the subjectivity and bias that infect other systems. As originally designed by PredPol, this "crime report" focus, as opposed to an "arrest" focus, may provide useful crime data without reifying biased policing patterns.

As other predictive policing models add additional variables to the equation, the questions get more difficult. Again, in cities in which race and poverty tightly correlate, the chosen risk factors might disproportionately impact communities of color. True, the algorithms purposely omit race as a factor, but in many U.S. cities, issues of race are bound up with issues of place. By law, practice, and custom, neighborhoods have been segregated by race and class.[70] Targeting areas with foreclosures or places of multifamily dwellings may too easily correlate with poor areas. Targeting areas with populations of returning citizens or probationers may not be severable from the policing strategies that caused those individuals to be in the criminal justice system in the first instance.

Importantly, the choice of crime to analyze can impact the discriminatory effect of predictive technologies. As stated, a predictive policing strategy that focuses on drug arrests will almost certainly replicate policing patterns independent of underlying drug use. Burglaries and car thefts happen across a city in rich neighborhoods and poor neighborhoods, so PredPol's red boxes for car theft might not all cluster in poor neighborhoods, reaching downtown parking lots and wealthy suburbs. Violent shootings tend to cluster in poor neighborhoods, so in cities in which poverty and race tightly correlate, predictive targeting of violence will appear more racially skewed than will predictive targeting of burglary. But then again, police usually just follow the bodies. The predicted boxes of heighted gun violence may correlate with poor communities of color, but that is also where the shootings happen. The bias lies not in the algorithm but in the real-world facts going into the system. Accurate predictive policing models, thus, might look discriminatory, but this uncomfortable result might better be explained by the socioeconomic realities and crime patterns of an area.

Constitutional Questions

Uncertainties about place-based predictive policing continue in the constitutional realm. Can location factor into a police officer's suspicion? Are there areas where police should be more suspicious? Known open-air drug markets? Abandoned buildings? The Supreme Court has held that police observation in a "high crime area" can be a factor in deciding whether the officer has reasonable suspicion or probable cause.[71] Rather unhelpfully, the Court has never defined a "high crime area," but as can be imagined, predictive policing technologies might be quite useful in mapping such areas.[72] After all, the algorithm is literally creating a predicted high-crime area with every digital map.

Two significant Fourth Amendment questions arise from the move to place-based predictive policing. First, how does the forecast prediction impact police officers determining whether they have reasonable suspicion or probable cause on the street? Second, how should judges evaluate the predictive tip in court?

Imagine you are a police officer in Santa Cruz, California. At morning roll call, you receive the daily predictive report. Ten red boxes mark ten predicted areas of crime. One of the boxes targets a downtown garage with a 10.36% risk of a vehicle theft between five and six p.m.[73] Predictive policing does not purport to tell you how to do your job, but the theory is that you should spend some extra time around the garage to deter potential car thieves. So, as a dutiful officer, you head out on your shift. At around five p.m., you circle around to the garage. You see a few men loitering about. You don't know them. You don't know what they are doing. One seems to have some tools, which is consistent with both car theft and lawful employment. You are suspicious because they don't look like they have a purpose at the garage. One of the men moves away, wanting to distance himself from the police patrol car. At any other place in the city, at any other time, police most certainly do not have enough suspicion to stop the individual. A police stop would be based on a hunch and, thus, violate the Fourth Amendment. But here we have an algorithmic nudge, a one-in-ten chance of a forecasted car theft. You have a suspect at the right time and location and with tools consistent with car theft. Further, the men moved away from the police presence. You can see the way the predictive forecast might influence the officer's judgment. Such suspicion can distort otherwise-innocent actions and justify stops where perhaps there otherwise should not be a stop.

As can be observed, a predictive policing algorithm has just created a mini-high-crime area, which as the Supreme Court has stated, can be considered as a factor in evaluating reasonable suspicion.[74] A judge reviewing whether the officer had reasonable suspicion to stop the suspected car thief must make an even more difficult judgment. Assume that after the stop, police recovered a "slim jim"—one of those thin metal tools to break open car doors. The man is charged with attempted car theft, and the constitutional question for the court is whether the stop and search violated the Fourth Amendment. How should a judge evaluate the predicted forecast of crime in relation to the stop? Is the data like a tip (imagine an informant stating that a car theft would occur at the garage)? Is the predictive forecast like a police colleague stating, "Hey, partner, next shift be on the lookout for car thieves at the garage"? Is a profile of an area similar to a profile of a person, which might lead to concerns about racial profiling (but is generally accepted by the courts)?[75] Whatever a judge decides (and all the options are consistent with current law), the fact is that predictive policing technology will impact the Fourth Amendment rights of individuals.

Stepping back, the conclusion that a computer algorithm could alter Fourth Amendment freedoms in certain areas and especially in communities of color should be of great concern. Issues of disparate treatment, accuracy, transparency, and accountability all demand attention. If walking through a predicted red box changes my constitutional rights to be free from unreasonable searches and seizures, then a higher level of scrutiny might need to be brought to bear on the use of the technology.

As of yet, only a handful of advocacy groups have raised the issue, with little attention being paid by courts or communities. Community teach-ins in Los Angeles brought concern about predictive policing and other surveillance technology to Skid Row. Led by organizations like the Stop LAPD Spying Coalition, activists and community advocates educated themselves and fellow citizens about constitutional impacts.[76]

The protests provide a voice of concern about growing use of aggressive policing practices based on data-driven justifications. Hamid Kahn, one of the leaders of the coalition, explained the community's fear: "Predictive Policing is yet another tactic in the long trajectory of failed and racist policing programs like broken windows and the war on drugs and crime. Wrapped in the fancy language of data analytics and algorithms, Predictive Policing is fundamentally a proxy for racism and a license to further strengthen the violent policing of black, brown, and poor bodies."[77] This is the underlying fear—that the history of unjust policing practices will be justified by technological spin. In communities marked by police-citizen tension and regularly beset with aggressive police patrols, the idea that a computer can improve police-community relations simply does not compute.

How Big Data Impacts Where We Police

Predictive policing literally changes where police go. In cities that have adopted the technologies, police investigate the red boxes on patrol. But the real change involves how predictive policing impacts what police do while on those patrols.

At an individual level, predictive policing impacts how police see neighborhoods. Quite naturally, police officers who are given official data to be on the lookout for particular crimes in particular places will be invested or encouraged to see the predicted crime. This is the danger of "high crime areas," as the chief judge of the Ninth Circuit Court of Appeals, Alex Kozinski, once wrote: "Just as a man with a hammer sees every problem as a nail, so a man with a badge may see every corner of his beat as a high crime area. Police are trained to detect criminal activity and they look at the world with suspicious eyes."[78] Individuals in the predicted areas—innocent or guilty—will be seen with the same suspicious eyes.

Such suspicion will result in additional stops, frisks, and physical encounters, which may increase the level of tension between police and citizens in those areas. The old adage of "what gets measured gets managed" applies to police. Told to police red boxes, police will do so. Told to target certain neighborhoods, police will do so. Informed that they need to up their "stats" (to show productivity), patrol officers will feel pressure to stop people even when the legal justification for the stop seems weak. This was one of the problems that led to the NYPD stop-and-frisk program being declared unconstitutional in 2013.

Predictive policing may, in fact, lead to additional police shootings and civilian unrest. In the targeted areas, police may feel additional license to investigate more aggressively. Because the areas have been designated as more dangerous, police may also respond in a more aggressively protective posture. While every police stop involves potential danger, the knowledge of being in an area of higher violence may alter the daily practice of officers, leading them to resort to physical force more often.

At a crime-strategy level, predictive policing may have distorting effects on traditional police practice. In one of the first iterations of Pred-Pol in California, officers had to be reminded to leave the predicted "red box" areas.[79] Apparently, police officers, instructed to patrol the predicted areas, never left. In explaining the San Francisco Police Department's concern with one predictive system, Susan Merritt, the department's chief information officer, recounted, "In L.A. I heard that many officers were only patrolling the red boxes, not other areas. . . . People became too focused on the boxes, and they had to come up with a slogan, 'Think outside the box.'"[80]

In the RAND Shreveport study, a similar distortion occurred. Researchers observed that patrol officers became more like detectives trying to figure out the crime drivers in the predicted area. Patrol officers got out of their cars more, engaged citizens more, and focused on "intelligence gathering."[81] Police officers stopped and questioned more people, ran people's records, investigated unreported narcotics use, and tried to understand who was involved in criminal activity. Ironically, this type of community investigation slowed responses to traditional calls for service, leading to complaints that police were unresponsive in emergencies.[82] Further, the investigatory tips generated about the targeted area were handed over to detectives without contextual information or active cases, burdening already-overloaded detectives and causing some internal resentment. The detectives apparently did not like the patrol officers acting like detectives. In both cases, police officers altered traditional practice to fulfill the metrics designed by police administrators.

Yet this change—while disruptive to traditional practice—may not have been such a negative thing. Changing officers' orientation from being focused on arrests to investigation and from reactive response to proactive deterrence may, in fact, be a progressive by-product of predictive policing. In an interview on the effectiveness of PredPol in Los Angeles, LAPD's Sean Malinowski stated that he saw a reorientation in his officers' attitude about the goals of policing:

> Malinowski said he noticed a shift in officers' behavior when they started using PredPol. They became less focused on arrests, which was desirable from his standpoint because the public might see that and be more willing to trust the police, and more focused on preventing victimhood. "They had to change their way of thinking, because for years they were rewarded on their productivity, which meant citations and arrests, and I had to convince them that's not what I'm rewarding you for." . . . "I'm interested in rewarding for fewer victims."[83]

Ironically, a data-driven policing system could—if so implemented—result in less data emphasis and more human interaction.

Two further concerns emerge from this evolution to data-driven police management. The first involves "data myopia," which is when data-driven administrators follow the data even when it no longer makes sense.[84] In the policing context, this can take the form of forgetting to think about the underlying "why" of any prediction. For example, if a predictive algorithm triggers an alert for a burglary because of a series of related burglaries in one neighborhood, normally it would make sense to follow up on the tip. But if the burglar had been caught in the last house and admitted to all the other burglaries causing the spike, the prediction will likely be wrong. The "why" for the additional risk (the burglar) had been taken out of the equation (he is in jail), but the algorithm may not know that fact.

The focus on "why" a prediction might work suggests a larger question about predictive policing: is risk identification enough? PredPol, HunchLab, RAND's model, and other predictive technologies all purport to identify higher-risk areas of crime. But knowing where these risks are does not necessarily inform police about how to approach those areas. Is just sending a police car to a predicted area enough? If environmental vulnerabilities encourage crime, changing the environment might matter more than policing the area. If abandoned buildings provide cover for drug dealing, you could put a police car out front for a temporary fix or rebuild the building for a more permanent fix. You could also address drug addiction and offer substance-abuse treatment. The predictive data identifies the problem but not the solution. Of the place-based predictive technologies, only RTM explicitly attempts to address and remediate "why" particular areas attract illegal behaviors.[85]

Without understanding why a prediction might work, data-driven projections can just serve to cover more aggressive and less constructive policing practices. This is one of the lurking dangers of predictive technologies: data can justify poor policy choices.

As one of the more self-defeating examples of this concern, the LAPD decided to adapt predictive policing theories using police helicopters.[86] To be clear, PredPol did not sanction the helicopter project, but LAPD blended elements of predictive deterrence theory with a long-standing reliance on helicopter air support. As might be evident, however, putting an LAPD air-support helicopter on top of a surgically targeted city block makes little practical sense. The reality of helicopters is that they are anything but surgical. Helicopters fly. Helicopters fly beyond the 500-by-500-foot predicted target area. Helicopters are loud, annoying, scary, and intrusive. Whatever you think of the risk-identification methods, the remedy is overbroad. Instead of a crime scalpel, police used a helicopter blade for surgery. The remedy also undermined the theory. In practice, to accommodate the flight path of helicopters, police had to expand the predicted areas (and thus the reach of predictive policing theory) to flight corridors spanning many city blocks. Obviously, the larger the area covered, the less accurate the targeted predictions will be. No predictive policing studies had ever been validated on large corridors of predicted crime, nor would they be since the whole value of the technology (and theory) was to narrow the geographic focus. In addition, in order to be an effective deterrent, helicopters had to fly low enough to be visible, which meant that all of the law-abiding citizens in those areas also became burdened by invasive and intimidating police surveillance.[87]

The true danger of the helicopter project, thus, involves how it was justified: by data. The argument for helicopter deterrence came from believing in predictive policing data. If police cars could deter, police helicopters could deter more. Whether that is true or not, the use of predictive policing theory to justify it is misleading. This concern of borrowing predictive data but applying an overbroad remedy runs throughout predictive policing. Confusing risk and remedy and relying on misleading data can undermine the positive insights available from predictive policing.

A final concern involves the limitations of adapting predictive tactics to different geographic areas. Police administrators must understand that even if a predictive policing system works in one city, it may not work in their city. What works in the sprawling sections of Los Angeles may not work in the vertically designed metropolis of New York City. What works in Chicago may not work in a smaller, more rural town. Data availability may also weaken the predictive values of the models. To be useful, police systems need sufficient data to work with, and some small towns do not have adequate data sets to build a strong model. Police administrators choosing among the various commercial products must be conscious of the differences of their cities or towns.

Despite questions about predictive policing's scientific backing, effectiveness, and discriminatory impact, anecdotal evidence has convinced many police chiefs and cities to buy into the idea. The lure of a black-box solution to stopping crime has won over skeptics. What police department does not want to be "intelligence driven" or "cutting-edge"? Smarter is usually better, even when smarter does not always work. As more police departments expressed interest in new technologies, major companies like Hitachi, Motorola, and IBM started to create technologies to compete against the small upstart companies.[88]

In part, the choice presented can be framed as whether the new predictive policing technology is better than the old way of doing things. From a management perspective, restructuring police districts, staffing, and patrols using data, computer maps, and predictive analytics speaks to a huge improvement over past practice. One likely apocryphal story of the old way talks about the "Bud-Shell Method" of creating the districts for police officers to patrol:

The "Bud-Shell Method" of creating police districts . . . describes a police administrator who sits down one night with a "six pack of Budweiser and a Shell station road map" and uses a magic marker to draw lines down major streets. If you have a major east-west artery and a major north-south artery—*voila!*—you have four districts! Never mind that one contains mostly upper-class residential housing and another contains a hospital, a high school, and a methadone clinic. It would probably be too much to say that the "Bud-Shell Method" was the predominant method of districting during the first 90 percent of the 20th century . . . but until the advent of affordable desktop geographic information system (GIS) software, the task was too difficult to accomplish any other way.[89]

Today, the data available about place—down to the granular crime patterns—makes such a process laughable. In terms of police administration, there is no question that predictive technologies and related crime mapping have vastly improved efficiencies in police patrol and personnel allocation. As long as crime continues to happen in particular places, understanding those places and the environmental risks associated with those places is a clear measure of progress. Place-based predictive policing has hit a nerve to offer technological solutions to places that need it most. These place-based solutions have also influenced where to locate new big data surveillance technologies, which offer real-time monitoring and investigation capabilities. This is the subject of the next chapter.

When We Police

Real-Time Surveillance and Investigation

Our officers are expected to know the unknown and see the unseen. They are making split-second decisions based on limited facts. The more you can provide in terms of intelligence . . . the more safely you can respond to calls.
—Fresno Police Chief Jerry Dyer[1]

Beware Your Threat Score

First responders operate largely in the dark. A 911 call for a disturbance or report of violence requires police to approach a home without much information. If you are that responding officer, you might want to know if the person behind the door is a gangbanger or grandmother, a felon or first-grade teacher.

Enter big data and the data brokers who have been collecting billions of bits of personal information about you, your family, and your home. Conveniently, this information is arranged by address and accessible in real time for police responding to your home. The same folks who know you have stable credit, two kids, and a good job and like fine wine and cooking magazines can also predict whether you will be a danger when you open the door. Through big data, police can get the information before they need to act.

Police in Fresno, California, piloted a service called Beware to give them real-time "threat scores" about addresses and people.[2] Beware searches through proprietary consumer databanks to provide a rough predictive judgment about the 911 caller, the address, or the neighborhood.[3] The predictions initially involved color-coded threat levels (red, yellow, or green) and provided some measure of risk assessment for police responding to a scene. Beware's data comes from commercially available records such as criminal records, warrants, and property records—in essence, most of the data populating consumer big data systems—and early versions also incorporated social media data, which might pick up on threatening statements, gang associations, or other violent comments.[4]

Not much is known about how Beware determines threat levels. The service is owned by Intrado, a subsidiary of West Corporation, and has kept the threat-score algorithm out of public view.[5] In community hearings about the technology, the Fresno police chief admitted that Intrado had not even informed the police about how the threat scores were calculated. But, like many things with big data, the secret is not really much of a secret.[6] Data about arrests, convictions, gun licenses, neighborhoods, crime rates, and the like remain readily available in the consumer data marketplace. In fact, if the same first responder simply typed the 911 caller's address into an existing police database, many of the same pieces of information could be obtained and the same inferences drawn.

Predictions, of course, have consequences. If police officers have information that a violent felon lives in a particular home, the officers are more likely to be on guard. Police are more likely to react to the danger and are more likely to shoot at a perceived threat. Thus, a high threat score might well produce hostile or even deadly results. A threat prediction literally and figuratively colors judgment about the relative danger.

Unsettlingly, the data can be wrong. In the same public hearing about the use of the technology, a Fresno City Council member asked the police chief to run his address through the Beware system. The council member's house came back with an elevated "yellow" threat level.[7] While no one suspected this particular official of being a danger, a responding police officer would still treat him as such. No one at the hearing could explain the elevated threat level. These concerns and other civil liberty issues caused the Fresno Police Department to back away from continued use of the Beware technology, reducing reliance on color-coded threat levels and social media information.

This chapter explores how new surveillance technologies shift when police act. Immediately available information, all-seeing surveillance, and large-scale tracking capabilities with automated alerts help speed up decision making. For police officers needing to make split-second decisions or investigators needing to sort through stacks of files, big data can offer significant efficiency benefits. But data available in real time helps only if the information is accurate. As with the Beware system, questions of reliability, transparency, and bias remain and must be addressed. In addition, constitutional concerns arising from video surveillance systems challenge traditional Fourth Amendment understandings of personal privacy in public.

Real-Time Domain Awareness

A car drives into lower Manhattan. A man with a red shirt gets out with a bag. He walks a few blocks and leaves the bag on the street. He hops in a different car and drives away. In any other city, this action would be one of a million anonymous acts, untraceable, lost in the bustle of a big city.

But not in New York City. Not with the Domain Awareness System (DAS)—a partnership between the NYPD and Microsoft. The DAS links approximately 9,000 closed-circuit surveillance cameras for real-time monitoring of lower Manhattan.[8] The video feeds go directly to a digital alert system that automatically tracks for suspicious behaviors (such as leaving a bag on the street). Cameras pick up images of the car and automated license-plate readers record every car that enters the area. These 500 license-plate systems connect with DMV records, police watchlists, open warrants, and terrorist databases and all of the personal information associated with these databases.[9] The recorded video can be replayed to track the direction, location, and movements of the suspect, and the technology can even search for descriptions, such as "all people wearing red shirts near the New York Stock Exchange."[10] Still photos of matching people can be pulled up with one search, tagged to location, time, and date.

Under the DAS, as soon as the man abandons the bag, an automatic alert triggers. Cameras within 500 feet of the location can be reviewed, and officers can play back the path of the man getting out of the car.[11] The car itself could be traced back to the point it entered the network of surveillance cameras, and using the automated license-plate tracking systems, information about the owner or whether the car was stolen could be obtained. Similarly, the getaway car could be tracked and analyzed. Camera data going back a month can be studied about the area, so that historical information about whether this was a terrorist or a tourist could be relayed to responding officers. To augment the data sharing, NYPD invested in 35,000 smartphones so patrol officers could have access to DAS on patrol.[12]

More limited versions of the circle of cameras have been tested in Los Angeles, Fresno, and other cities. Fresno even sought to link police body-worn-camera videos to the network of surveillance.[13] With such linked camera systems, the normal limitations of human observation and memory become all but irrelevant. All-seeing digital technologies speed up police reaction time and also prolong investigative capabilities.

For first responders, real-time surveillance can provide a wealth of helpful information. Police can know who is on the scene, what has happened, and whether anyone poses a danger. Police regularly must sort out friend and foe, victim and offender, in the middle of highly emotional incidents, so visual assistance from supervisors able to review what actually happened before police arrived can help make better decisions. In addition, other first-responder medical services can be provided before police arrive, shortening ambulance calls or the time to receive emergency services.

Police response time improves through automation. Automated suspicion algorithms using artificial-intelligence capabilities can turn surveillance cameras into digital spies able to recognize suspicious patterns and alert the police to the crime.[14] The same type of pattern-recognition algorithm that can identify an abandoned bag on the street can also identify other suspicious human activities. For example, in East Orange, New Jersey, police adopted Digisensory Technologies' Avista Smart Sensors to automatically monitor the streets.[15] These smart cameras have been trained to look for patterns of suspicious activity, processing 60 billion instructions a second.[16] For example, repeated, frequent hand-to-hand transactions on a corner may signify a drug dealer. A quick movement toward a person and then running away might signify a robbery. Sensors monitor the actions on the street and then alert police if the pattern observed matches a pattern the sensor has been trained to identify. Once the sensor triggers, the nearest two officers are automatically alerted to the potential crime, time, and location. Cameras can trace back the scene, so commanders at headquarters can make sure the algorithm got it right. These automated suspicion algorithms guide police to the scene, providing clues that would be missed by routine police patrols.

Similar algorithms exist to identify gunshots from audio sensors. One technology—ShotSpotter—provides automated reports of gunshots, alerting police to possible violent crime before it is reported by human witnesses.[17] As soon as the highly sensitive microphone hears the sound of a gunshot, police are dispatched to the targeted location. Victims can be found faster, perpetrators caught, and witnesses interviewed. These automatic sensors have been deployed in Washington, D.C., Boston, Oakland, San Francisco, and Minneapolis.[18] Crime is being responded to in real time, usually more quickly than any human could react.

Tracking Cars, Faces, and Spaces

License plates are unique identifiers, linking cars to their owner. Automated license-plate readers (ALPRs) are camera-like devices that can scan a license plate and automatically compare the license to a database of active warrants, stolen cars, unpaid tickets, or any other variable.[19] Affixed on the top of police cars, ALPRs can scan thousands of license plates a day. In practice, a police officer can drive on a highway, pass a car associated with an open warrant or registered as stolen, and immediately receive a real-time alert.[20]

The digital record of ALPRs has grown exponentially, as police vehicles record millions of license plates each year. Sophisticated enough to read one license plate every second, ALPR systems can generate city-wide maps of car locations. By driving through parking lots, apartment complexes, and ordinary streets, the system automatically memorializes where particular cars were at particular times. An aggregated ALPR map can, thus, link cars and owners by time, date, and location. Over time, the accumulated tracking of cars provides clues about travel patterns, habits, and the actual location of cars at certain times.[21] If police suspect that a particular house is used for drug dealing, the repeated sighting of a license plate might be a clue to suggest involvement in the drug trade. In emergency rescue situations like an "Amber Alert" child abduction, searches for car license plates can lead to clues about the location of the suspect. For investigations, police can find possible witnesses to a crime. Such a database of locational information, of course, presents a real privacy problem because everybody with a car can be sucked into the data stream. Journalists have requested their own ALPR data and found their personal car tracked, with photos of their car and family and a revealing pattern of personal activities.[22]

What ALPR does for cars, facial-recognition technology does for people walking on the street. Advanced surveillance cameras in Los Angeles have the capabilities to scan and compare live facial images to mug shots in police databases.[23] These fixed cameras can scan faces from 600 feet and can match faces with anyone in the police database.[24] Like a car with a license plate, a person wanted for criminal activity can be automatically identified using facial-recognition technologies. In addition, a digital map of past sightings is available for later investigatory use, so that should a crime occur near a camera, police can scroll back the video and identify all the people who walked past the camera at the relevant time.

Facial-recognition technology offers virtual fingerprinting for anyone in front of a camera. The FBI possesses a database of 30 million photographs.[25] State databases contain millions more.[26] Some photographs come from civilian drivers' license photos, meaning that millions of innocent people are regularly put in virtual criminal photo spreads.[27] Many other photographs result from criminal arrests. In just under five years, the FBI requested 215,000 searches of facial-recognition databases, with 36,000 searches of state driver's license databases.[28] When connected with real-time video capabilities and sophisticated facial-recognition technologies, a new web of visual surveillance may soon spread over cities.

The growth of police-worn body cameras provides additional identification capabilities. Police-worn body cameras are small cameras usually affixed to the front of a uniform, and some police departments even have adopted software that allows personal smartphones to double as body-worn cameras.[29] These cameras create a continuous feed of the people police come in contact with during their daily routines.[30] The video can be used to identify who, where, and when police made contact with a particular person. Next-generation body cameras will include real-time facial-recognition technology that will allow police to know about active warrants, prior violence, or generally peaceful conduct (just like the fixed cameras).[31] While current limitations on battery power and computing requirements have made facial recognition through body cameras more aspirational than real, companies promise that in the next few years this capability will be operational.[32] In addition, the facial-recognition technology itself is growing more sophisticated by the month. Facebook's facial-recognition program DeepFace boasts of a 97% accuracy rate of identifying faces across its platform, with new improvements happening every year.[33]

If DAS and body cameras are not invasive enough, aerial cameras provide the ultimate mass-surveillance tool. Flying high overhead, able to record entire neighborhoods for hours at a time, aerial cameras like Persistent Surveillance Systems can watch crime in real time and record the patterns of all vehicles, people, and events below.[34] *Washington Post* reporter Craig Timberg vividly described the plane's observational capabilities:

> Shooter and victim were just a pair of pixels, dark specks on a gray streetscape. Hair color, bullet wounds, even the weapon were not visible in the series of pictures taken from an airplane flying two miles above.
>
> But what the images revealed—to a degree impossible just a few years ago—was location, mapped over time. Second by second, they showed a gang assembling, blocking off access points, sending the shooter to meet his target and taking flight after the body hit the pavement. When the report reached police, it included a picture of the blue stucco building into which the killer ultimately retreated, at last beyond the view of the powerful camera overhead.[35]

Add sophisticated audio capture, and these aerial camera systems or drones provide the potential for cities to be surveilled in real time and for days at a time. Similar to the Domain Awareness System, police can roll back the tape and watch how the crime developed, where the suspects fled, and patterns of behavior before and after the suspects got to their supposed safe houses. Persistent Surveillance Systems planes have flown missions over Baltimore, Los Angeles, Indianapolis, Charlotte, and other cities.[36] Cars or people can be digitally identified and tracked over time. Time and movement can be reduced to searchable data points. A digitized history allows time's normal passing to be recaptured. And all of the information (tens of thousands of witnessed moments) can be (and has been) turned over to police interested in solving crimes.

Real-Time Investigation

The first 48—homicide investigation lore holds that the first 48 hours of an investigation remain the most important. If you speed up the investigation, you close more cases.

Across the country, police departments are developing real-time operations systems to investigate crimes. These nerve centers centralize information gathering,[37] linking video feeds, calls for service, crime maps, and real-time police patrols to allow commanders to respond to ever-shifting crime patterns immediately. An uptick in robberies in the afternoon can lead to additional police patrols at night.

But the game-changing technology involves big data networks of investigative leads. Sarah Brayne conducted a groundbreaking two-and-a-half-year case study of the LAPD's embrace of data-driven technology.[38] Brayne describes how larger and larger data sets have made police investigation faster, more accurate, and data centered.[39] She describes a homicide investigation that began with a body dumped at a remote location. The victim appeared to be a Los Angeles gang member, but no witnesses could be located. Fortunately, an automated license-plate scanner recorded license plates near the location. By narrowing down the time of day, police focused on a single license plate from Compton, California. By running the tags in a database and cross-checking the owner's name with a gang database, police generated a suspect who happened to be in a rival gang from the person killed. The suspect's vehicle was searched, and incriminating evidence was recovered linking the suspect to the victim.[40] Case closed.

Networked systems allow police to process more data, much more quickly. Palantir developed an integrated data system that allows LAPD to search for people, automobiles, homes, cellphones, email addresses, locations, friends, associates, family, or employment from among the various data sources already in the possession of the department.[41] If any link can be connected between two of these things, it can be digitally mapped. If investigators want to extend out a second or third link, entire groups can be connected. Gang members, people with open warrants, and others targeted for investigation can all be linked together, so you could see all the home addresses of a particular gang or the travel patterns of three known drug distributors.[42] For big-picture investigation, this allows police to see the nature of crime networks in the city (and across multiple jurisdictions).[43]

Non-law-enforcement data also populates the investigative databases. Information from social services, health services, mental health services, foreclosures, social media, utility bills, and even stored phone records from pizza chains (used to speed pizza delivery) can all be potentially linked up.[44] Such a comprehensive data-aggregation system might run into privacy issues, and the inclusion of health information would certainly add additional legal complications; but as a technical matter, this data is available and can be integrated into aggregated police systems.

At a minimum, the LAPD database can be used to target particular crimes. If, for example, police wish to track a car suspected of being involved in human trafficking, police can find all the times the automated license-plate reader tagged the car. The pattern can be visualized on a map. This connecting thread might lead to finding trafficked people or routes used for smuggling people between houses. Or if police learn about three particular houses used for prostitution, a "geofence" (electronic sensor that alerts when crossed) can be created around the houses,[45] such that if any single car shows up at all three houses, an inference can be drawn that the individuals in the car are involved in the suspected trafficking activity.

All of this can be done in real time. Instead of conducting a stakeout, an automatic alert system can be created to ping the officer that a particular car has entered an area or person has come into contact with police. Literally, an email goes out informing the officer that the wanted person has just made contact with a police sensor. In addition, similar to the Beware system, all of this accumulated data about a location can inform officers responding to a 911 call or effectuating an arrest. Data about the area, the people who live at an address, past crimes in the neighborhood, and other data that has been entered into the system can be provided almost instantaneously. Automation pushes out tactical information constantly, quickly, and conveniently to officers in the streets.

Race for Data

Proactively studying crime means mapping it. In the most heavily surveilled areas of Los Angeles, field contacts, ALPR, and facial-recognition records pinpoint the location of people and cars. As data points, these basic locational facts can be studied over time. As clues to solve crimes, these facts can be useful for identifying witnesses, tracking suspects, and even providing (or debunking) alibis. Further, because the information is not only individualized but associational, link analysis can connect many other people to the groups involved in particular group crimes.

Communities of color bear the brunt of these tactics. By and large, it is poor people from minority backgrounds who are stopped by police. By and large, it is people of color who are populating the growing police databases. If these racially skewed databases of past police contacts become the justification for future police contacts, then biased data collection will distort police suspicion. Worse, when linked to commercially available big data systems, citizens might be inappropriately stereotyped based on overbroad generalizations.

Similarly, the choice of where to place the surveillance systems can be seen as discriminatory. The Stop LAPD Spying Coalition argued that by targeting Skid Row, the facial-recognition technology mapped only poor people of color living and working in the community.[46] In Baltimore—home to a police department under federal investigation for racial discrimination—the police used data from the aerial Persistent Surveillance Systems over West Baltimore (a predominantly African American community).[47]

The choice of targeting communities of color matters, because race actually distorts the accuracy of certain technologies. For example, facial-recognition matching works by creating models of faces, digitally broken down into tiny pixelated nodes.[48] With current technology, every face can be digitally deconstructed to 80 nodal points and thus matched with other faces in a database system. Facebook recently developed technology that can identify a face out of the 800 million photographs on its network in under five seconds.[49] Facial-recognition algorithms are trained by looking at faces, but because algorithms are trained on existing photos, certain racial bias seeps into the process.[50] As Clare Garvie and Jonathan Frankle wrote in the *Atlantic*,

> Algorithms developed in China, Japan, and South Korea recognized East Asian faces far more readily than Caucasians. The reverse was true for algorithms developed in France, Germany, and the United States, which

were significantly better at recognizing Caucasian facial characteristics. This suggests that the conditions in which an algorithm is created—particularly the racial makeup of its development team and test photo databases—can influence the accuracy of its results.[51]

Another study of facial-recognition technology found racial disparities between African Americans and Caucasians. The technology failed to identify the correct person twice as often when the photo was of an African American subject.[52] This inaccuracy can have one of two results. First, because the facial-recognition technology cannot find a match (even though there is a match in the data set), a person who should be identified is not identified (the guilty go free). Second, because the facial-recognition technology cannot find a match (because there is no match in the data set), the algorithm nevertheless suggests the person who is the closest match (an innocent is flagged). This closest match becomes the target of investigation,[53] and in the United States, due to the embedded racial disparity of who gets arrested (and thus who is in the data system), this error will fall on racial minorities more than on whites. In any algorithmically dependent project, these errors can have discriminatory impacts about who is stopped or even arrested.

Race does not need to have a distorting effect on policing. In New York City, the Domain Awareness System focuses its attention on downtown New York, in the financial center. Such placement avoids direct allegations of racial (or economic) bias correlating with minority communities or that the cameras were intended to target high-crime areas (assuming Wall Street does not count as a traditional high-crime area). Because of the commercial nature of the area and the terrorist attacks of September 11, 2001, use of the Domain Awareness System in Manhattan has avoided much of the criticism heard in Los Angeles.

Race, policing, and surveillance collide when police use mass-surveillance technologies to monitor domestic political unrest. In both Ferguson, Missouri, and Baltimore, Maryland, the FBI used sophisticated aerial surveillance to monitor protesters challenging police use of force.[54] These surveillance flights—initially secret—were eventually exposed by curious citizens who saw small planes flying in odd patterns. In Baltimore, federal agents accompanied by local police flew planes equipped with high-tech cameras to provide live video feeds and even lasers to capture photographs in darkness.[55] According to the *Baltimore Sun*, the surveillance aircraft made ten flights over the protests during the days following the death of Freddie Gray in 2015,[56] confirming activists' complaints of ongoing surveillance and tracking by federal law enforcement agencies.[57] Obviously, use of such technologies against peaceful protests raises difficult constitutional questions about the limits of police surveillance, the importance of free speech, and the need to ensure civil order. These questions are made more difficult because of the racial cast of the surveillance, targeting not just communities of color but members of the Movement for Black Lives.

Unreal Reliance

Big data technologies are changing the pace of police response. Driving these technologies are automated capabilities that can search information faster than human investigators can and that can make that information usable in real time. The timing of when we police, however, has its downsides as speed does not always encourage accuracy.

Denise Green learned the hard way that automated suspicion can fail. One night, Green, a 47-year-old African American woman, was driving her burgundy 1992 Lexus ES 300 on Mission Street in San Francisco.[58] A police cruiser with ALPR technology passed by and alerted to a stolen car. Green's license-plate number was 5SOW350, but the ALPR misread the license plate as 5SOW750. Due to darkness, the photograph normally used to confirm the automated report was "blurry and illegible."[59] The officer driving the cruiser radioed ahead regarding the stolen car, and a second officer, without double checking the license plate (or the fact that the stolen tag 5SOW750 corresponded with a gray GMC truck, not a burgundy Lexus sedan) performed a "high-risk stop." This stop entailed Green being forced out of the car at gunpoint. Green, a municipal driver for the city with no convictions, was required to kneel in the middle of the street and be handcuffed by six armed officers.[60] She sued the police for the violation of her constitutional rights as a result of the mistake. While police protocols did suggest double checking and confirming the license plate before stopping the driver, police just deferred to the automatic alert without a second thought.

"Garbage in, Garbage out. Everyone knows that much about computers; you give them bad data, they give you bad results."[61] So begins another federal case—written by then-judge Neil M. Gorsuch—dealing with the accuracy of a computerized state license-plate database. In this case, a state trooper in Kansas stopped Antonio Esquivel-Rios because his car's temporary Colorado tag did not show up in the database that was routinely used to search for licensed cars.[62] It turns out, however, that temporary tags from Colorado could not show up in the Kansas database because temporary tags were not routinely loaded into the Kansas system.[63] The police officer based his stop solely on the database response, but the database was an unreliable source of information. In fact, only at the subsequent court hearing did it come to light about the types of licenses included in the shared database and the fact that such temporary tags were never loaded in. The police officer, however, did not know that fact and relied on the incomplete information in the database, resulting in the erroneous stop. Such database errors are unfortunately common. Over the past few years, the U.S. Supreme Court has decided four cases involving arrests based on faulty arrest warrants in police databases.[64] Data-driven suspicion is only good as the data in the system.

Accuracy concerns also exist with consumer data repurposed for criminal investigation. The Beware program in Fresno, for instance, relies on similar commercial data compiled by data brokers. While data brokers have proven quite useful in making sure we have the appropriate catalogues in the mail, it does not matter very much that they occasionally get things wrong. But when the Beware system provides inaccurate (or merely out-of-date) information to police responding to an emergency, the errors can turn deadly. If, for example, a 911 call returns information that a violent felon lives in the house, any responding officer would be wise to pay attention. But the heighted vigilance could turn tragic if the data is wrong, is dated, or causes the officer to overreact out of fear in a situation that did not call for it. Maybe the felon moved away. Maybe the address had merely been given to receive mail, and his grandmother lived in the house. Maybe the former felon had turned his life around. The consumer data captures none of these realities and yet directly impacts how police perceive the situation and how they respond.

Similarly, facial-recognition technologies have yet to be adequately tested for accuracy. The Government Accountability Office (GAO) issued a critical report on the FBI's facial-recognition technology policies, castigating the FBI for failing to assess the accuracy of its searches.[65] The FBI did not assess the "false positive rate," did not conduct operational reviews of the actual use of the technology, and did not assess the accuracy of external face-recognition systems from partners.[66] Simply stated, the most advanced and sophisticated user of facial-recognition technology could not validate the accuracy of the system. In 2016, the Georgetown Law Center on Technology & Privacy issued a nationwide report titled "The Perpetual Line-Up" detailing the growth of facial-recognition technologies.[67] The report found that 117 million (one in two) Americans have their images in these law enforcement database systems.[68] Many driver's license photos now can be used in police photo arrays to match against suspected criminals. These local, state, and national databases of images (of largely innocent people) remain unregulated with few legal (or even regulatory) protections.[69] Using this system, police conduct automated searches for suspects every single day.

The automated nature of the information creates two interrelated problems. First, the officers relying on the automated tips or matches have no way to double check the black-box data. This is a real "black data" problem, as the systems have not been designed to explain the match or data hit but only to flag the information. Almost by design, police can only defer to the data since there is no way to see beneath the result.

Second, the speed at which the information is supposed to be used reduces the ability to check for accuracy. In a non-big-data world, while it is certainly possible for a police officer to obtain bad information about who lives at a particular address, the usual human process of obtaining that information (asking fellow officers, looking through records, personal observation) might provide more contextual understanding than an automated color-coded threat score. With automated threat scores or automated license-plate scans or automated facial-recognition alerts, police will have a tendency to simply accept the information as true without questioning it or the assumptions behind it. Worse, they will lack the ability to interrogate why or how the data was created.

The Time-Machine Problem

Stephen Henderson examined the technological future and realized we have a "time machine problem."[70] Available mass-surveillance technologies, like Persistent Surveillance Systems, now can observe, record, and digitize movement in real time and thus can be used to investigate after the fact. Police can see into the past, piecing together data about cars, people, and movements. Drones, ALPR, the Domain Awareness System, and old-fashioned surveillance cameras all provide wonderfully helpful digital time machines.

Such surveillance capacity presents a real threat to privacy, because in order to collect the time-machine data on a particular suspect, the rest of the population also must be recorded. Associational freedoms can be threatened by the mere possibility of such mass surveillance. As Neil Richards has written, "The gathering of information affects the power dynamic between the watcher and the watched, giving the watcher greater power to influence or direct the subject of surveillance. It might sound trite to say that 'information is power,' but the power of personal information lies at the heart of surveillance."[71] With all-seeing surveillance, police power expands, and citizens' freedom shrinks.

Big data police surveillance, thus, presents a stark privacy problem. The digitization and ability to search and recall particular data points changes the traditional physical limitations of policing. In doing so, it also distorts the constitutional protections of citizens.

Traditionally, the U.S. Constitution through the Fourth Amendment has not provided much protection for activities that occur in public.[72] Think about it: if you walk outside your house, why should you expect any privacy? You are in public, and a nosy neighbor, paparazzo, or police officer can observe what you do. So for years, police could set up surveillance cameras, trail you in unmarked cars, and watch with whom you meet without any constitutional concerns. Most modern police investigation takes advantage of this absence of constitutional protection from ordinary observational surveillance in public.

The question becomes, does this analysis change with pervasive surveillance?[73] After all, police have the technology to record your every public movement (with drones), listen to every public conversation (with high-tech audio devices), and track your every movement (with

GPS technology). The fact that police can obtain this information as a technical matter does not mean that they should be able to obtain this information from a constitutional point of view. This was—more or less—the issue presented in a recent Supreme Court case, *United States v. Jones.*[74]

Antoine Jones owned nightclubs and other business interests in Washington, D.C. He was a successful man about town but also, according to police, a major figure in a drug distribution ring.[75] The difficulty for police was being able to connect Jones to the drugs. In an effort to make that connection, police attached a GPS device to Jones's Jeep Cherokee and monitored it for 28 days. As the Court explained, "By means of signals from multiple satellites, the device established the vehicle's location within 50 to 100 feet, and communicated that location by cellular phone to a Government computer. It relayed more than 2,000 pages of data over the 4-week period."[76] Fortunately for police and prosecutors, the GPS coordinates of the Jeep linked Jones to one of the stash houses suspected of containing the illegal narcotics.

During the criminal prosecution against Jones, he challenged the use of the GPS device placed on his Jeep. He argued that this type of tracking without a valid warrant constituted an unreasonable search and, thus, violated his Fourth Amendment rights. The government responded that all of Jones's movements were in public, so Jones really should not have had any expectation of privacy in his travels. After all, police could have followed him using old-fashioned surveillance techniques on public roadways without any constitutional concern.

Jones presented the Supreme Court with a choice between the traditional understanding that people do not have much expectation of privacy in public and the potentially invasive 24/7 surveillance capabilities of new tracking technologies. If the Court sided with the government, it would mean that police could track all cars at all times without any judicial approval. It could mean that big data monitoring in public would have no constitutional limit.

The Court unanimously rejected the government's argument, although it divided on its reasoning. The majority of the Court, led by Antonin Scalia, held that placing the GPS device on the car was a search because it physically invaded Antoine Jones's property.[77] By physically attaching the GPS device to the Jeep, police trespassed on Jones's private property. Other justices took a more technologically sophisticated view of the problem. These justices reasoned that the long-term nature of the tracking violated the Fourth Amendment because it violated Jones's reasonable expectation of privacy. These justices, led by Sonia Sotomayor, offered the first real analysis of the danger of the time-machine problem.[78]

The privacy fear, as articulated by several justices, stemmed from the long-term aggregated nature of the data collection and use. The justices reasoned that long-term surveillance made almost effortless by new technology presented a different privacy threat than old-fashioned surveillance in public did. As Justice Sotomayor summarized,

> GPS monitoring generates a precise, comprehensive record of a person's public movements that reflects a wealth of detail about her familial, political, professional, religious, and sexual associations. . . . The Government can store such records and efficiently mine them for information years into the future. . . . And because GPS monitoring is cheap in comparison to conventional surveillance techniques and, by design, proceeds surreptitiously, it evades the ordinary checks that constrain abusive law enforcement practices: "limited police resources and community hostility."
>
> Awareness that the Government may be watching chills associational and expressive freedoms. And the Government's unrestrained power to assemble data that reveal private aspects of identity is susceptible to abuse. The net result is that GPS monitoring—by making available at a relatively low cost such a substantial quantum of intimate information about any person whom the Government, in its unfettered discretion, chooses to track—may alter the relationship between citizen and government in a way that is inimical to democratic society.[79]

Justice Samuel Alito also echoed this concern that big data technologies required a rethinking of Fourth Amendment protections:

> In the pre-computer age, the greatest protections of privacy were neither constitutional nor statutory, but practical. Traditional surveillance for any extended period of time was difficult and costly and therefore rarely undertaken. The surveillance at issue in this case—constant monitoring of the location of a vehicle for four weeks—would have required a large

team of agents, multiple vehicles, and perhaps aerial assistance. Only an investigation of unusual importance could have justified such an expenditure of law enforcement resources.[80]

A majority of the Supreme Court, thus, agreed that the type of digital time machine at issue presented a threat to Fourth Amendment principles. Yet, despite the awareness of the dangers of mass surveillance, none of the justices offered a clear answer about the future. Five of the justices were in agreement that long-term (28-day) GPS tracking for a drug crime violated the Fourth Amendment because it violated a reasonable expectation of privacy, but no further specifics about other technologies, other time frames, or other crimes were offered. The Supreme Court answered the question before it and nothing more, leaving for another day how it might address the growth of big data surveillance technologies. We do not know if surveillance for 14 days or four days might change the Court's analysis or if a different crime (murder, terrorism) might affect the outcome. We know that technology has changed the Fourth Amendment but just not how much.

The big data surveillance capabilities detailed in this book vastly exceeds the rather-simple GPS location-tracking device used in the *Jones* case. Fourth Amendment questions will arise from use of ALPR devices and facial-recognition cameras. Fourth Amendment concerns will impact DAS and drone surveillance. But as of now, these constitutional issues remain unresolved, and Congress has largely failed to act.

Future threats of mass surveillance are only growing. *Wired* magazine reported that technology now exists that potentially could link 30 million private CCTV surveillance cameras together in a truly massive surveillance system.[81] Private towing companies have begun equipping their trucks with ALPR scanners to assist with repossession claims and have been willing to share that data with law enforcement.[82] Cities have seen the capabilities of the Domain Awareness System and are looking to purchase it. In combination, this surveillance network provides a real-time map of our daily activities without any guide to future privacy protections or constitutional limitations. This is the Fourth Amendment question for the future, one that threatens to rewrite existing constitutional understandings of liberty, autonomy, and freedom from government monitoring.

How Big Data Impacts When We Police

Changing "when we police" is not just about real-time investigative capacities but also signals a commitment to proactive information gathering. Constant collection of data to understand community networks of criminal activity has altered what police do on a daily basis.

In doing fieldwork with the LAPD, Sarah Brayne observed the effect that new pre-crime data collection had on policing. Central to the LAPD's data-collection effort were "field interview cards."[83] Police on patrol would fill out these cards, which included personal information such as name, address, sex, height, weight, "descent" (presumably ethnicity), date of birth, aliases, probation/parole status, phone numbers, and Social Security numbers.[84] Additional information about "personal oddities," union affiliation, or gang or club membership can be added on the cards. Other information about the subject's vehicle (including damage, custom accessories, or stickers) and persons found with the suspect can be memorialized. Importantly, the location and time of the contact (geocoordinates) are recorded, so that all of this information could be saved for later investigative use and uploaded to the system to link suspects together. So, for example, if two people were observed on two separate days in the same vehicle, that link—once reduced to digital form—could be observed in the data. Or if several field interview cards identified individuals from the same gang, the location of these gang members could be digitally mapped over time.

In some cases, the field interview cards were bundled into formal "Chronic Violent Crime Offender Bulletins," which became one-page dossiers about high-risk individuals.[85] These bulletins would include a photograph of the subject with identifying information but also would list the history of prior contacts between police and the individual (and his associates). These bulletins were not intended to replace arrests warrants and had no independent legal significance but did end up having a real tactical impact. In practice, the Chronic Violent Crime Offender Bulletins were operationalized into Project LASER (Los Angeles Strategic Extraction and Restoration),[86] the goal of which was "to target with laser-like precision the violent repeat offenders and gang members who commit crimes in the specific target areas. The program is analogous to laser surgery, where a trained medical doctor uses modern technology to remove tumors or improve eyesight."[87] Like priority targets in New York City, these men became the focus of police attention before any report of a completed crime.

This move to collect data through field interview cards began to have an outsized role in policing. Each police contact ratcheted up the likelihood of future suspicion, because each contact counted toward an informal threat score. So just by being the recipient of police attention, one's threat score increased. Or, in other words, police could increase suspicion just by being suspicious. Second, the push for contacts encouraged officers to initiate physical conversations and stops with those who were targeted. Even if consensual, these stops felt like seizures for those people being stopped. And information that a person was a "Chronic Violent Crime Offender" likely would tip the balance into finding some reasonable suspicion for a stop. After all, if you are a police officer on patrol and you receive a "Chronic Violent Crime Offender Bulletin" with a photograph of someone who lives on your patrol route, you are going to be suspicious of that person.

This pre-crime information also impacts how police treat citizens. Police approaching someone considered a "Chronic Violent Crime Offender" might reasonably use significant caution and perhaps force, including physical force, to ensure their safety. From the perspective of the suspect, such treatment will be considered demeaning, frightening, and unnecessary. While the suspect may well have gang affiliations and a prior record and may be under court supervision, it might be the case that at that particular time, the suspect is trying to go home, get a job, or care for his family.

To be clear, these police contacts do not involve investigating ongoing crimes or making arrests of completed crimes (there is neither reasonable suspicion nor probable cause). They involve pre-crime data collection, transforming police officers into data collectors for a larger system of information control. Police are policing before the crime and building the investigative network to solve future crimes. While no doubt these regular police contacts also impose a measure of social control over a population likely to be involved in crime, the focus is really about proactively developing data, rather than responding to reported crimes.

A real-time data-collection focus makes the job of a police officer far more complex. In addition to doing all of the normal day-to-day tasks, police officers must also become data-entry experts, interpreters, and technicians. Data in a data-driven policing system comes from the officers collecting it. As can be seen in the push for data from field interview cards with the LAPD, this means a lot of data entry. While certain start-up companies like Mark43 have offered new digital software to speed up data entry and automate police reforms,[88] for most officers, the paperwork system is not too different from their father's police force.

Besides the time-consuming nature of the data-entry process, this data focus requires police to see things as the data fields consider things. The cards reduce individuals to categories of race, gang affiliation, gender, and the like, rather than thinking about the individuals as individuals. Suspects become data points as much as people. The focus becomes one of tagging individuals rather than seeing the environments in which they operate. By design, the LAPD system is trying to mark people in time and place, so police become hunters, geotagging suspects for the larger data net. Every patrol becomes a data-gathering mission, rather than a crime-suppression mission.

With more information, police officers must become fluent data interpreters. A constant flow of new information is available to police. Before knocking on a door or stopping a car or talking to a person on the street, a wealth of data must be interpreted. Much of this instantaneously available information is imperfectly sourced, contradictory, and overwhelming. Imagine: a police officer stops a car owned by a convicted violent felon, but one who appears to be employed and lives in a big home in a nice neighborhood. Is he dangerous? How does the additional information help the officer sort through the risks? How can the officer check the reliability of the information? Adding a Beware "threat score" filled with miscellaneous consumer data (or the equivalent) only complicates the decision.

Of course, police have always had to make difficult decisions, but the inputs of traditional policing were much narrower. When Officer McFadden watched John Terry, he saw what he saw with his own two eyes.[89] His prior experience could inform his personal observation, but much of his decision making came from inside his head and gut. But in a big data world, McFadden would be burdened with all sorts of externally derived facts. He might know the type of neighborhood, down to last week's robbery stats. He might know about John Terry, receiving not just the available law enforcement information but also what the data brokers have on him. He might have information through cameras about where Terry was beforehand. All of these additional inputs probably assist in assessing whether reasonable suspicion exists for a stop, and most are probably quite helpful; but all are new burdens for officers forced to evaluate the reliability and credibility of the information.

Police officers must become sophisticated data consumers. All the data in the world does not help anyone if line officers do not access the information. NYPD's handheld devices become expensive phones if officers do not master the skills of querying the data. These soft computer skills might also have to go beyond merely using police data to the world of social media or data mining. This reality involves not just technological competence and familiarity but the ability to articulate why officers did what they did and why the data can be trusted. Police officers on the witness stand at a suppression hearing will not do well if their answer to "why did you stop the suspect?" is merely "because the computer told me to." Instead, officers will need to be able to articulate how the data informed their professional judgment and why it makes sense to rely on this type of data for this type of case. Only then will courts accept the value of big data policing to determine the fate of criminal defendants.

The growth of pervasive surveillance capabilities, big data analysis technologies, and aggregated personal information threatens to radically expand when (and how) police investigate cases. A single drone with sophisticated video, audio, and tracking capabilities could change crime patterns and privacy protections in one figurative sweep. While the technology does not quite exist yet, one would be hard-pressed to think of a crime that occurs in public that could not be observed and then investigated with an all-seeing drone. Like the ground-level DAS system, police could digitally search for all hand-to-hand transactions and then observe which ones involved drug dealing. Police could (again with not-yet-operational video capacity) identify the individuals and identify where they came from (their home) and their daily patterns. Big cases like bank robberies or murders could be watched, with all of the players tracked back not just to their home but for the past week. Such a time machine might deter a significant amount of crime. With digital mass collection, the time for police to use this information changes, allowing quicker responses to emergencies but also longer-term investigations of criminal patterns on the streets.

But the cost of such surveillance is our privacy, because that same technology also monitors political protesters, religious dissenters, and everyone else. This is the dilemma of the "collect it all" mind-set. To catch the bank robber, you also need to capture the photo of everyone who uses the bank. Constitutional and statutory law has yet to navigate big data technologies' privacy-eroding potential, but the two are on a collision course with an uncertain future.

6

How We Police

Data Mining Digital Haystacks

Our work is very challenging. We are looking for needles in
a nationwide haystack, but we are also called up to figure out
which pieces of hay might someday become needles.
—FBI Director James Comey[1]

Cellular Circuits

The High Country Bandits robbed 16 small-town banks over the course
of two years.[2] Two men dressed in ski masks, jackets, and gloves pulled
off one armed robbery after another across rural Arizona, Colorado,
and New Mexico. In a posted "Wanted Bulletin," the FBI described the
bandits' modus operandi: "The unknown male identified as suspect
number one often enters the banks in rural locations near closing time
and brandishes a black semi-automatic handgun. Suspect number one
then demands all the money from the teller drawers. He obtains an
undisclosed amount of money, puts it in a bag, orders everyone on the
ground, then exits the banks with a second suspect."[3] The bank robbers netted small amounts of cash and disappeared. Over and over, they
managed to stay one step ahead of law enforcement, tacking back and
forth through small towns in the West. They forgot just one thing. They
were being tracked by their data.

The FBI caught the bandits with a relatively simple digital search.[4]
First, the FBI obtained a court order for all of the cellphone-tower records from four of the most rural victimized banks. Since all cellphones
regularly check in with the nearest cell tower, a continuous log of nearby
cellphone numbers can be obtained. FBI agents figured that if any single
phone number showed up at each of the robbed banks, they would have
their suspect.[5] And they were right. One Verizon cellphone number
popped up (out of the 150,000 numbers collected) near three of the four

banks (Verizon did not have a tower near the fourth bank).[6] Another cell number popped up in two of the four bank locations. And that second number had called the first number on repeated occasions.[7] The FBI went back to the judge and obtained another court order seeking locational data from the two cellphones in question. By examining the cell-tower records, the FBI could demonstrate that one or both of the cellphones had been near most of the 16 bank robberies. The FBI then tracked the phones to their subscribers, Joel Glore and Ronald Capito, and ended the criminal careers of the High Country Bandits.[8]

A more sophisticated cellphone investigation broke open the largest cash theft in Swedish history.[9] In a crime right out of the movies, a well-financed ring of international thieves used a stolen helicopter, fake bombs, and armed robbers rappelling down ropes into a locked vault to walk off with 6.5 million in Swedish kronor. As described by Evan Ratliff in his spellbinding article *Lifted* in the *Atavist* magazine, the robbers targeted a cash depot holding the equivalent of $150 million.[10] The plan involved a coordinated assault via helicopter, high-power explosives, and a violent attack that overwhelmed the guards at the depot. The plan worked flawlessly, except that despite the gloves, masks, stolen getaway vehicles, and other precautions, the criminals could not escape their data trails.

Unlike the High Country Bandits, the international thieves had the good sense not to bring along their personal cellphones to the heist. Instead, they used disposable prepaid phones ("burner phones") to hide their contacts.[11] But even disposable phones leave data trails. One of the Swedish police investigators, Jonas "Jocke" Hildeby, decided to find the needles in the haystack of phone calls. He collected a list of all of the phone numbers processed by cell towers near the cash depot at the time of the robbery. The list included 300,000 calls and 18,000 telephone numbers. Hildeby's goal was to find a closed loop of disposable phone numbers that communicated only with each other and only around the time of the heist. His theory, which turned out to be correct, was that the robbers would be given burner phones to communicate, only use them to plan the robbery, and then ditch them once the robbery was over. In combing through the data, Hildeby found one such closed circuit of 14 phones. These phones spoke only with each other, did so only in the weeks leading up to the robbery, and stopped immediately after the robbery. In triangulating the location of those 14 phones, investigators could actually map out the path of the different participants during the course of the robbery.[12] For example, police knew that the helicopter had been stolen from a particular hanger and could track one of the burner phones to that location. Essentially, a digital map could be reconstructed with cellular locational data that mirrored each step of the robbery.

The next step required connecting the burner phones used in the robbery to actual people. The police had identified two potential suspects but needed to connect those men to the phones. Again, data trails revealed the link. Police traced the suspects' personal cellphones using the same tracking technology. Lo and behold, the suspects' personal cellphones were located at the exact same place as the burner phones (before the robbery). The suspects had used personal phones to make personal calls and burner phones to further the conspiracy, but the data trails put both sets of phones at the same place at the same time. At trial, the suspects tried to explain away the coincidence, but the data trails undermined their efforts. Using these cell-tower links, as well as other surveillance, digital, and biological evidence, prosecutors were able to convict the men of the crime.[13]

Big data policing takes advantage of these cellular, digital, and biological data trails by creating new ways to search for connections. This chapter explores how data can be mined to aid criminal investigations. But it also addresses the problems with data error, the racial bias infecting data-driven systems, and the temptation of pure probabilistic suspicion.

Cellular Haystacks

In the United States, police have used cell-tower searches in thousands of criminal cases.[14] In some instances, police simply subpoenaed the phone numbers from cellphone companies, and in other cases, the police directly intercepted the cellphone numbers using "cell site simulators."[15] Cell site simulation technology, formally known as an International Mobile Subscriber Identity catcher (IMSI-catcher) but informally known as a "stingray device" or "D[i]RT-box," mimics a cell tower and tricks cellphones into thinking it is an official tower.[16] Once tricked, the cellphone reveals its unique identifier, and the cell site simulator captures the location, time, date, and duration of the call.[17] The device is precise enough to find a phone within a few feet.[18]

The difficulty is that in order to capture a targeted cell number, the stingray device also has to capture all the other phone numbers in the area.[19] To find the guilty needle in the haystack, you have to collect a lot of innocent hay. And because cell site simulators collect data from all phones in the area, they create massive cellular nets of personal information.[20] These simulators can be fixed but also have been mounted on planes, which allows the capturing of cell data from thousands of phones. For example, the *Wall Street Journal* reported that U.S. marshals used small Cessna planes outfitted with DRT-box surveillance tools to find wanted suspects down below.[21]

Sifting through cellphone data can result in remarkably effective policing. On May 9, 2009, an employee at the Central Booking Station at the Baltimore Police Department discovered that her car window had been smashed and her cellphone stolen.[22] In a city plagued by serious crime, and without witnesses or clues, these petty thefts generally remain unsolved. Two days later, the thief had been caught. The secret? Baltimore police used a stingray device to locate the stolen phone. But there was a problem. The secret was a secret.[23] The Baltimore police had signed a nondisclosure agreement with the FBI at the behest of Harris International (the maker of the stingray device), which prohibited the police from mentioning the device's use in any public manner.[24] So investigators did not mention how they discovered the phone in the police reports. Prosecutors could not reveal the information to the defense lawyers or the judge. This secret surveillance caused problems for criminal prosecutions, and in a few cases, judges threw out the charges because the nondisclosure agreement restricted police officers from testifying truthfully about using the devices. In other cases, prosecutors dropped or reduced the charges.[25] In the Baltimore cellphone case, prosecutors dismissed the charges after a few months.

The scope of this cellular sleuthing is growing with the technology. In litigation over the use of IMSI-catchers, a Baltimore police detective testified that the police had used the technology 4,300 times since 2007.[26] Some of those cases involved serious charges such as homicide, shooting, or rapes, but others fell on the petty-theft side of the line.[27]

In Florida, court records show that police have used the devices 1,800 times.[28] In Tacoma, Washington, police used it 170 times.[29] The federal government currently owns over 400 cell-site simulation devices and spent almost $100 million on the technology between 2010 and 2014.[30] Other jurisdictions also own the technology but have maintained secrecy about the scope of its use.

Metadata

When you know a phone has been stolen, it makes sense to search for the phone's location (and thus the thief). But what if you do not know whether there was a crime, but you suspect that watching patterns of communications could reveal a crime? The capturing of the entire haystack of phone records can be wonderfully revealing for police investigators, because the metadata connecting those numbers reveals otherwise-unseen connections. Metadata is "data about data," which in the phone context means the number, contacts, time, date, and location of the call (but not the content).[31] Metadata is a big data creation, only useful because powerful computers can crunch the 3 billion phone calls made to or from the United States *each day*.[32] Metadata is also created by internet and computer usage, social media posts, digital photographs, and pretty much every digital activity done today.[33]

The popular discussion of telephone metadata begins with Edward Snowden's revelations that the National Security Agency (NSA) had been collecting phone-record metadata.[34] Although the NSA is focused on the collection of foreign—not domestic—intelligence, through the agency's telephony metadata program, the NSA collected locational data about calls, the IMSI identity of the callers, and the duration of the calls but not the content of the calls.[35] NSA would query the data for information about specific, targeted phone numbers. Connections between targeted numbers could be linked in "hops," meaning linking all of the numbers connected to the target phone number. So, for example, an international terrorist target's phone number could be linked to all the people he called, as well as all the people they called (one hop), and then linked to all the people the secondary group called (two hops). The network map "hops" outward, expanding to reveal other possible connections between suspected intelligence threats.

In the litigation over the constitutionality of the NSA program, Edward Felten, director of the Center for Information Technology Policy at Princeton University, detailed the revealing nature of metadata.[36] In a legal declaration filed in federal court in the Southern District of New York, he wrote,

> Although this metadata might, on first impression, seem to be little more than "information concerning the numbers dialed," analysis of telephony metadata often reveals information that could traditionally only be obtained by examining the contents of communications. That is, metadata is often a proxy for content. In the simplest example, certain telephone numbers are used for a single purpose, such that any contact reveals basic and often sensitive information about the caller. Examples include support hotlines for victims of domestic violence and rape, including a specific hotline for rape victims in the armed services. Similarly, numerous hotlines exist for people considering suicide, including specific services for first responders, veterans, and gay and lesbian teenagers. Hotlines exist for sufferers of various forms of addiction, such as alcohol, drugs, and gambling.[37]

Felten also detailed how calls to certain numbers can reveal charitable and political donations, connections to activist organizations, employment, and friendships.[38] Sometimes a series of calls can reveal intimate or embarrassing details. "Consider the following hypothetical example: A young woman calls her gynecologist; then immediately calls her mother; then a man who, during the past few months, she had repeatedly spoken to on the telephone after 11pm; followed by a call to a family planning center that also offers abortions. A likely storyline emerges that would not be as evident by examining the record of a single telephone call."[39]

A Stanford University study confirmed the invasive power of telephone metadata.[40] The study involved 823 volunteer participants who provided access to metadata information on 251,788 calls and 1,234,231 text messages.[41] The study sought to create a data set that could test just how revealing a NSA-like metadata program could be. The study provided four main takeaways relevant to big data policing. First, even a "two hop" constraint resulted in linking almost all of the quarter million telephone numbers. Certain "hub" numbers (for example, telemarketers) contacted so many people that almost all other people could be linked through those shared connections. Second, even though the phone numbers did not have names attached, through the use of publicly available social media and internet searches, the deidentified numbers could be reidentified to find real people. The researchers concluded, "Telephone numbers are trivially identifiable." Third, by studying the patterns of calls, researchers could determine revealing insights about people's lives. For example, by studying the pattern and time of phone calls, researchers could determine who was in a romantic relationship. Finally, and most interestingly, the metadata revealed sensitive personal information. The study describes being able to diagnose illnesses, medical conditions, and an interest in firearms just from the numbers called.[42] Researchers could even develop suspicion hinting at particular crimes, such as calls to a hydroponics store, a head shop, a locksmith, and a hardware store all in under three weeks, which could lead to the inference that the caller had an interest in growing marijuana.[43]

Despite such privacy concerns, the government has consistently argued that the metadata program—because it was a non-content-based collection system—did not reveal constitutionally protected personal information.[44] Further, it has argued that because of restrictions on access to and dissemination of the data, as well as the program's focus on identifying unknown terrorist operations and preventing terrorist attacks, the program did not violate the constitutional rights of United States citizens. Both points are legally important. If metadata does not reveal private data, then it would be hard to claim that the Fourth Amendment's protection of the reasonable expectation of privacy should apply. Not only did the phone user knowingly share the information with a third-party provider (the phone company), but the collected information does not target personal content (all that is revealed is the data around the phone numbers).[45] Second, the government argued that a vast amount of data collection was reasonable based on the limited way it was used and the significance of the government's interest.[46] While Congress has since banned the bulk collection of telephone metadata under NSA's previous program, domestic law enforcement can obtain access to metadata for specific cases.[47]

But, really, one does not need the NSA to collect the information. NSA collected the raw information from telephone companies such as AT&T, which maintained telephone metadata for years.[48] Literally, trillions of records of phone calls exist in searchable form. Certain law enforcement agencies like the DEA have access to this super database of metadata through a still-secret program called the Hemisphere Project.[49] The Drug Enforcement Agency has even allowed AT&T employees to work beside DEA agents to more efficiently search the database.[50] The Hemisphere Project database has been called "a super search engine" or "Google on Steroids" that allows investigators to search connections between numbers and locations on any call that passes through AT&T switches.[51] Without a judicial warrant, law enforcement can obtain targeted information using an administrative subpoena or equivalent judicial order. This metadata connects the dots of social networks and locations of people suspected of criminal activities.

Social Media Mining

A shooting outside a club, a mass protest, a citywide celebration—these events generate instant social media commentary, photos, and video. Individuals at the events can post public comments or images from the events. What if police could zero in on the geographic location and view all of the social media commentary happening in real time, identifying both the people present and the content of the communication? Police in Austin, Oakland, San Diego, San Jose, Santa Clara, and Philadelphia have experimented with Geofeedia,[52] a software program that allows users to tag, search, and sort social media content for investigation. Other companies such as BlueJay or SnapTrends offer similar social media scraping services.[53]

The possibilities for investigating social media are alluring to police. Imagine that moments after a club shooting, police use a Geofeedia-like tool to isolate the geographic area around the club and search all of the Twitter, Facebook, Instagram, Picasa, and Flickr posts in real time.[54] These public comments could be searched for key words ("gun," "suspects"), and the people in the area could be geotagged, thus memorializing witness locations in real time. Communications between individuals could be linked so that investigators could see who was associated with whom at the scene, and videos and photos of the crime scene could be saved for future use at trial. Police could create a searchable database of all posts within that geographic boundary, and they could track all future posts of suspects initially identified as being at the scene.[55]

Social media surveillance can also help police investigating high-crime areas. For example, if police suspect a particular housing project as being the home of a drug gang, police can conduct long-term monitoring, intercepting all the social media posts coming from that geographic area. Police can identify all the people posting from the area (both those living there and visiting friends), and police can link those posts to others contacted through social media (developing a web of relationships). The result is a social media surveillance program that can monitor the public content to see if activities, threats, or social commentary suggest criminal activity.

Police in New York and Chicago have long monitored social media, including watching YouTube videos to determine the composition of gangs and related gang activity.[56] As most gangs involve youth who are fully immersed in social media culture, it is not surprising that gang life bleeds into the digital space. Gangs have used social media to threaten rivals and to stake out turf.[57] Gangs boast and insult others online, and sometimes threats in videos lead to real-world consequences. Ben Austen in *Wired* magazine interviewed a few of the digitally oriented detectives involved in policing the social media beat, examining the almost "entrepreneurial" way the gang unit in Chicago approaches social media threats.[58] "The police in Chicago now actively look for inflammatory comments around specific dates: the anniversary of a homicide, say, or the birthday of a slain gang member, the sorts of events that have often incited renewed rounds of violence."[59] As an example, he described how a police gang unit notified a 12-year-old's parents that their son had foolishly insulted a well-known gang member in a posted rap video. Police went so far as to relocate the family temporarily from their home and then watched as angry gang members stalked the young boy's home. Police believe that this type of preventive, real-time intervention saves lives.[60]

Academics have also begun studying Twitter to predict crime. The idea is that Twitter represents society's current views, organized by location and content, and thus could be useful for identifying future risks of violence. In an interview with NPR's *All Things Considered*, Desmond Patton, a professor of social work at Columbia University, explained how he has developed an algorithm to mine tweets for predicted violence: "One idea is that if we can decode the language, then perhaps we can send triggers to social workers, violence workers who are embedded in these neighborhoods already, so that they can utilize the strategies they already have to reach out to youth before the post becomes an injury or homicide."[61] While this type of algorithmic mining of content is still in its infancy, one can see that it could offer insights to police about patterns of youth activity in a city. Even something as simple as where the hot parties or hangouts will be on a weekend night might allow police to respond more effectively to prevent out-of-control situations in the immediate future.

But, of course, like in the cellular collection situation, in order to monitor the individualized risks, police and researchers also have to collect everyone's data. The haystack keeps growing, with billions of bytes of data being shared every day. To find the violent tweets, police also must collect the other content being shared on social media, and this can include First Amendment–protected public speech. In fact, Geofeedia was used to track and arrest young people in Baltimore protesting the death of Freddie Gray.[62] Similar concerns have arisen after the FBI and the Boston Police Department declared an interest in monitoring public social media posts for investigative purposes.[63]

Data Mining

"Data mining" involves the search of large data sets to discover new insights.[64] In policing, this means using data searches to help solve past crimes or uncover ongoing ones.

Data-mining searches have been conducted for years by law enforcement.[65] Police routinely search for fingerprints or DNA evidence in large national databases,[66] meaning that pattern-matching software sifts through collected fingerprints or DNA profiles to find a match. The FBI has augmented its search capacity by building a sophisticated biometric database that includes DNA, fingerprints, palm prints, face prints, tattoos, and iris scans.[67] This Next Generation Identification (NGI) system builds on big data capabilities to allow over 18,000 law enforcement entities to search the growing database.[68] Similarly, the FBI, the U.S. Treasury, and the Securities and Exchange Commission (SEC) rely on financial algorithms to track unusual or structured cash deposits, international transfers, or stock manipulation.[69] These pattern-matching investigative techniques look for suspicious movements in the flow of money and are expanding in sophistication alongside improved technologies.

Data mining also allows for more unstructured searches. For example, when the Richmond Police Department queried its correctional database to study stranger rapes, it found that "a prior property crime was a better predictor of a stranger rape than a prior sex offense."[70] As the chief of police explained,

> Upon further examination of the property crimes committed by some stranger rapists, we noted that many of their burglaries differed in that they seemed to preferentially target occupied dwellings and frequently stole property with little value, if they stole anything at all. Using this type of anomaly detection, we can identify unusual or suspicious incidents that are worthy of additional investigation and have been able to successfully identify cases associated with an increased risk for escalation based on subtle deviations from normal.[71]

This data-driven insight was both counterintuitive and critical to understanding criminal behavior. The result is also something that would have remained hidden in an era without large, searchable data sets.

Data reveals previously unseen connections between places, people, or acts. For example, sex trafficking is a vast and transient business, making it difficult to find the locations of trafficking victims. In response to this challenge, the Polaris Project, a national antitrafficking group, partnered with big data companies to begin geotagging the locations of hotline calls requesting help.[72] From a data set of 75,000 calls, the Polaris Project began identifying organized networks of trafficking across America.[73] Each call could be tagged by location and included the victim's age, immigration status, language needs, and shelter requirements.[74] Patterns emerged of certain truck stops that served as the location points for forced trafficking.[75] Certain cities at certain times (like during Super Bowl week) emerged as places to focus law enforcement attention.[76] Data mining allowed a geographically fluid and otherwise-secret network to be mapped and financial patterns to be exposed. For example, in targeted areas, nail salons that regularly processed numerous $100 charges after 11 p.m. were investigated as fronts for illicit prostitution businesses.[77] Fake entertainment companies used to cover trafficking could be targeted for tax-evasion or money-laundering investigations.[78] By tracing movement and money through data, a global and quick-moving criminal network could be monitored and prosecuted.

Data mining has also helped police address domestic violence. In New York City, data helped identify those men most likely to escalate violence on their partners.[79] Over a one-year period, NYPD officers responded to 263,207 calls for reported domestic violence.[80] Knowing that precursor acts of domestic violence tend to escalate into serious assaults and even homicides but not knowing which of those reports to prioritize, police turned to a computer program to scan the police complaint reports. The algorithm looked for words like "kill," "alcohol," or "suicide." In addition, police studied the addresses of stay-away orders and used those clues to prioritize certain households for additional attention.[81] Building off the data, police created a program whereby designated houses predicted to be the source of future domestic violence were visited and the victims interviewed.[82] Police conducted tens of thousands of precautionary follow-up visits to deter future acts of violence.

Finally, consumer purchases can be mined for possible clues about illegal activity. For example, one Kentucky study found that sales of over-the-counter cold medicine with the active ingredient pseudoephedrine directly correlated with an increase in meth-lab seizures and drug arrests.[83] As reported in the Los Angeles Times, "In any given county, an increase in pseudoephedrine sales of 13 grams per 100 people translated to an additional meth lab busted. The results suggest that the computer databases could actually be used to predict where drug busts are most likely to take place."[84] More basic correlations can also be made about individuals. By studying the purchase of anyone who bought lye, iodine, ephedrine (Sudafed), Drano, brake fluid, and lighter fluid—all component parts to making crystal meth—police might be able to see future criminal acts from otherwise-lawful purchases.[85] From the data of ordinary customer receipts, a pattern of criminal activity might emerge.

Of course, many innocent people with colds, injuries, and plumbing or car problems may also buy those fairly basic (and legal) consumer items.

The correlation, while suspicious, is not criminal. And this brings up one of the fundamental questions with algorithmic investigation: can correlation replace causation when the underlying data remains imperfect?

Can Algorithmic Investigation Be Trusted?

The rise of big data policing rests in part on the belief that data-based decisions can be more objective, fair, and accurate than traditional policing. Data is data and thus, the thinking goes, not subject to the same subjective errors as human decision making. But in truth, algorithms encode both error and bias. As David Vladeck, the former director of the Bureau of Consumer Protection at the Federal Trade Commission (who was, thus, in charge of much of the law surrounding big data consumer protection), once warned, "Algorithms may also be imperfect decisional tools. Algorithms themselves are designed by humans, leaving open the possibility that unrecognized human bias may taint the process. And algorithms are no better than the data they process, and we know that much of that data may be unreliable, outdated, or reflect bias."[86]

Algorithmic technologies that aid law enforcement in targeting crime must compete with a host of very human questions. What data goes into the computer model? After all, the inputs determine the outputs. How much data must go into the model? The choice of sample size can alter the outcome. How do you account for cultural differences? Sometimes algorithms try to smooth out the anomalies in the data—anomalies that can correspond with minority populations. How do you address the complexity in the data or the "noise" that results from imperfect results? The human world remains both complex and imperfect.[87] The choices made to create an algorithm can radically impact the model's usefulness or reliability.

To examine the problem of algorithmic design, imagine that police in Cincinnati, Ohio, have a problem with the Bloods gang—a national criminal gang originating out of Los Angeles that signifies membership by wearing the color red. Police use a social media scraping tool like Geofeedia to target possible gang members involved in drive-by shootings. They search key terms like "gang," "car," "gun," "hit," "cap," "park," "run," "drive," "shoot," "strike," "red," and "colors." A series of tweets and social media posts pop up, and police begin tracking links between the various social media users. On the basis of the identified problem (shootings), the identified targets (people using social media and making gang-related comments), and the location (Cincinnati), the software program comes up with a list of suspects to target. But unfortunately for the accuracy of the computer program, many people in Cincinnati might be talking about the local baseball team—the Reds—using words like "hit," "run," "strike," "cap," "park," and other baseball terms to discuss sports. The correlation might be very accurate given the search parameters and algorithmic design but overbroad with regard to finding the actual targets.

Similarly, the data mining of precursor crimes—if designed poorly—can lead to unhelpful and overgeneralized results. PredPol, which has successfully tested place-based predictive policing models of property crimes, attempted to use a similar approach for homicides.[88] PredPol's starting point, rather commonsensically, was that if you traced the prevalence of handguns, you could predict future shooting deaths. Find the guns, and you will find the bodies. Using Chicago as its laboratory, PredPol compiled a data set consisting of 38,740 violent crimes during the years 2009, 2010, and 2011. Looking at crimes with "handgun" in the descriptive field, the researchers isolated 17,020 robberies, 6,560 assaults, 8,252 weapons violations, 5,274 batteries, and 303 criminal sexual assaults.[89] The researchers then compared those precursor handgun crimes to the 1,331 homicides during that same time frame. In a white paper published on the results, the company claimed, "PredPol successfully predicts 50% of gun homicides by flagging in real-time only 10.3% of Chicago. . . . Crimes involving guns continue to have an impact on future gun homicides for 30–100 days and risk spreads over as much as 1/2 mile in area."[90] Pulling that conclusion apart, however, demonstrates the misleading utility of the analysis. First, predicting a shooting one month to three months out does not provide much guidance to police on the streets every day. When during that three-month time period should police be vigilant? What would they be looking for during that time? Also the area (10% of Chicago) is a vast area—approximately 23 square miles.[91] Again, without more granular information, this correlation—even if 100% accurate, does not offer enough insight to improve policing.

Algorithms can also just get it wrong. Pedro Domingos, a professor of computer science at the University of Washington and author of *The*

Master Algorithm, recounted an important lesson of mistaken machine learning.[92] In an article in the *Washington Post*, he explained how a colleague had created a computer algorithm to tell the difference between wolves and wild dogs (which can look quite similar).[93] During testing, the algorithm performed perfectly, too perfectly. Only upon further inspection was it revealed why the computer did so well. All of the photos of the wolves had been taken with white snow in the background, and none of the photos of the dogs had snow in the background. The computer had simply learned to identify snow, not wolves.[94] Similar dangers face predictive algorithms; false flags might prove correlations but only because of a poorly designed model.

Is Big Data Racist?

Sometimes, the machines get it wrong because of racial or gender bias built into the model. For policing, this is a serious concern. As Frank Pasquale has written in his acclaimed book *The Black Box Society*, "Algorithms are not immune from the fundamental problem of discrimination, in which negative and baseless assumptions congeal into prejudice. . . . And they must often use data laced with all-too-human prejudice."[95]

Solon Barocas and Andrew Selbst are scholars who study the disparate impact of big data technologies.[96] In an article on why big data discriminates, they articulate the four root problems of all algorithmic decision making: (1) definitional bias, (2) training bias, (3) feature selection bias, and (4) proxy bias.[97] Combined, these problems contribute to largely unintentional algorithmic discrimination in many big data "supervised learning" models.[98] Supervised learning algorithms are those that create rank-ordered targets, useful for hiring or matching the probability that someone will commit a crime.

Think about the design problem from a computer scientist's perspective. Imagine that you are called into an office and told to build a big data system to predict crime. You know how to create a model that predicts outputs from inputs, but there are some big design questions to answer. First, there are definitional questions. Are the inputs crime? Criminals? Patterns? How do you label the crime? What constitutes a burglary (some states include breaking into outbuildings and even cars as burglaries)? What class of crime does the act fit with? Is a burglary a nonviolent or violent crime? What are the target variables? Do you focus on arrests (which are only allegations of crime) or convictions (which might be resolved only months or even years after the incident)? What types of crime do you care about? The algorithm to predict burglary will look a lot different than the one to predict sexual assault. If you pick a place-based property-crime algorithm to guide your policing strategy, you may be ignoring other crimes in the area that are harder to track. How do you define the location of a crime (block, address, GPS coordinates)? The level of locational precision may impact how useful the resulting prediction model will be for police. These "target variable" and larger "definitional labeling" problems must be answered. Choices must be made. Human decisions impact "target variables" (the answers sought) and "class labels" (the menu of possible answers), and bias from those choices can impact the ultimate algorithmic model.[99]

To build a model, you need to use training data to "train" the model.[100] Algorithms and machine-learning models learn by analyzing past data. This means that the mathematical model's only ability to learn is to sort through historical data to determine a correlation. Inputs go in, and generalizations come out, so that if historical crime data shows that robberies happen at banks more often than at nursery schools, the algorithm will correlate banks with robberies, without any need to understand that banks hold lots of cash and nursery schools do not. "Why" does not matter to the math. The correlation is the key.

Of course, algorithms can replicate past biases, so that if an algorithm is built around biased data, analysts will get a biased result. For example, if police primarily arrest people of color from minority neighborhoods for marijuana, even though people of all races and all neighborhoods use marijuana at equal rates, the algorithm will correlate race with marijuana use. The algorithm will also correlate marijuana with certain locations. A policing strategy based on such an algorithm will correlate race and drugs, even though the correlation does not accurately reflect the actual underlying criminal activity across society. And even if race were completely stripped out of the model, the correlation with communities of color might still remain because of the location. A proxy for racial bias can be baked into the system, even without any formal focus on race as a variable.

In building a model and training the data, the system requires human judgment. Analysts must make decisions about how to use the data. "Feature selection" has the potential to create bias,[101] meaning that the features you choose for the model will alter your result. Again, take the relatively simple model to predict the location of a crime. You can build the crime-prediction model, collect the data, and train the data, but how do you define the resulting output? How big is the predicted high-crime area? Do you choose a 500-by-500-square-foot box, or a half-mile radius? The data could fit both, but the effectiveness and adverse impacts could be quite different for actual policing. How long does the targeted area remain "hot" (a month, a day), and does the strength of the prediction decay over time? Which crimes are weighted as more important to track? These are choices independent to the data but critical to the usefulness of the model.

Finally, proxies for racial bias can infect the data. Barocas and Selbst discuss the problem of "redundant encodings," when "membership in a protected class happens to be encoded in other data."[102] It may be that the data has been trained to look only at neighborhoods, but if city neighborhoods have been segregated though racially discriminatory zoning laws or have been economically fractured such that poverty, race, and place correlate, then a place-based predictive model may unintentionally discriminate. Data-based systems import the biases of their builders and the larger society. Data is not blind. Data is us, just reduced to binary code.

These concerns with predictive big data technologies appear in most big data policing models. Worse, the bias in the system can justify unequal or unfair treatment by police. If the algorithm is guiding policing, then police administrators and patrol officers are likely to follow. Thus, as Jules Polonetsky, Omer Tene, and Joseph Jerome have recognized, "big data could have the perverse result of *exacerbating* existing inequalities by suggesting that historically disadvantaged groups actually *deserve* less favorable treatment."[103] If one does not see the potential bias in the inputs, all that is left is a seemingly neutral objective output.

As algorithms become more central to our lives, the racial biases built into them have been exposed. Notorious examples involve an experiment by Harvard professor Latanya Sweeney, who demonstrated that Google's AdWords sales program discriminated by race.[104] Sweeney studied 120,000 internet-search ads promoted by data services that provided criminal background checks. When names associated with someone of African American descent were queried, the ads displayed for criminal background checks. When names associated with the white community were queried, no such ads displayed.[105] Another Google algorithm has been called out as sexist. Researchers at Carnegie Mellon created a tool that showed that Google search queries promoted prestigious job openings to men more than to women.[106] This was not because Google programed its search algorithm to be intentionally sexist, but the underlying data reflects existing gender bias in society. Simply taking gender or race out of the model does not cure the underlying bias. As mathematician Jeremy Kun has written, "It's true that an algorithm itself is quantitative—it boils down to a sequence of arithmetic steps for solving a problem. The danger is that these algorithms, which are trained on data produced by people, may reflect the biases in that data, perpetuating structural racism and negative biases about minority groups."[107] Big data policing involves a similar danger of perpetrating structural racism and negative biases about minority groups. "How" we target impacts "whom" we target, and underlying existing racial biases means that data-driven policing may well reflect those biases.

Probabilistic Suspicion?

Data mining cell-tower numbers or metadata or crime data all rely on the same principle: there is a high probability that suspicious linkages will connect a suspect to a crime. The probability that the High Country Bandit's cellphone coincidently would be at each of the banks at the exact time of the robberies is just too high to ignore. The probabilities suggest criminality and to a high degree of certainty.

But should an algorithm be sufficient to generate probable cause for an arrest? Should an algorithm that alerted police to your purchase of fertilizer, propane tanks, and matches, plus a rental truck, be sufficient to generate an arrest warrant on the suspicion of creating a truck bomb like that used for the Oklahoma City bombing of the Alfred P. Murrah Federal Building? While everyone might want the danger investigated, does it rise to the level that you can be actually handcuffed and brought to jail? Or stopped on the highway? What if the algorithm said it was a

90% certainty? Can any well-designed, well-trained, bias-free algorithm with high levels of accuracy be enough to generate an arrest warrant to result in a physical, real-world detention? This is the ultimate data-driven policing puzzle.

Two contradictory intuitions collide when thinking about pure probabilistic suspicion. The first involves acknowledging that prediction has long been a part of law enforcement, and predictions, almost by definition, can be wrong.[108] The second involves the discomfort felt about generalized suspicion. When it comes to liberty, mere correlation or a mathematical probability should not, the thinking goes, be enough to justify police action. Both sides can claim some support from the case law, and neither side has won the day in court.

First, unquestionably, the Fourth Amendment recognizes the need for predictive suspicion. When police officers draft a search warrant, they are making a prediction that contraband will be located at that particular place.[109] The judge must determine whether "there is a fair probability that contraband or evidence of a crime will be found in a particular place."[110] It is always possible that the contraband will be gone or was never there in the first place. Predictive suspicion is, thus, not a new concept, tracing its roots back to the words "probable cause" in the text of the Fourth Amendment. As the Supreme Court stated, "In the typical case where the police seek permission to search a house for an item they believe is already located there, the magistrate's determination that there is probable cause for the search amounts to a prediction that the item will still be there when the warrant is executed."[111]

Probable cause, as the term suggests, turns on probabilities. And these predictive probabilities are not necessarily the stuff of fixed numbers. In fact, the Supreme Court has refused to provide clear percentages as to the certainty required for probable cause.[112] The Court has stated, "The probable-cause standard is incapable of precise definition or quantification into percentages because it deals with probabilities and depends on the totality of the circumstances."[113] The reason for this lack of guidance is largely because judges must make quick decisions with imperfect information, and holding courts or police officers to a particular percentage seems both unfair and unrealistic.[114]

This deference continues on the streets, where investigative detentions (police stops) also involve quick predictive judgments. The standard from *Terry v. Ohio* states that to justify a stop, police must "be able to point to specific and articulable facts which, taken together with rational inferences from those facts, reasonably warrant that intrusion."[115] In other words, police must articulate why they predict a certain person is involved in criminal activity. Again, the prediction can be wrong, but at its core, it is a predictive, probabilistic judgment.

Predictions also underlie forensic investigation. A DNA match is, in reality, a probability that the two biological samples match.[116] The prediction can be quite strong (with a low chance of error), but it is still a prediction. Strong predictions can even be used to justify an arrest warrant—for example, in a "cold case" where a DNA match is the only thing linking the suspect to the crime scene. Police reliance on predictive theories and technologies are thus neither new nor necessarily controversial.

Background principles about prediction, however, run into our discomfort of generalized suspicion. In each of the examples just given— arrest warrant, *Terry* stop, DNA match—the prediction is linked to an individual person suspected of a crime. There is a reason why this person or that house or that biological material should be searched. But what about a situation in which all you have is a generalized suspicion, albeit with a high probability of accuracy? In an article on the Fourth Amendment, Arnold Loewy offered an intriguing hypothetical question on this point: "Suppose that in a particular city block of Main Street, between Fourth and Main and Fifth and Main, it could be established demographically that nine out of every ten men on the street between 6 p.m. and 10 p.m. are carrying drugs. Would that create probable cause (or reasonable suspicion) to arrest any man found on that block of Main Street at the requisite hours?"[117] By any measure, a 90% probability would easily surmount the probable cause standard required by the courts. Yet something feels wrong. The generality of the suspicion, which very likely will target innocent people (one in ten are not guilty), cuts against the support of otherwise-strong probability-based suspicion.

What is wrong is the lack of individualized suspicion. As Loewy answered his own question, "The answer, I believe, is 'no.' Probable cause and reasonable suspicion require more than demographic probabilities. There must be something specific to the defendant to create the probability as to him (perhaps a furtive gesture, an informant's tip, excessive nervousness, etc.)."[118] Something more than generalizations about the "high crime" location or the "hot" people who frequent the area must be established. As the Supreme Court said in another case, "probable cause requires 'that the belief of guilt must be particularized with respect to the person to be searched or seized.'"[119] Or as Tracey Maclin put it in historical context, "It is a fair summary of the history of the Fourth Amendment to say that the provision reflected the Framers' desire to control the discretion of ordinary law enforcement officers and to eliminate governmental intrusions lacking particularized suspicion."[120]

Applying this principle of particularized suspicion to the problem of pure probabilistic data mining, courts may be reluctant to allow generalized suspicion (even with a high degree of accuracy) to constitute probable cause. Something more, individualizing the suspicion to a person, may be necessary to satisfy the Fourth Amendment. So database suspicion alone should be insufficient to meet the constitutional threshold.

But this requirement presents difficult questions. For example, imagine that an algorithm alerts when any white man between 40 and 60 years old files bankruptcy, receives emergency psychiatric services, and buys a gun in the same week, on the theory that in combination, those life stresses and actions are statistically more likely to result in impulsive, emotional acts of violence. Assuming that there is clear data that such clusters of events result in violence (as of now, there is no such data), should police act to stop, seize, or even arrest the suspect? One difficulty is that the judge or arresting officer will have no way to test the accuracy of such a correlation. The numbers remain a black box. Another is that the generic suspicion that may attach to such a cluster may not attach to this particular suspect. An innocent man who is facing already-significant life issues will now face criminal suspicion. A third issue is that no one in the system knows what to do with the information. One solution, of course, would be to have the alert lead only to a contact, not any actual criminal action. Police might call or inquire but not do anything more invasive. In this way, the algorithmic alert would serve more of a public health function, rather than a law enforcement function. But, again, one can only imagine the response of this already-stressed individual when the police knock on the door to "talk" about his problems.

Other scholars have pushed back against the whole conception of individualized suspicion.[121] After all, if you consider how police really make decisions, they routinely generalize and use intuitions from past experiences to predict future actions. Individual judgments, in truth, are just reflections of generalizations from past experience.[122] For example, our understanding of concepts like "pretty" or "ugly," "suspicious" or "innocent" only come from our own personal algorithm of accumulated past experiences and intuitions. Bernard Harcourt and Tracey Meares detail a more accurate reality of police suspicion:

> Suspicion attaches to a group trait that an individual displays, such as having a bulge in one's pants pocket, fitting a description in the vicinity of a recently committed offense, throwing away a plastic vial at the sight of a police patrol car. . . . These are group-based determinations often made irrespective of the officer's knowledge of whether a specific offense has been committed, and suspicion potentially attaches to all individuals within these categories. Suspicion in these cases is "individualized" only in the sense that it attaches to an individual because he or she is a member of the suspect group. In other words, in most cases of policing, suspicion does not originate at the individual level.[123]

In other words, individual suspicion really incorporates generalizations about group action. Police use these cognitive shortcuts all the time, and if police can use these group traits for suspicion, why should algorithms not also be able to draw similar group correlations together? The difficulty, as has been discussed, is that these shortcuts or generalizations include implicit (and sometimes explicit) bias, and the same problems that infect human generalizations can also infect algorithmic generalizations. Just because police generalize does not make it permissible to design an algorithmic system to mirror the same biases.

The legal question about pure algorithmic suspicion remains open. Daniel Steinbock has argued, "Predictive profiling is not inconsistent with the Fourth Amendment, [and] the factors used must indicate to the investigating officers (and, later, the reviewing court) the requisite degree of suspicion. Nothing suggests that these actors should defer to a computer algorithm for projecting that level of suspicion, but nothing rules out that possibility either."[124] Perhaps improved big data technologies will allow us to feel more comfortable with this type of generalized but accurate correlation. I have my doubts, as the human requirement to confirm suspicion seems necessary in a human system of law enforcement. Even if the algorithm or alert system can help find the needle in the haystack, a human should confirm that the correlation makes sense in this particular case. But courts have yet to answer this question, and the existing law may well allow it. This will matter because the rise of data mining and the ease of matching those data-driven clues to real people will only increase in the future.

How Big Data Impacts How We Police

Data collection, data mining, and data analysis shape both police investigation and police practice. The work involves technical expertise and a significant investment in technology.

For investigation purposes, the move toward data mining opens up a new type of suspicion. Data creates the clues. Data generates the leads. Human suspects emerge only after the data has been queried. As Erin Murphy has recognized, "The use of databases to generate suspects represents a new kind of investigation altogether—whether based on particular information (e.g., "who called this number") or upon predefined algorithms (e.g., "who has traveled to these three countries and bought these two items within a one month period")."[125] This type of suspicion offers the ability to develop targets without the report of a crime. Building off the proactive, intelligence-led investigative model, this type of predictive suspicion will result in more surveillance and a greater need for police to collect data. If you combine the various different surveillance technologies discussed in this book, you can see that a huge change awaits law enforcement. Although analyzed separately, each of these technologies—person based, place based, real time, social networks, aerial surveillance, and so on—can be aggregated in ways such that data mining will offer new possibilities to develop suspicion.

More practically, police administrators will need to begin hiring more technologically savvy data geeks. Unless police agencies wish to outsource their investigation to private companies and consultants to manage the technology, then in-house officers will have to be trained (and retained). Currently, the public-private partnerships between LAPD and

Palantir or NYPD and Microsoft (which built the Domain Awareness System) appear to be working, but one can imagine all sorts of problems in the future. The private company could decide not to continue working in the policing space, abandoning the technology and the city contract. The private company could itself be suspected of criminal activity (creating a major conflict of interest). Budget issues could require police to scale back the participation arrangement, and without continually trained, data-smart officers, a data-dependent policing system could fail.

Changing how we police also involves a change in mind-set. Police administrators face a big challenge to get officers to buy into big data's potential. Policing is a status quo job, which by design and tradition protects the status quo. Many police officers have practiced within traditional policing structures for decades, so moving to a data-driven system brings resistance, distrust, and tension.[126] Early versions of predictive policing technologies have been met with skeptical tolerance, with senior officers thinking the technology adds little to their own professional knowledge of the area and others thinking that the products are more magic than science. Police administrators thus must educate officers of the value added by data-mining technology.

Finally, data-driven policing will require a focus on precision. Police administrators will need to develop quality-control mechanisms for data-mining systems. Big data in the consumer space does not need to be perfectly accurate to be helpful, but big data in the policing space does not have the same luxury to tolerate error. As big data systems grow in scope, more errors will be included, and government officials must be able to cleanse, cure, and trust the data. It cannot be the case that a chief of police has no idea of the content or reliability of the information that is influencing his or her officers. It should not be the case that the police cannot reveal the nature of the technological tools used to capture information. As attractive as new surveillance tools may be, police must take ownership of their use and be able to defend their legality. Police departments cannot live in the dark.

7

Black Data

Distortions of Race, Transparency, and Law

Seeing in the Dark

In the near future, the innovations of big data policing will amplify "who," "where," "when," and "how" law enforcement targets crime. While not all jurisdictions will utilize all of these new technologies and while new technologies will continue to develop, every police force using big data techniques will share one thing: a "black data" problem.

"Black data" denotes three overlapping concerns with the rise of data-driven policing, involving race, transparency, and constitutional law. First, data comes from the real world, weighted with racial disparities and a history of unfair application. Second, new data technologies are secretive, scary, and unfamiliar. There exists a darkness. A void. A fear. We cannot see into the future. And, third, what we do see regarding privacy or constitutional protections seems distorted.

The tensions inherent in black data will shape perceptions about new policing technologies. At this moment, at the intersection of new technology and old policing problems, black data must be illuminated. This chapter seeks to examine the future of big data policing through the lens of black data. Only by confronting the issues of race, transparency, and constitutional distortion can a future vision of big data policing become clear. Like one's eyes adjusting to a dark room, seeing in the darkness of black data allows a differentiation of those shapes that one should be scared of and those that are harmless or even helpful.

Black Data and Race

Big data's claim to objectivity and fairness must confront the racial history of American policing. Police data remains colored by explicit and implicit bias. Police data is racially coded, shaded by millions of distrustful looks and thousands of discomfiting physical encounters. The data incorporates the lived experience of African Americans, Latinos, and other people of color who have rightly or wrongly felt discriminated against because of society's suspicion.[1] In short, big data policing must acknowledge that race is still part of modern policing. Even as code, the data is black.

Acknowledging the "blackness" of police data serves two very useful goals. First, this admission pushes back against the facile claim that the issue of race can be removed by "objective," data-driven policing or that new big data technologies avoid racially biased effects. Second, the acknowledgment forces a serious examination of the very human injustices that still stir resentment and distrust in minority communities. Police can develop technologies to address and overcome these racial tensions, but first the adopters of data-driven systems must acknowledge and design around this racial reality.

As detailed throughout the book, big data policing reifies many of the systemic inequalities of traditional policing. Place-based predictive systems culled from unrefined crime statistics reflect policing patterns, not necessarily the underlying crime patterns.[2] The choice to send undercover narcotics investigators to inner cities as opposed to Ivy League colleges ensures drug arrests of the poor instead of the privileged. Targeting high-risk blocks because of the number of returning citizens or people on probation living there encodes the prior decisions of a criminal justice system that disproportionately punishes people of color. Suspect-based predictive policing, because it takes into account prior arrests, suspected gang associations, and the like, cannot help but also reflect the socioeconomic impacts of traditional policing patterns.[3] As none other than Jeff Brantingham, the father of modern predictive policing, warned about person-based models, "These 'person-centric' models are problematic . . . because they carry an elevated margin of error and can legitimize racial, gender-based and socioeconomic-driven profiling. As a scientist you better be damn sure the model of causality is right or else it's going to lead to a lot of false positives."[4]

Other systemic racial inequalities exist. One can see how the pressure to collect "field interview cards" can create a self-fulfilling system of suspicion for those high-risk individuals targeted.[5] Official policies of aggressive stops in minority neighborhoods generate future suspicion shaped in part by the number of prior contacts. Even pure algorithmic suspicion, which should avoid charges of racial bias, can be found to be infected with biases due to the way the models are built or the data collected and trained. If facial recognition, pretrial risk assessments, and Google search query technology cannot avoid race-based disparate effects, then all data-driven technologies must be alert for potential bias.

So, while promising a clean start, big data policing cannot—in truth—escape a long history of racial discrimination. Instead, it must confront an uncomfortable tradition of social control in minority communities. As Sandra Bass has summarized,

> The interactive relationship between race, space and policing has been of social and political significance since the earliest days of American history. Monitoring the movement of slaves was a central concern for plantation masters and slave patrollers. The desire to regulate and subjugate the behavior of newly manumitted slaves was the primary impetus for creating new legal rules against vagrancy and loitering in the post-antebellum South. The rise of Jim Crow and the location and construction of urban ghettos and public housing were deliberate efforts to promote social control and isolation through racial containment. For the better part of our history, race has been a central determinant in the definition, construction and regulation of public spaces.[6]

For over a century after the Civil War, local police enforced racially discriminatory laws.[7] Police captured escaped slaves. Police enforced economic peonage. Police failed to protect civil rights protesters.[8] Police allowed violence, lynchings, and prejudice to undermine the criminal justice system.[9] It is no accident that the major urban riots from the 1960s to the present day all arose in anger to instances of police brutality.[10] The petty harassment of Ferguson, Missouri, or the repetitive disrespect of NYPD's stop-and-frisk program or the death of unarmed men in police custody all reclaim—in the present day—a shared history of racial discrimination at the hands of the police.

And these dark marks exist branded with official sanction. The racial harm was inflicted knowingly. In *Terry v. Ohio*, the case that constitutionalized stop-and-frisks in 1968, the Supreme Court conceded the future racial impact on overpoliced minority communities: "The frequency with which 'frisking' forms a part of field interrogation practice ... cannot help but be a severely exacerbating factor in police-community tensions. This is particularly true in situations where the 'stop and frisk' of youths or minority group members is 'motivated by the officers' perceived need to maintain the power image of the beat officer.'"[11] The NYPD stop-and-frisk program, declared unconstitutional in 2013, systematized a modern version of this "power image of the beat officer." The constitutional wrong involved a system of control using the legal authority and physical force of police against particular communities.

This "black" reality of social control literally and figuratively colors the introduction of big data technologies in the modern era. The history of American policing includes the history of surveillance of African American communities and civil rights protests.[12] The FBI in the 1960s specifically targeted civil rights protesters for government surveillance[13] as agents of the state imprisoned Martin Luther King Jr. and many others in order to silence a message of racial equality. Phones were bugged, lives examined, meetings infiltrated. From W. E. B. Du Bois to Fannie Lou Hamer to the Movement for Black Lives, police have sought to monitor threats to social order through surveillance.[14] So why should big data technologies be different when they emerge from such a dark history? How can big data surveillance avoid the traps of the past, when initial uses—"predictive heat lists" filled with nothing but poor people of color, African American activists monitored on social media, sentencing risk assessments found to be racially discriminatory, and surveillance flights only over West Baltimore—all point to a high-tech form of parallel discrimination?

Answering these questions will shape the future of big data policing. Fortunately, the questions are starting to be addressed. In 2016, Paul Butler and Alvaro Bedoya hosted a conference, "The Color of Surveillance," at Georgetown University Law Center that focused on the intersection of surveillance and race. Scholars, activists, technologists, the general counsel of the FBI, and a national audience began the process of acknowledging past police practices with an eye toward the technological future. Bedoya explained the purpose of the conference:

We're having the most intense surveillance debate in a generation. But that debate largely misses the point that when everyone is watched, not everyone is watched equally. The burdens of surveillance have historically and to this day been disproportionately borne by African Americans and other "others" that society deems dangerous. The justification for that surveillance has been both law enforcement and national security. If we want to create meaningful protections for privacy and civil liberties, we have to reckon with the color of surveillance.[15]

These types of events, engagements, and forums will ensure that big data policing does not remain anchored to the past. By acknowledging the impact of race on black data policing, a space can open for discussion. Or as Butler reflected, "The race crisis in criminal justice is not just about police and incarceration, it's also about surveillance in its more technological forms. The voices, history, and moral authority of African Americans are crucial to the discourse on privacy and technology."[16]

Acknowledging race in policing data requires new technological capabilities. Both the inputs and outputs of big data policing must be monitored for a disparate impact on communities of color. Clearly, explicit uses of race can be kept out of computer models, but race is too easy to mask as something else. Choices must be interrogated to ensure that race does not impact police decision making, which is easier said than done. Arrest statistics might be simple to collect and measure, but a system that looks only at arrest statistics applied to a city like Ferguson, Missouri, will lead to racial inequity.[17] Such a system would measure arrests at the expense of actual crime drivers. Such a system would confuse a desire for municipal revenue (in the form of arrests/ fines) with actual crime, thus disproportionately impacting people of color.[18] Changing the inputs from arrests to reported calls for service (reported crimes) or removing low-level arrests from the inputs could alter the outcomes.

Designing data systems to avoid racial bias has begun in other professional fields.[19] Private companies now use algorithms for hiring decisions, because sorting through a stack of applicants can be done relatively easily by a computer model that examines past successful hires and then looks to replicate those hires from résumés submitted. Of course, bias can creep in; if most of the company's past hires were white, Ivy League–educated men, then training the data to match past hires could result in a racially imbalanced hiring strategy. Recognizing this reality, scholars like Ifeoma Ajunwa have proposed a system to examine hiring algorithms and evaluate them for racial bias.[20] Using such a technique, companies can be comforted that the hiring algorithm did not unintentionally discriminate based on race or gender, and if bias is identified, the model can be modified. Such a process, because it focuses on the model itself, as opposed to the inputs, might also be applicable to policing models. Cities could request that companies certify that their predictive policing systems avoid disparate impacts.[21]

The blackness of big data policing cannot be easily fixed. But one important lesson can change how big data policing moves forward in the future. The lesson is simple: remember race. Despite the temptations to focus on the math or the technology or the futuristic sound bite, big data policing will remain black (and brown). Being conscious of potential racial bias does not delegitimize big data policing but merely offers a constant corrective reminder that the implicit and explicit biases that impact policing on the streets also impact the black data in the system.

Black Data and Transparency

Beyond race, big data policing also suffers from a transparency problem. With the exception of data analysts, almost all data systems are black-box mysteries to the user.[22] Proprietary predictive algorithms protect their secrets.[23] Open-source predictive algorithms remain inscrutably complex. Even simple databases cannot be easily understood by the end user. Policing is not a field that typically requires PhD-level technological expertise, and while some data scientists participate in developing police strategy, the vast majority of police administrators and patrol officers do not have the code-writing capacity to look under the big data hood. In addition, the black data being used by police to monitor criminal activity needs to remain secret enough to be effective. For both officer safety and tactical advantage, data secrecy matters.

The concept of black data symbolizes this problem of transparency and lack of accountability. If police, courts, or citizens cannot understand the technology and if lawyers, journalists, and academics cannot interrogate the data, then how can anyone trust it?

Big data policing must address this opacity. Secrets live in the dark. Secrecy distances citizens from publicly accountable government entities and heightens confusion about the technology. Black data policing, thus, creates a legitimate fear that secret systems will impact people's lives and liberty. Citizens rightly may question why the tools used to protect them cannot be explained to them. Communities may fairly express skepticism that secret technology that cannot even be revealed in court (like the stingray device) works to their benefit.

Police seeking to overcome the black data transparency problem must first orient citizens to the fact that big data policing is not too different from other algorithmic decisions in their lives. Algorithms are already controlling what we read on our Facebook feed, what our credit looks like at the bank, what opportunities exist in the job market, what medicines are prescribed, who gets audited by the IRS, which insurance rates cover us, what consumer coupons we receive, and even the answer you get when you query Google for "what do algorithms control in daily life."[24] Admittedly, with the exception of the taxman, none of those other decisions inflict as much physical or psychological discomfort as may arise after a visit from the police, but acknowledging this reality may allow people to come to terms with the fact that much of our lives are controlled by nontransparent algorithms and scoring systems.[25]

Second, police must see that the response to a lack of transparency is not more information but more accountability. Citizens do not necessarily need information about the mathematical formula underlying the algorithm but do need explanation about why the algorithm is being used and what mechanisms exist to hold the creators accountable. Revelations about secret stingray devices or the secret NSA metadata program generated far more controversy than the equally privacy-invasive Domain Awareness System in New York. The outrage came from the secret nature of government surveillance, more than the actual technological surveillance capacities.

The public health model of identifying environmental health risks provides a helpful analogy. Imagine that a city realizes that its public water supply is potentially contaminated with lead pipes installed in poor neighborhoods. The pipes are hidden, irregularly placed, and limited to only some homes. The city knows the likely risk of homes by reviewing old work contracts, shipping supply receipts, out-of-date plumbing maps, and a host of other imprecise variables. The identification process is a guessing game ordered by a simple algorithm to figure out the risk of homes and then separately the risk of children of a certain age in those homes. Creating a secret, largely incomprehensible algorithm to rank children most at risk of developing lead poisoning would be seen as unobjectionable even though personal data is exposed, children are targeted, the math is complex, the formula is hidden, and the outcome is perhaps racially skewed to impact poor children of color. Yet a similar algorithm to identify young men who might be victims of violence triggers fear and questions about transparency. The issue—in reality—is not the transparency of the algorithm (in both cases, we might not understand the math) but the transparency of how the program is explained to the public and, of course, what is done with the information.

An emphasis on algorithmic transparency, thus, may be misplaced for two separate reasons. The first is political, the second technological. Politically, as seen in the public health example, what matters is the reasons given to the community for why the algorithm is used. The issue is explaining not the mathematical formula but the reasons why a mathematical risk assessment is necessary (to find those who are most at risk of lead poisoning). Transparency in explanation for why the nontransparent algorithm is being used may be more valuable than the actual schematics for the computer model. Sitting down with a mother and explaining why her son's three prior arrests, friendship with a homicide victim, gang ties, and truancy from school make him a target of violence provides the transparency needed. His raw "heat-list score" provides very little additional clarity and the underlying rank-ordering formula even less. In Chicago, the plan for individualized meetings, custom notification letters, and personalized threat assessments recognized the value of procedural fairness and communicating the reasons behind the targeting system to the targets.

The second reason why demanding algorithmic transparency may be misguided is that as a technological matter, it may be impossible. Many of the predictive policing technologies are owned by private companies whose business models depend on keeping proprietary technology secret.[26] Revealing the source code means revealing the company's competitive advantage in business. Other algorithms are built using machine-learning tools that by design learn from prior modeling and, thus, never repeat the same calculations.[27] In artificial intelligence, machine-learning models, the analysis will be different each time because the machine will have learned from the last time it processed the information.[28] Doing calculations millions and millions of times means that the last calculation is different from the one before. Such a constantly evolving technology means that one cannot—even with the technical abilities—see the underlying formula because the system is not static. Nor can you audit the artificially intelligent model in the traditional way because the model will always be a moving target.[29]

Calls for transparency, thus, may not be possible in the sense of revealing the inner workings of the machines. But such calls also may not be necessary. What matters is not the math but the design and proving that the design of the model is fair, is accurate, and works. A group of computer scientists and scholars—Joshua Kroll, Joanna Huey, Solon Barocas, Edward Felten, Joel Reidenberg, David Robinson, and Harlan Yu—collaborated on an article that addresses this challenge of looking for transparency in an ever-evolving black-box system.[30] They propose a solution that involves designing computer systems with "procedural regularity," which means revealing how a computer system makes decisions and then creating mechanisms to test whether the computer system worked as designed.[31] Using tools of computer science—complicated things like "cryptographic commitments," "zero-knowledge proofs," and "fair random choices"—a predictive model can be designed to be tested for fairness without having to give up the source code.[32] For our purposes, what needs to be understood is that computer scientists can test whether a model works, even if they do not know exactly how the model works. By designing a model that can be tested, the most advanced machine-learning systems can be held accountable, even though they remain decidedly not transparent.

In the end, all of the fancy math comes down to the question of accountability. Does the model work, and how can we be convinced it does so in a fair manner? Accountability rather than transparency provides a way out of the black data opacity problem. Accountability by design will require big data policing to confront the problems raised in this book about bias, fear, and fair application. Some of this accountability may require additional communication—for example, explaining the inputs, explaining the design, and explaining how the system was designed to avoid racial or other bias—but this does not require complete transparency. True, certain predictive models may fail this basic requirement. Those companies or programs that refuse to disclose inputs, theories, or how they avoid bias may not be able to overcome the black data problem. But others may rise and succeed precisely because they embrace the challenge to explain how their predictive models work and why they should be trusted.

Black Data and Law

The law must also confront the distortions of big data policing. Data-driven changes of police role, practice, and culture have blurred traditional legal analysis and weakened existing constitutional protections.

Police action ends up in court. Policing technology gets litigated in court. Judges, prosecutors, and defense lawyers will be confronted with the problem of black data in the near future, and their jobs will be made more difficult because big data surveillance threatens to significantly reshape the existing Fourth Amendment doctrine.

As has been discussed, new surveillance technologies alter understandings of a reasonable expectation of privacy. With a Domain Awareness System recording your movements 24/7 or ALPR tagging your car everywhere you drive or facial-recognition technologies marking your location, how can one claim any expectation of privacy in public?[33] Five justices of the U.S. Supreme Court expressed a willingness to protect long-term (28-day), aggregated surveillance through GPS tracking, but real questions remain about short-term surveillance.[34] We simply have no clear answer to whether things like pervasive, high-altitude video surveillance violates the Fourth Amendment. Nor has Congress stepped in to provide statutory clarity.

Big data also skews the reasonable-suspicion decision to stop individuals on the street. The algorithmic decision to place someone on a Chicago-style heat list could mark that person for less Fourth Amendment protection.[35] After all, how does a judge deny the reasonable and articulable suspicion of an officer who sees the "number four"–ranked person in all of Chicago and stops that person on suspicion of being involved in violence? As a constitutional matter, the ranking should not be enough to justify the stop, but as a practical matter (in the crush of criminal court), it will likely influence the judge to find suspicion. With more information about individuals, the rather-weak limitations of reasonable suspicion will fall away. Innocent factors cobbled together (friendships, neighborhood, clothing, social media connections) will be crafted into suspicion as necessary. The result of a "small data" doctrine confronting a big data world will be less constitutional protection.

Similarly, the predictive policing technologies that can mark out areas of suspected crime may also mark out areas of lesser Fourth Amendment protection.[36] The "high crime" designation may merge with the predictive forecast, and suddenly an algorithm will alter the constitutional protections in a neighborhood.[37] Again, what is a judge expected to do when she learns that the stop occurred in a predicted "red box" of crime and the officer based his suspicion in part on that prediction? Factoring in that information to the totality of circumstances will add weight to the officer's otherwise-unconstitutional hunch. Predictive technology will impact the Fourth Amendment protection for all persons located in that targeted area.

Finally, questions of probabilistic suspicion will bedevil courts. Precise algorithms providing accurate but generalized suspicion will make decisions on probable cause very difficult. Metadata will provide actionable clues that police will want to act on in real time. Courts will have a difficult time saying highly predictive, pure-probability suspicion is not good enough. Unmediated social media threats or admissions of guilt will raise new issues of whether personal online communications are enough to support probable cause. Warrants for cell towers, stingray intercepts, and biometric samples will become more and more routine. Each of these technologies will face a certain legal challenge and an uncertain legal future.

Fortunately, the constitutional problem is probably the easiest of the black data problems to solve. Courts have regularly faced new technologies. Cars, telephones, and smartphones were all once "new."[38] While slow, judges have largely managed to adapt old law to new technology. In fact, courts are pretty well suited to the slow evolution of legal principles and are certainly well practiced. Legislative responses on occasion have also filled in the legal gaps, and law professors like myself have made careers theorizing how the Fourth Amendment fits these new technologies. While it is true that the fear of the new is disorienting, as in the past, the Fourth Amendment will adapt and change and respond to the challenge.

Overcoming Black Data

Big data policing is here to stay. Beyond being helpful, the technology is simply too innovative and futuristic to ignore. The appeal of new technological solutions goes deep in our psyche. Americans in character and temperament remain fascinated by "the next new thing." Splashed across every magazine, newspaper, and television news show is a headline about the "next breakthrough in science or technology." A country of upstart rebels, restless innovators, and progressive thinkers has always had one eye on the future, which is why police, like the rest of us, have embraced the idea of big data so effortlessly. The insights and advantages of new data-driven policing remain just too tempting to ignore.

To get to that promising future, police must overcome the black data problem. Black data policing must absorb the complexity of new technologies and old practices. Police must respond by acknowledging challenges and addressing the complexities of racial bias, a lack of transparency, and legal distortions—good and bad. The black data problem can be overcome but only by confronting the complexities rather than blindly pretending to turn the page to something new. In this way, a light can shine on the blackness and reveal a deep and much-less-frightening future.

Big data's potential, however, goes further. The next chapter examines how big data could revolutionize policing practice, by inverting the architecture of surveillance to collect blue data systems of police misconduct and racial bias.

8

Blue Data

Policing Data

Blue Risk

The lens of big data policing generally points outward—toward crime and criminal activity. But, big data technologies also provide valuable internal lessons. Police can learn a lot about the profession by studying the insights coming from big data surveillance.

This chapter examines the role big data technologies can play in improving police effectiveness, reducing police violence, and strengthening training and accountability. These blue data innovations mirror the surveillance technologies developed to police society, including crime mapping, heat lists, real-time monitoring, data mining, probabilistic suspicion, and predictive targeting.

On a national level, blue data remains relatively sparse, with data-collection systems being the exception rather than the rule. Despite concerns over police shootings, at the time of the Michael Brown protests in Ferguson, Missouri, no law enforcement database catalogued the number of police deadly force incidents across the nation. As then attorney general Eric Holder complained, "The troubling reality is that we lack the ability right now to comprehensively track the number of incidents of either uses of force directed at police officers or uses of force by police. . . . This strikes many—including me—as unacceptable."[1] Despite concern over racially discriminatory stops, no national, government-run police database exists to measure racial profiling. Local data-collection systems are equally poor.

While many jurisdictions have experimented with "early warning systems" to flag officers who might be at risk for citizen complaints or violence, other jurisdictions have failed to institute any serious internal disciplinary system.[2] Department of Justice investigations found that many troubled policing systems had no functioning internal review process.[3] Only a few cities have countered that trend, trying to get ahead of the problem, and usually only as a result of a court order requiring such data collection (after police have run afoul of constitutional rights). Systems to track officers who disproportionally or unlawfully use force simply have not been successfully implemented in most police departments.

This lack of attention to police accountability may be changing. In 2014, Congress passed the Death in Custody Reporting Act, which requires reporting of the death of any person "who is detained, under arrest, or is in the process of being arrested."[4] In 2015, President Barack Obama launched the White House "Police Data Initiative" to create financial incentives and organizational capacity to start studying police data.[5] Federal leadership and money, in partnership with local data scientists, could—if prioritized—result in the development of new forms of risk assessment.[6] In late 2016, the Department of Justice announced a pilot project to begin collecting national statistics on police use-of-force incidents.[7] While still in development and subject to political priorities and funding, the idea that blue data matters has grown from a hope into a national plan.

The rise of big data offers a new opportunity to collect blue data. Parallel to the innovations to monitor and understand crime patterns, police can now map and track police patterns to better understand police practices and predict future personnel problems. The goal is to systemize but also to solve recurring problems in modern policing.

Full Crime Maps

Place-based predictive policing tracks crime using geolocational data.[8] Police administrators can visualize crime patterns and hot spots in particular neighborhoods. But crime mapping and predictive policing focus on only half the picture; we know where *the crime* occurred but not where *the police* were when the crime occurred. We have a crime map with only half the relevant information. If a robbery happens at a particular alley and police happen to be two blocks away, examining this near miss could be very helpful to stopping future robberies or designing patrols. Or if the robbery happens and police are nowhere in the area, this big miss might reveal a larger resource-allocation error. Or if robberies routinely happen just after police leave an area, police administrators might see that the criminals have been monitoring police routines waiting for opportunities.

In prior eras, police administrators had a sense of where police officers drove on patrol. Police had routines and communication points and used radios to make sure that dispatch knew where they were in order to respond to a crime scene. But generally, after roll call, police headed out on their own, using their discretion and professional judgment to patrol, respond to calls for service, or investigate as they thought necessary. The same occurred with foot patrols, with very limited tracking of where police officers were at any given time. Today, better information about these patrols and the resulting police-citizen interactions now can be visualized through contact cards. For example, in New York City, police fill out a UF-250 card memorializing the exact location of every police-citizen interaction.[9] This data (like the LAPD's field interview cards) are uploaded to a database that can be used to track patterns of police contacts. Similar systems exist in other big cities, providing a useful *ex post* understanding of locations of police-citizen contact that can be mapped out after the fact.

New GPS tracking technology, however, changes what police administrators can know about these discretionary patrol patterns in real time. Just as crime mapping went from retrospective hot-spot mapping to real-time visual mapping, so too can police mapping. Today, many patrol cars have GPS tracking, second-generation body cameras have GPS tracking, and police departments like the NYPD, which recently gave out thousands of handheld devices to its officers, now have the capability to track officers at a granular geolocational level.[10] If police administrators wished, they could have a real-time, precise digital map of every officer walking or driving every beat in the city. Police-citizen contacts could be tracked in real time. This full crime map (live monitoring of crimes *and* officers) could produce valuable data about the interrelation between crime and policing. It would also improve police efficiency and effectiveness and provide community accountability.

At an operational level, police administrators could see the locations of available officers to send backup when necessary and to respond to crime scenes. This is already happening in some departments that have the capacity to switch patrol patterns on the basis of daily crime figures and problems. An uptick in car thefts in the morning means redeployment in the afternoon. Next-generation technologies might allow immediate redeployment based on newly identified environmental risks. Using full crime maps augmented with information about hot spots or environmental crime drivers, police administrators could direct extra patrols after a shooting or during the hours most likely to see young people on the street. Or police commanders could combine social media feeds with officer GPS to direct police officers toward groups communicating from particular locations at protests, parties, or other large events. The real-time tracking could monitor not only the watched but the watchers as well.

At an individual level, police administrators could monitor particular officers to evaluate effectiveness. Does one officer follow the exact same patrol route each day, spend too much time at the local coffee shop, or stay in his car rather than engage the community? Supervisors might well suspect that such suboptimal policing is happening, but now it can be monitored. Like worker-surveillance technologies in other industries,[11] police can adopt mechanisms to ensure compliance with specified work goals (number of blocks walked, number of businesses checked, number of hot spots monitored). While obviously invasive and perhaps unwelcome for line officers, big data's tracking capabilities are tracking them anyway (with their personal smartphone), so this just gives supervisors the information. Again, if Google knows, why should police administrators not also know where police are during their official patrol shifts?

At a systemic level, mapping police patrols over time can provide a revealing insight into the effectiveness of patrol design. Imagine a month's worth of patrols superimposed on a digital crime map of the city. Each patrol officer is a colored line following a path of daily activity. Together, the colored lines would overlap to show the frequency of coverage. Where are police actually patrolling? Are certain neighborhoods being patrolled too aggressively? Are other neighborhoods being neglected? And how do the lines match up with the crimes? Do any of the resource decisions reflect an unintentional racial bias? Can they be justified to communities concerned with policing patterns and resources? In the same way that predictive policing allows commanders to more effectively use resources to do more with less, this type of tracking of officers will allow commanders to more effectively use police officers' time and skills.

Finally, monitoring real-time deployment could offer a new way to measure the efficiency of 911 call response times.[12] One complaint in many communities of color is that police do not respond quickly enough to 911 calls. Despite complaints of high levels of police saturation patrols, in an emergency, no police are available.[13] Patrol data could identify problems of 911 response times and reduce resource inefficiencies.[14]

Risk Flags

Person-based predictive policing recognizes that certain individuals can be predicted to be more at risk for bad behavior.[15] The algorithms do not predict who will commit a criminal act but analyze risk factors that make such behavior more likely. The same insight can identify police officers who are more at risk for negative civilian interactions or the use of force.

Studies show that only a small number of officers create a disproportionate number of "use of force" complaints.[16] In Chicago, 124 out of 12,000 police officers were responsible for one-third of all police-misconduct lawsuits over five years.[17] The ten worst offenders averaged 23.4 complaints a year.[18] In Orlando, Florida, only 5% of police officers were responsible for a quarter of the 3,200 use-of-force incidents.[19] The difficulty for police chiefs has always been predicting who the "problem officers" will be before something bad occurs.

Enter big data. What if risk factors could flag officers before they crossed the line and inappropriately used force? What if police supervisors could intervene, warn, and retrain officers before a shooting? Rayid Ghani, director of the Center for Data Science and Public Policy at the University of Chicago, has begun to experiment with a big data solution.[20] Ghani teamed up with the Charlotte-Mecklenburg Police Department for a real-world experiment about how to identify at-risk police officers. To build the risk model, the Charlotte-Mecklenburg Police Department provided 15 years' worth of personnel records[21] and data about arrests, stops, dispatches, and other police actions.[22] The research team settled on an algorithm that crunched 300 data points to find predictors of negative police-citizen interactions.[23] Everything from the time of day to the neighborhood to the type of case was sorted for analysis. As Ghani explained, "The idea is to take the data from these police departments and help them predict which officers are at risk of these adverse incidents. So instead of the systems today where you wait until somebody—something bad happens and, again, the only intervention at that point you have is punitive, we're focusing on, can I detect these things early? And if I can detect them early, can I direct interventions to them—so training, counseling."[24] The process directly parallels the evolution of early focused-deterrence programs, emphasizing risk and rehabilitation rather than punishment.

The new system tried to isolate hidden variables that might increase police overreaction or poor decision making.[25] In comparison, the old early-warning system in Charlotte-Mecklenburg flagged an officer if he or she had three use-of-force incidents in the past 180 days, so that anyone with three hits got referred to internal affairs for further investigation.[26] Officers did not like the system because it was punitive and looked at only one data point to identify "hot cops," ignoring other factors like the types of patrols or cases, the time of day, or other things that might add stress.[27] "The old system was also over-inclusive identifying more than half the police force for further investigation."[28] Ghani's predictive system offered a more targeted approach that isolated previously unrecognized patterns: "One of the things we're finding—a few predictors we're finding are that stress is a big indicator there. For example, if you are an officer and you have been subject to—you know, you've been responding to a lot of domestic abuse cases or suicide cases, that is a big predictor of you being involved in an at-risk incident in the near future."[29] Other insights included that many domestic violence responses ended in police violence due to the highly emotional nature of the situation, which officers could not control. Police realized that by sending three or four officers to control the scene rather than one or two, they decreased the likelihood for violence.[30]

Similar to the public health approach to violence, the goal of the blue data project was to identify environmental risks so as to change policies, training, or services to better address the stress that police face. The goal was not, as it was in the old system, to investigate for purposes of internal affairs discipline. This systems-based approach, focused on minimizing foreseeable risk, rather than punishing past conduct, parallels the proactive, predictive model of other big data policing strategies.

Such risk-based assessments to find "hot cops" are not new. Over 20 years ago, the Chicago Police Department came up with an algorithm that studied an officer's past history of complaints and personal stressors like debt or divorce.[31] But two years after launching the program, the system was shut down over protests by police unions and the Fraternal Order of Police.[32] The concern had been—ironically parallel to modern concern about predictive technologies—that such predictive judgments were unfair to officers since they were being punished for something they had not yet done. The system that replaced the Chicago Police Department's early-warning system has been less than effective.[33] Notably, according to analysis of recent police-misconduct data, the existing system failed to flag 161 out of 162 police officers with ten or more misconduct complaints from 2011 to 2015.[34] The 2017 Department of Justice investigation into excessive force in Chicago found that the Early Intervention System "exists in name only" and does not assist supervisors in correcting behavior.[35]

It remains to be seen whether other police departments will welcome analysis of blue data as Charlotte-Mecklenburg has. The focus on proactive risk identification with training, education, and empathy as the goal, rather than professional punishment, might mollify some who would resist a call for more accountability. Clearly, privacy issues arise, and police, like all workers, will probably resent overly intrusive workplace monitoring. But just as employees in other professions have learned the hard way, big data may be too attractive to resist for managers looking to find efficiencies and improvements in lean times.[36]

Algorithms seeking at-risk police officers could also—in theory— incorporate consumer big data insights. The Charlotte-Mecklenburg project focused on police data arising from professional activities. For privacy reasons, the individual backgrounds of officers were omitted from the analysis. But, while highly controversial and personally invasive, other forms of consumer data could also be mined for risk-based insights about individual officers. Credit scores could alert supervisors to high levels of financial distress. Social media posts could be studied for racial or gender bias or expressions of stress or violence. In a 2017 DOJ investigation into the Chicago Police Department, federal investigators found troubling social media posts that demonstrated animus toward Muslims and repeated racial insensitivity toward African Americans.[37] Even hobbies could be flagged for contributing to potential problems. One expert identified participation in mixed martial arts or Muay Thai (a combat sport) as a predictive factor for increased use of force on the job.[38] It may be the case that police officers will feel this type of big data surveillance too invasive, but as with the rest of consumer surveillance, the creepy nature of the personal invasion does not necessarily undermine its predictive value.

Data Mining Police Practice

The next stage of blue data collection will involve the mining of otherwise-mundane police data to find efficiencies, bias, and ways to improve accuracy and fairness in the routine practice of policing. Like the power of consumer data mining, discovering these hidden correlations and efficiencies can add value to policing.[39] This section explores three ways researchers have suggested police data can be used to improve police practice. Parallel to the black data discussion, these projects focus on ways to address error, racial bias, and opacity.

Stop-Level Hit Rates

What if there was a way to calculate the likelihood that a particular stop-and-frisk would be successful or whether a particular practice of stop-and-frisks would discriminate against racial minorities? The *Floyd* litigation involving the NYPD stop-and-frisk practices revealed that most police frisks recovered no weapon (the success rate was only 1.5%).[40] Further, the statistical data and supporting trial evidence demonstrated that racial bias infected the practice.[41] Building off these revelations, a multidisciplinary group of scholars—David Sklansky, Sharad Goel, Ravi Shroff, and Maya Perlman (a law professor, an engineering professor, a data scientist, and a law student)—have shown that big data can improve the predictive accuracy of stop-and-frisks.[42]

Using the data from the NYPD litigation covering the years 2008–10, the researchers created what they call a "stop-level hit rate" (SHR), which can calculate before the stop-and-frisk the numerical likelihood of a successful search for a weapon.[43] The SHR was calculated by crunching the data from 472,344 UF-250 cards to see what attributes lead to a successful seizure of a weapon and what attributes do not help the police recover weapons.[44] Because police officers were required to fill out the UF-250 card articulating their suspicion for the stop, a database of official justifications already existed (the suspicious factors included things like "furtive movement," "high-crime area," and "suspicious bulge"). In crunching the data, the researchers simply compared which of these justifications actually helped police make accurate stops and which did not. The model examined demographic information about the suspect, location information, date, time, year of the stop, the context of the stop (radio run, uniform patrol), and how long the officer observed the suspect and then weighted this data with other information about the area of the stop. The model eventually included 7,705 predictive features to figure out the key factors to the successful recovery of a weapon.[45]

Next, the researchers took the predictive model they created and applied it to the 288,158 stops conducted in the years 2011–12 to see if the predictions tracked the success rate in the real world.[46] As applied to the data set, the model correctly predicted which stops would successfully find a weapon 83% of the time. More importantly, the model predicted which factors did not correlate with a successful recovery of a weapon. From the findings, a claim of "furtive movements" statistically offered no support for eventually finding a weapon. Strikingly, 43% of stops had less than a 1% chance of turning up a weapon.[47] Operationalizing this data means that police could reduce the number of stops but maintain the same number of recovered weapons. Further, the data showed that "49% of blacks and 34% of Hispanics stopped under suspicion [of carrying a weapon] had less than a 1% chance of possessing a weapon, compared to 19% of whites."[48]

The SHR method provides a way that police data can be made to improve policing practices. By studying police data using methods like SHR, police can refine which suspicious behaviors actually correlate with criminal behavior and which do not and can design training or strategies to avoid unnecessary stops. Further, this method could be developed into a predictive guideline to help police think through their stop-and-frisk decisions before they go out onto the streets.[49] By studying blue data, new efficiencies can be discovered and old biases reduced. Blue data could be used in court cases to prove or prevent racially grounded equal protection violations and for training purposes to make sure systemic inefficiencies do not burden communities of color.

Hit-Rate Percentages

Data could also be collected and used to determine which police officers were better (more accurate) in stopping suspects. In most Fourth Amendment suppression hearings, a police officer testifies about the suspicion that gave rise to the police stop at issue. The judge listens to the testimony, considers the evidence, and then decides whether the Constitution was violated or not. Because of the nature of how the inquiry arises—after contraband has been found and in the middle of a pretrial suppression hearing—judges tend to credit the suspicions of the police officer and deny the motion to suppress the evidence. After all, the officer got the question of suspicion "right" this time (contraband was recovered). This process, while understandable and quite typical, misses an important fact that is never considered: how many times did the police officer get the question of suspicion "wrong" before this particular correct stop?

Max Minzner has proposed a more individualized, data-driven test for stop-and-frisks, suggesting that judges review the accuracy of an officer's prior success in recovering contraband.[50] As a matter of course, judges would examine historical hit rates and include them in the Fourth Amendment analysis. As Minzner explains,

> When deciding whether a baseball player is likely to get a hit, we look at his history of success at the plate. When deciding whether to listen to the advice of a stock analyst, we look at whether the prices of her past recommendations rose or fell. But when police officers claim that they have probable cause to believe a certain location contains evidence of a crime, we do not look at whether they have been right or wrong when they have made the same claim in the past. This is a mistake.[51]

With accurate blue data collection systems, such probability statistics could be determined with little difficulty. In some cities, the data already exists; in others, it could be collected. Judges could examine the success rate of the particular police unit or the particular officer and then "increase their scrutiny of search types that are particularly unlikely to recover evidence and officers who, especially in relative terms, are less capable than their colleagues."[52]

The result of Minzner's proposal could have both individual and systemic impacts. Individually, the use of statistics could provide some additional information to a judge making a decision about reasonable suspicion or probable cause. Obviously, the information would be only one factor and maybe not even a big factor, as prior success rates give only a general sense and do not directly bear on the particular circumstances of a case. Homerun sluggers do strike out, and terrible hitters do get on base. But in the totality of circumstances, knowing whether an officer was particularly good at finding contraband (success rate of 80%) or horribly bad (success rate of 1%) might impact the final decision.

Systemically, if police officers knew that their hit-rate pattern could impact their credibility in courts, it could alter how they conduct stop-and-frisks. Police officers and administrators would try to ensure a level of accuracy by curtailing unnecessary stop-and-frisk practices. Police officers might study the information that could help them get better and improve their scores. High percentages could create an incentive for improvement, and this type of historical information might also rebalance the deference given to police officers in suppression hearings. Currently, judges see the cases only when officers recover contraband. In a judge's eye, the officer always hits a homerun. Knowing the overall statistics of all of the misses or pattern of errors would rebalance the presumption of accuracy that occurs because of the way cases come before the court for Fourth Amendment challenges.

Data for Change

Data-driven insights about accuracy and racial bias can be found in a groundbreaking 2016 study—*Data for Change*—from Stanford University.[53] The research team led by Jennifer Eberhardt collaborated with the city of Oakland to study real-world policing data from the Oakland Police Department.[54] The data-mining process was as sophisticated as it was innovative. First, the researchers used computer tools to analyze "stop data" from 28,119 forms that police filled out after stopping pedestrians and drivers over a two-year period.[55] Second, they used search tools to analyze the language captured from body-worn cameras, studying 157,000 words spoken by officers during 380 of the stops during one month. Third, they used programs to analyze the written narratives from 1,000 police stops.[56] The goal was to examine the collected police data to see who was being stopped, searched, and arrested and how they were treated by police.

After reviewing data from close to 30,000 stops and conversations from body-worn cameras, along with interviews and surveys of police and community members, the researchers concluded that the culture of the Oakland Police Department resulted in a racially discriminatory practice of stops, searches, arrests, and the use of handcuffs.[57] The study showed that the Oakland Police Department stopped more African Americans than whites over a year period, even controlling for neighborhood crime rates and demographics. In real numbers, 60% of the stops were of African Americans, although they made up only 28% of the population.[58] Again, this fact of racial bias existed even when controlling for the high-crime nature of the area and demographic factors. Further, African Americans were more likely to be handcuffed and arrested than whites were, and the language and tone used toward African Americans tended to be less respectful.[59]

The Stanford study provides a model of how to mine blue data. In *Data for Change* and the companion report, *Strategies for Change*,[60] the Stanford researchers provide some novel data-driven methods for studying just how police interact with citizens. For example, going beyond just the decision to stop, the data explored the use of handcuffs as a measure for differential treatment depending on race. The study found, "African American men were handcuffed in one out of every four stops, as compared to one in every 15 stops for White men. Even after controlling for neighborhood crime rates, demographics, and many other factors, our analyses showed that [Oakland Police Department] officers handcuffed significantly more African Americans than Whites."[61] Also of interest, 20% of the officers did 67% of the handcuffing, meaning that not every police officer reacted to similar situations the same way.[62] Yet the researchers cautioned that their findings revealed a discriminatory culture—a systemic problem—which should not be written off as the work of a few bad apples:

In a 13-month period, for instance, three-quarters of all OPD officers who made stops never handcuffed, searched, or arrested a White person, but the majority of officers who made stops did perform these actions with African Americans. These findings are not evidence of a few or even many bad apples, but of pervasive cultural norms (that is, the unwritten rules of how to behave) about how to police people of different races. Focusing on individual officers, rather than on the culture as a whole, would likely allow racial disparities in policing to persist.[63]

As another example of the possibilities that exist for data mining, the researchers explored the language used during traffic stops. Data collected through body-camera recordings could be searched with automated programs, so that researchers could query whether honorifics were used ("sir" or "ma'am") or whether apologies were given ("sorry" or "apologize").[64] The study examined whether different types of words were used when speaking to people of a different race. Researchers found that police did speak differently to people of color, and they even set up an algorithm that could predict with 68% accuracy whether the person was white or black depending on the words used. The researchers found no use of racial or derogatory words and no curse words, but other differences were uncovered about the time taken for explanations and the questions between the officer and the citizen. As might be imagined, this ability to search for the language used between officers and citizens opens up a whole world of data-driven possibilities for training or identifying risk factors for future problems. Similar data-mining systems can search through police reports, affidavits, or even testimony,[65] creating a future where big data search tools can be used to study the words, justifications, or reasons given for a search.

Andrew Crespo proposed a similar big-data-inspired investigation into the way police officers justify their suspicion. In an article in the *Harvard Law Review*, Crespo suggested thinking about the information in court files, arrest-warrant affidavits and returns, suppression-hearing transcripts, and administrative metadata not as distinct bits of data but as "systemic facts"—a revealing (if untapped) treasure trove of information.[66] For purposes of examining blue data, it can offer a new measure of accountability and transparency for traditional police actions.

For example, ordinarily a judge making a probable-cause determination reviews a written affidavit in support of a search or arrest warrant. The affidavit usually includes a narrative story that follows traditional patterns or "scripts."[67] These scripts are familiar fact patterns that tend to result in the recovery of contraband. For example, a warrant affidavit seeking to search a drug dealer's apartment might read, "upon information and belief, the affiant believes that drug dealers usually stash money and weapons in their homes." What Crespo proposes is to study the scripts using data-mining techniques. Tens of thousands of such scripts exist in every court system yet are never consulted to determine accuracy or consistency. As Crespo explains,

> A judge asked "to determine whether a police officer complied with the Fourth Amendment" will typically "listen to the officer tell the story of an individual incident and then" decide "whether that officer" has or "had enough information to disturb the target's privacy and autonomy." A judge armed with the searchable database of systemic facts just described, however, can do much more than that. Specifically, she can assess the *consistency*, the *descriptive accuracy*, and even the *predictive accuracy* of the probable-cause scripts that are routinely presented to her as justifications for the programmatic Fourth Amendment events carried out by police officers within her jurisdiction.[68]

In studying the data, certain omissions or contradictions in the current practice become exposed. Crespo points out that to justify a search warrant, police officers in the District of Columbia regularly state in sworn affidavits that suspects arrested for drugs routinely *possess records, proceeds, and firearms in their homes.*[69] It turns out that officers also regularly state in separate sworn affidavits that suspects arrested for drugs routinely *do not possess records, proceeds, and firearms in their homes* but in certain stash houses, homes of friends, or homes of relatives.[70] Conceptually, one of these alternatives might be true in a particular case, but as routine scripts, they reveal contradictory statements of fact. Sworn affidavits exist claiming both that suspects arrested for drugs routinely have drugs at home and that they routinely do not have drugs at home. In the individual case, the judge never sees the contradiction. Only by data mining the contradictory claims can the systemic facts be revealed.

Similarly, in studying a database of warrants, one could divine legally cognizable "high-crime areas."[71] In many warrants, a claim is made that the area is a high-crime area, but the fact gets lost because no one tracks the consistency of the claims. Studying affidavits alleging that a particular home is in a high-crime area could allow a mapping project of court-approved high-crime areas.[72] A judge could look through the past areas to see if in fact the affidavit fit the pattern. For blue data purposes, these contradictions or errors could be corrected. Training could be conducted to ensure that truthful and consistent statements were provided to the court. Scripts could be studied to determine effective warrant arguments and those that failed to create probable cause. In fact, one could run a similar experiment like the stop-level hit rates but with arrest-warrant success rates. The point is that systemic facts can be data mined to reveal patterns of police behavior in order to improve practice.

Police Awareness System

In the future, the ability to monitor cities in real time will also allow police administrators to monitor police officers on the street. Imagine if the Domain Awareness System (DAS) in New York City changed its focus from thwarting terrorist plots to instead holding police accountable for unprofessional acts, unconstitutional stops, and acts of violence.

Such a police awareness system would need continuous real-time video surveillance, callback capabilities, real-time monitoring of police cars, video from body cameras, and personalized GPS location from handheld devices—exactly the capabilities currently available through DAS and the 35,000 smartphones handed out to NYPD officers.[73] An administrator using these capabilities would be able to monitor all police officers at all times, to review uses of force, examine treatment of citizens, and evaluate training protocols.

The problems destabilizing policing in the United States—poor community relations, constitutional violations, use of force, racial bias, lack of transparency, and lack of data could all potentially be solved, ironically enough, by the very surveillance designed to create order on the streets. While very few jurisdictions have embraced big data policing as fast or as broadly as New York City has, it—perhaps accidently—provides a model for a new form of blue data accountability.

The tinder for the firestorm against policing pre- and post-Ferguson involves daily police stop-and-frisks. The act is disempowering. Police ask for identification, frisk for weapons, or simply intrude on the daily business of life, generating fear, resentment, and distrust.[74] Part of that fear comes from the fact that police hold seemingly unreviewable state-sanctioned power (including the use of force). Resistance can lead to violence, and stopped individuals feel isolated and unable to challenge the act, complain about their treatment, or provide another side of the story. For this reason, the advent of citizen cellphone videos following police confrontations and the push for body-worn police cameras have been seen as a means to alter that power imbalance. But the fortuity of a camera is not necessary in a DAS world. Administrators can watch in real time the interactions of police and citizens.

Imagine the practice of stop-and-frisks at the height of the NYPD program. As detailed by the *New York Times*, relatively inexperienced officers would aggressively patrol targeted areas, systematically stopping and frisking young men of color.[75] These routine "surge patrols" probably fall on the unconstitutional side of the line but happened so frequently and to individuals without political power that the stops became a significant source of community-police tension.[76] In one particular eight-block area of Brownsville, Brooklyn, police stopped 52,000 people over four years.[77] One 26-year-old legal assistant reported being stopped between 30 and 40 times.[78] But with real-time DAS, police administrators could see what their junior officers were doing.[79] Administrators could observe stop after stop. They could evaluate which officers conducted the stops. They could inquire about the legal justification for the stop. They could train individuals and groups when they observed unconstitutional actions. Further, by reviewing body-camera footage, they could confirm language, tone, and levels of respect or hostility.

This type of police monitoring could also be very useful for data collection. Do police disproportionally stop people of color? How often? Can police observations of "furtive movements" or "bulges" (signifying a gun) or "flight" be corroborated by visual evidence? The same digital recall technology that can identify all people with red shirts can also identify every time a police officer draws a weapon. Electronic data-collection cards recording the legal justification for the stop could be filled out on handheld devices and uploaded in real time. It is hardly

a radical proposition to suggest that instead of measuring productivity by citations or fines, police administrators monitor productivity by
actually watching police do their jobs. One of the perverse incentives of
the early NYPD CompStat practice was to encourage citations as measures of productivity, irrespective of their utility in stopping crime,[80] so
a focus on observing actual police behavior, as opposed to proxy metrics
like citations, could change incentives and, thus, police interactions with
citizens.

Such DAS monitoring could also improve the constitutionality of
policing. In the cities required by court order to keep data about police stops, a consistent theme of unconstitutional policing emerges. In
Philadelphia, Pennsylvania, a team of lawyers led by David Rudovsky
found that over one-third to one-half of police stops fail the reasonable-
suspicion standard, even under the police officer's own version of the
relevant facts.[81] In Newark, New Jersey, the Department of Justice found
that local police failed to adequately articulate reasonable suspicion for
75% of the stops.[82] In Albuquerque, New Mexico, DOJ found that police
unconstitutionally used excessive force in more than half of the deadly
and nondeadly use-of-force cases over a three-year period.[83] All of this
court-ordered compliance involving data collection could be done much
more efficiently and quickly if the policing (and thus data) were immediately visible. Supervisors would not have to re-create the *ex post*
legal justification of officers when they could evaluate the stop that same
day. Access to data that raises constitutional concern would give police
departments the opportunity to correct problems before they become
systemic. Prosecutors and defense lawyers would also have access to
video footage of some of these stops, adding an additional level of accountability to policing. Litigating what the officer saw on the street can
be made much easier by actually seeing the reality of the police stop
through video in court.

If you asked police administrators to respond to claims about the
perceived unconstitutionality of stop-and-frisk practices, most would
truthfully say supervisors train as best they can but cannot be out on the
street holding the hands of officers as they do their jobs. Yet with DAS
and real-time policing, supervisors can be virtually present. With certain nonemergency situations, police officers on the street could obtain
legal permission by supervisors (or even lawyers) in the central com-

mand center. Imagine that a police officer is watching a house thinking that the people leaving have likely purchased drugs.[84] He wants to stop the next person. He can now communicate with central command for advice. They can see what he saw by reviewing the video. Does he have enough legal justification? Or does he need more information? More details about the suspicious nature of the house (via law enforcement or data-broker records) or any of the people leaving it could tilt him toward reasonable suspicion. Or administrators could say, "No, do not stop anyone because you would be violating the Fourth Amendment." All options could be possible with DAS and real-time communication.

The same type of real-time accountability can reduce tensions involving police use of force. Citizen cellphone videos have opened a window into these events, but the truth is that many more deaths every year remain hidden from public discussion. Because of the prevailing distrust, without objective evidence, lawful uses of police force get lumped into the same narrative as police misjudgments or crimes. The lack of clarity means police agencies remain defensive, and citizens remain distrustful. But with a DAS network, all police officers' use-of-force events would be captured. Not only would you have the body-camera footage, but you would be able to see the "before" and "after" of the event, so you could trace through the hour leading up to the violence and the aftermath. No longer could either side make up a narrative to fit a position. Claims that the victim "had his hands up" (as was the initial reporting in the police shooting of Michael Brown) could be debunked in real time (rather than waiting months and only after an exhaustive independent federal investigation).[85] While video does not always tell the full story, the transparency of the process will be much improved. All of this is technically possible with DAS.

Community Collection

Blue data does not have to come from law enforcement. Academics, journalists, and activists have begun collecting information on policing practices, using big data technologies that allow data collection to be crowdsourced, aggregated, and queried in untraditional ways.

Academics like Phillip Atiba Goff, president of the Center for Policing Equity, now oversee a new "National Justice Database" that seeks to track and standardize national statistics on stop-and-frisks and police use of force.[86] The project, funded by the National Science Foundation, is working with dozens of law enforcement jurisdictions to collect data. The project is just beginning but has pledges of cooperation from the law enforcement community. The Center for Policing Equity's first report, *The Science of Justice: Race, Arrests, and Police Use of Force*, surveyed 12 jurisdictions on racial disparities of police use of force,[87] finding that "even when controlling for arrest demographics, participating departments revealed racial disparities across multiple levels of force severity."[88] Stanford University's School of Engineering has launched a "Project on Law, Order & Algorithms" to use big math to study policing patterns.[89] Sharad Goel and his team have already collected data on 50 million traffic stops from 11 states with the hope of getting a database of over 100 million stops.[90] The project's goal is to see if big data strategies can determine racial or other systemic bias in police practice.

Journalists at the *Washington Post* and the *Guardian* have begun collecting data about police shootings in an effort to understand the extent of the problem.[91] The journalists built a website and have undertaken a public education campaign to highlight the human stories behind the shootings.[92] Other journalists and news organizations like the Marshall Project, ProPublica, and Nate Silver's *FiveThirtyEight* website have exposed the lack of empirical data behind police violence and other criminal justice problems.[93]

In addition, mobile applications created by national advocacy groups like the ACLU and small start-up entrepreneurs allow citizens to report police abuse, upload videos, and learn about constitutional rights on their smartphones. The ACLU's Stop & Frisk Watch app allows people in participating cities to document police abuse,[94] and because the information is digital and thus able to be aggregated, a national map of police incidents can be tracked using the system. As more and more police-citizen incidents get uploaded, a parallel, community-driven blue data source can be created. These types of parallel data sources serve not only as a resource for the community but also as an incentive for police to gather and maintain their own data that can be used to counter narratives they believe to be incorrect.

New technologies have even sought to restructure the metrics being assessed when it comes to policing. Instead of CompStat, which collects crime statistics, Chicago and other cities have experimented with Respect-

Stat, which collects community-sentiment data from citizen surveys about police treatment.[95] The idea behind RespectStat was to assess police officers by evaluating their level of respect, helpfulness, and competence.[96] Police supervisors would thus have another metric to decide how police officers are doing their jobs, and measuring respect might shift the "productivity goals" from stops and arrests to something more community friendly.

Systems of Blue Data

What all of these blue data innovations have in common is a systems-oriented approach to police practice. Mapping, tracking, mining, or watching police officers do their jobs opens a window to see that the recurring problems—police violence and unconstitutional stops—are not the fault of a few bad apples. Instead, these mistakes result from unaddressed systemic forces that heighten the risk of "accidents" in an inherently high-risk job. Policing systems create foreseeable environmental risks that result in misjudgment and misconduct, and blue data exposes these risks and offers opportunity for reform.

Seeing things systemically marks a change in how we think about the profession of policing. Being a police officer appears to be a chaotic, contingent, systemless, dataless profession. There are so many types of policing, so many ways a day can be spent, and so many different quirks and oddities that thinking systemically seems impossible. On any patrol, an officer might be in a city or a rural desert, arresting a murderer or delivering a baby, saving a life or taking one. Because of the randomness, policing remains localized and largely unexamined by data-driven systems. This does not mean to ignore the libraries of books on policing theory, policing practice, training manuals, and general orders for police to follow, but good data is hard to find. Information exists on how to do the job, but information does not exist on how the job gets done.

In this seemingly dataless world, police can be joined by doctors, airline pilots, and other high-risk professionals who also work in chaotic environments and who initially resisted data collection and analysis.[97] Doctors argued that every surgery was different, with unique patients, health histories, and diagnoses, such that no system could improve on their expert judgment.[98] Pilots argued that every flight presented a different test of weather, technology, and planning, such that no system could address the particular flight plan.[99] Doctors and pilots preferred to see themselves as artists, not scientists, masters of the system, not part of a larger system of doctors and pilots all doing more or less the same thing. As a result, when things went wrong—mistakes made on the operating table or before a crash—the cause was thought to be isolated errors, not systemic problems. This turned out to be wrong. The mistakes were never a single misjudgment but a cascading series of little errors that resulted in a major surgical mistake or crash.[100] The artistry and ego common to professional experts hid the recurring avoidable small errors that resulted in avoidable tragedy.

Over time, the high-risk professions of surgeons and pilots came to embrace a "systems analysis" of error.[101] Those professions changed to collect data about what was happening in the operating room or cockpit and then invited other players in the system (nurses, mechanics, supervisors, and auditors) to expose systemic risks and study recurring errors. In doing so, harmful, sometimes deadly risks were minimized and systems improved. Today, both doctors and pilots have come to share a safety culture that addresses and proactively seeks to prevent risk before the error occurs.[102]

James Doyle, a lawyer and criminal justice expert, has been applying that systems approach to improving the criminal justice system.[103] For two years, he led a National Institute of Justice project examining lessons that could be learned from studying errors in the criminal justice system. The NIJ project, supported by then attorney general Eric Holder and a host of leading criminal justice experts, pioneered the idea of holding "sentinel event" reviews of errors arising from wrongful convictions and other known injustices.[104] These sentinel events bring together all of the stakeholders to evaluate in a nonjudgmental manner the cause of the error and then to strategize systemic ways to address future risks and threats. The core idea, again, is that any single catastrophic error is really the product of many smaller cascading system errors.[105] The failure is not personal (the detective screwed up) but systemic, an organizational accident (the system of checks and accountability measures failed). Viewing errors as the collective fault of many different actors intersecting with structural risk factors makes it easier to fix the systemic problems. By studying the data collected, the "sentinels" can see that the doctor did not choose to err but that a combination of circumstances built within a flawed system led to error. Borrowing from the medical profession, where such sentinel events are used to study medication errors or "near misses" (almost operating on the wrong patient), Doyle has applied the lessons to wrongful convictions and other police errors.[106]

Similar to the NIJ work, John Hollway, the director of the Quattrone Center for the Fair Administration of Justice at the University of Pennsylvania Law School, initiated a series of national discussions about systems-based change of the criminal justice system.[107] Errors in the criminal justice system, including policing error, can be analyzed using "a root cause analysis." This process, similar to a sentinel event, seeks to create a blame-free space to understand how error occurs in high-risk systems. Looking to find the "root cause" of the problem, the goal is always to promote learning, not punishment.[108] All parts of the problem (the system) get broken down and examined by a team looking to see what parts failed, with the ultimate goal to see if there are changes, training, or improvements that will prevent the error from ever occurring again.

Visualizing police mistakes as a systems problem can open the door for dialogue about how to reduce the risk of recurring problems like the unnecessary use of police violence. The shooting deaths of Michael Brown, Tamir Rice, and Philando Castile—all tragic endings resulting from relatively petty wrongdoing—cannot be simplified to a single bad act of a single bad actor fueled by racial animus. The errors were more ordinary, overlapping, and cascading. Racial bias—implicit or explicit— may have played a role. But in addition, officers received partial, imperfect radio dispatches of criminal activity. Officers were isolated, approaching the suspects without adequate backup. Officers confronted men perceived to be a physical threat without any knowledge of who they were or the danger they posed. Officers did not have acceptable other nonlethal weapons, and officers erred in the proportionate response to the perceived threat. These errors can be reconceptualized as structural risk factors (involving communication, awareness, bias, training, hiring) that, if not remedied, will lead to a deadly situation. By studying police practices, collecting data, and visualizing the events not as isolated mistakes but as part of a flawed system, a new approach to structuring high-risk encounters can be created.

Similarly, the conflict over aggressive stop-and-frisks in New York City did not result from individual police officers going out to intentionally racially harass young men of color. Instead, a systemic, "cultural" policing problem existed. Since *Terry*, the Supreme Court has allowed stops based on an indeterminate and undefined Fourth Amendment law, meaning that reasonable people can disagree on the definition of "reasonable suspicion." Police receive little clear guidance, and in fact, training on the standards can be confusing or even wrong, as demonstrated in one of the companion NYPD lawsuits, in which the court found that a training video used to teach police about Fourth Amendment seizures was legally incorrect.[109] This training video had been shown in almost every precinct and to every patrol officer.[110] Further, in New York, systemic pressures to show "productivity" in the form of citations or arrests encouraged unnecessary confrontations, while tensions of race, class, and neighborhood, along with a history of police violence, seeded resentment. Most importantly, a culture of aggressive policing was encouraged, both explicitly and implicitly, with the police seeing the need to establish social control on the streets.[111] The list goes on, with all of these latent risks heightening the possibility of an organizational accident in every new stop-and-frisk. To say that a police officer acting aggressively and unconstitutionally in this environment made an isolated error in judgment is to miss the deeper systemic flaws. The systems and culture of aggressive policing—identified through data—exposed an unnecessarily high level of constitutional risk.

Using blue data to reveal these systemic weaknesses provides an opportunity to address the risks. Three changes can be made. First, blue data like the type of data discussed throughout this chapter can be collected and analyzed. Without the data collection, the component parts of the system cannot be examined. Second, a systems approach focused on improving organizational culture and reducing latent risks needs to be adopted. Blue data provides the visualization tools to see the entire system, but police administrators and other stakeholders must want to make a cultural change. Finally, when the organizational accident occurs—and it will—the parties need to be willing to hold open and nonjudgmental sentinel events to study the problem using the data collected.

The Future of Blue Data

The future of blue data faces traditional headwinds. Police, like all professionals, would rather not be micromanaged or surveilled. Police, like all people, would rather not have their personal lives invaded or professional judgments analyzed to see if an algorithm deems them "at risk." Police unions and organizations representing their members will, as they have in the past, push back on more oversight.

Oversight has, however, proved valuable in the past. The idea of collecting police data is not exactly new.[112] The Department of Justice has overseen and investigated dozens of police departments.[113] Civil rights injunctions under 42 U.S.C. § 14141 have led to decades of data-intensive investigations.[114] Formal consent decrees resulting from private settlements regularly require data collection as a remedial measure.[115] Private police lawsuits under 42 U.S.C. § 1983 have also resulted in data collection of police practices as a remedy.[116] Adapting these data-collection mechanisms to big data technologies may simply augment the capacity of civil rights advocates and agencies trying to monitor a diffuse and geographically disparate set of problem jurisdictions. Big data oversight may—assuming the political will—be able to add value to the existing systems working to improve policing.

Despite resistance, data collection and analysis, as in other professions, will likely force their way forward. This push, and the larger push for blue data, was helped by the Obama administration. As mentioned, the Obama White House Police Data Initiative envisioned an ambitious collaboration between government, academics, and the private sector.[117] Over 50 local jurisdictions have opened 90 data sets for study.[118] The federal government through the Department of Justice Office of Community Oriented Policing Services (COPS) agreed to fund training and technical assistance for local police departments that want to engage with the Police Data Initiative. In addition, private companies and nonprofits like the Police Foundation, the International Association of Chiefs of Police, the Sunlight Foundation, and others have agreed to provide additional technical and digital tools to allow more people to access and use the data.[119] The key to policing is legitimacy, and being smarter about systemic problems can both help solve these problems and improve legitimacy. Police chiefs see the need for transparency and trust, and the hope is that blue data can lead the way.

Bright Data

Risk and Remedy

Illuminating Risk

Big data policing technologies all share one thing in common: the identification of predictive risk factors that correlate with criminal activity. As described throughout the book, risk identification technologies have led to a host of innovative policing strategies to address crime. But this new data-driven ability to identify risk does not necessarily require a policing remedy. Risk is severable from remedy. Big data insights do not have to be addressed by the police. Counterintuitively, a predictive policing approach may be just as effective without direct police involvement.

This chapter examines big data's approach to risk and remedy. It suggests decoupling the automatic assumption that a crime problem needs a policing solution. While big data policing has largely been funded and promoted by law enforcement, it need not be controlled by the police. This chapter seeks to shine light on what I call "bright data remedies"— "bright" because they are smart (precise and focused) and "bright" because they are illuminating (revealing hidden problems and patterns).[1] Bright data remedies offer a contrast to big data policing because they remain purposely agnostic about the role of the police. In some cases, police may be necessary to address the identified risk, but in other cases, a nonpolice response might suggest a better, more long-lasting solution. In all cases, the big data identifies the risk but not necessarily the remedy.

Bright Data and Place

A predictive policing algorithm can forecast a particular likelihood of crime in a particular place. But identifying risky places does not determine the appropriate remedy to fix the crime problem.

Take, as an example, a modified version of the RTM car-theft case study in Colorado (discussed in chapter 4 on placed-based prediction). One winter morning, imagine that the algorithm predicts a heightened likelihood of car thefts at a particular apartment complex. The reason, as discussed, is the problem of "puffers"—the phenomenon where people leave their cars running on cold winter mornings out of sight of their apartments. A predictive algorithm might forecast that on a particularly cold morning, a particular parking lot has a high risk for car theft.

PredPol or HunchLab might respond to such a prediction by directing a police car to patrol the area during the high-risk morning hours to deter potential thieves. RTM proposed a more holistic approach that involved intensive police patrols but also enforcement of existing municipal regulations (traffic offenses, housing violations), all of which should reduce the risk factors and make the location less attractive for criminals. Another predictive company might suggest a foot patrol in the parking lot or installing a real-time video surveillance feed to police headquarters. But all of these remedies involve the police. Because predictive policing grows out of a law enforcement culture and because police agencies control the technology, the solutions focus on what the police do best—police.

Yet the bright data insight is not that there needs to be more police in the parking lot. Nor is it that there needs to be more citation enforcement around the risky area. Instead, the insight of the technology concerns a pattern of human action (starting your car in the cold) in a place with certain environmental vulnerabilities (distance of one's apartment to parking lot, available places to loiter, and lack of security). Many other nonpolice measures could be taken to remedy the environmental vulnerability that leads to puffing. Everything from physical changes to the parking lot (installing gates, locks, security passes) to educational outreach to the neighbors (explaining the dangers of leaving your car running unattended) to civilian/community watches in the morning to technological fixes (quicker heaters in cars) to structural fixes (rebuilding the parking lot underground) could all address the specific risk identified without burdening police.

Now expand the lens of big data outward. Think of the existing consumer data about that particular crime location.[2] Data brokers know who lives in each apartment and what types of cars they drive. Matched with crime patterns showing preferred cars to steal or easiest cars to steal, particular vehicle owners could be specifically warned about the risk. Certain cars come equipped with smart sensors emitting geolocational data, and such cars might serve as both a deterrent before the theft and an aid to investigation after the theft. Social media trackers know who is communicating from that area and when, so that individuals who are regularly at the location in the morning could be identified for community patrols. Community listservs could share information. Surveillance cameras could be purchased by the apartment's leasing company. These technological or community-based interventions can occur with or without police assistance to remedy the same environmental risk.

The choice to use police presence as the remedy must be seen as a choice—a policy choice—not one driven by predictive data. True, police may be the primary actors in the system to solve crime, but they do not have to be the primary actors in the system to reduce risk. Other institutions, agencies, and community groups might be able to reduce the risk without police intervention. Simply stated, the insight that predictive policing data can identify the problem does not dictate the choice of remedy.

An even bigger question involves whether a police-focused remedy helps or hurts the larger goal of reducing the environmental vulnerabilities that encourage crime. Even a week or two of successful police deterrence provides only a temporary fix. Next month or next winter, the problem might reoccur. While holistic plans to strengthen police presence through traffic citations or to reduce abandoned buildings through zoning enforcement might have a longer-term impact, neither would have as much of an impact as permanently improving the physical environment. The danger is that by thinking police can fix the problem by following the data, the community stops looking for longer-term solutions. After all, the real crime driver involves the structural poverty that causes someone to need to steal a car in the first place. In thinking of predictive policing as only a policing tool, the community may fail to see other solutions to the identified environmental risks.

Bright Data and Patterns

Big data patterns can help visualize the societal risk factors that encourage crime. Current crime maps record reported crimes, but big data technologies could also create a sophisticated *risk map* that displays social needs.

Imagine a digital map that took all of the consumer data provided by a data-broker service like Beware,[3] but instead of identifying homes *of danger*, the algorithm identified homes *in need*. Which families need educational assistance, financial assistance, or mental or physical health assistance? Which people in those families have the highest level of need? What if you had a risk map that showed all of the children not getting enough food to eat? Then, one could overlay that map with existing available services. What if you could show a mother a digital map with the closest food pantries? What if you could precisely target your social-service employment resources to a particular single father? One thing you would likely see on that map is that the social-services providers are not where the people are located. Further, you would likely see that there are too few resources available for the need. But a map showing the imbalance would effectively highlight the need for more funding and more resources. Patterns of social problems could be visualized (in addition to crime) on citywide risk maps.

Visualization matters. Before the advent of crime mapping, police knew that crime happened. Mayors knew crime happened. Communities knew crime happened. The mapping did not stop crime or solve crime, but it did allow for more focused attention to the particular areas of higher crime. The same visualization can happen with social need. The idea of a bright data risk map would be to make that social need visible, targetable, and, thus, the focus for remedial action. Just as police managers relentlessly used data to drive down crime numbers, demanding concrete, numerical improvement, so too could city managers drive down poverty figures in similar targeted fashion. This idea of turning CompStat-like data collection into bright data strategies for social and governmental accountability has been pioneered by Robert D. Behn, at Harvard's Kennedy School of Government. Behn created the idea of "PerformanceStat" as a data-driven leadership strategy to show the potential of data-centered governance.[4] Oversimplifying a bit, the same data-driven accountability mechanisms used to track crime reduction can be redirected to track and improve city problems from street lights to homelessness.

These risk maps of social problems could also help police officers do their jobs. Every day, police confront a series of social problems from poverty-driven crimes (urination in public, trespass, disorderly conduct) to mental-health-driven incidents (public displays of anger or confusion) to youth offenses (truancy, graffiti, school assaults). Many of these minor incidents never rise to the level of criminal prosecution (or even a citation) but do exist as part of the mosaic of urban life. Mapping these social problems would be very helpful to identify the problem spots and to catalogue what police do every day. The gaps of service and the repeated patterns in need of attention could be visualized with cold, hard data. In the same way that you could see the hot spots of crime, you could see the hot spots of social need (or social decay) and provide appropriate proactive intervention. Again visualization matters. These hot spots of social need are etched in the mind of every police patrol officer who knows his or her neighborhood. Officers know the homeless veteran, the begging runaway with his dog, and the mentally ill personalities. But these interactions are not measured or monitored because police data collection focuses on crime, not the myriad other public health functions police play on a daily basis. Mapping social problems with data could change the level of awareness about what first responders do every day.

As an example of mapping bright data, the District of Columbia Fire and Emergency Medical Services Department (Fire & EMS) and the Department of Behavioral Health (DBH) interact with a host of health-related data points on a daily basis.[5] Every drug overdose involves ambulance runs, hospital visits, mental-health or substance-abuse referrals, arrests, and social-service calls. In the typical overdose case, a 911 report brings police and emergency personnel to a location. The patient is treated and taken to the hospital. The forms are filled out, the services contacted, and the case closed. This is so even if the same drug user regularly overdoses. This is so even though all of the different agencies and first responders know the pattern will repeat. This is so even though the few people burdening the system with repeated emergency calls can be identified and assisted.

In the summer of 2015, D.C. Fire & EMS decided to change that reality by mapping data about drug overdoses. At the time, Fire & EMS was responding to an average of 15 suspected synthetic-cannabinoid overdoses and six suspected heroin overdoses every single day. In a pilot program, Fire & EMS started transmitting the name, location, and overdose history of every suspected heroin-overdose patient in real time to DBH. The two agencies set the goal of ensuring that every identifiable person in the city who appeared to overdose on heroin would receive a follow-up visit from a professional team (trained in substance-abuse counseling) within seven days of the overdose event. The team would offer the overdose victim a voluntary screening, brief intervention, and referral to drug treatment. Treatment options, including a free van ride to a treatment facility, would be offered on the spot. During the two-month pilot program, 84 individuals were referred to DBH for intervention.[6] These individuals had collectively been responsible for over 1,000 prior EMS responses over the past eight years. The DBH outreach team was able to locate 39 of the individuals, and over half (21) completed the voluntary screening and agreed to substance-abuse treatment, including eight individuals who literally got in the van and went directly to the treatment facility.[7]

Perhaps just as importantly, the data sharing between Fire & EMS and DBH enabled District of Columbia health officials to update their assumptions about the population at risk for opiate overdose and thus create more effective public health strategies.[8] Analysis of the addresses of locations where the overdose victims were found revealed that there was a strong correlation between repeat overdose and residence at a handful of specific homeless shelters, thus enabling D.C. officials to target their outreach and intervention efforts where they would achieve the most impact.[9]

Of course, the blurring of public health with law enforcement creates serious privacy issues. In the pilot project, D.C. Fire & EMS did not share the names or home addresses of drug-overdose victims with law enforcement. Information about the location and types of overdoses encountered was deidentified and aggregated to unit blocks or similar geographic subunits before being mapped and shared with law enforcement. Due to privacy concerns, locations, not people, were targeted.

Finally, imagine using a powerful video surveillance system like the Domain Awareness System to track not only terrorists but people in need.[10] The current tracking system focuses on patterns of suspicious activities (an abandoned bag, a hand-to-hand transaction, flight), but the same technological tools also could be used to track patterns of poverty or social need. DAS could be used to identify homeless youth in order to offer housing services. DAS could be used to identify people with mental illness to offer psychological assistance. DAS could automatically alert on particular patterns like a highly intoxicated woman being dragged from a bar or someone passed out from an overdose. The only change is widening the focus from identifying crime to a system that automatically alerts to the social forces that drive crime.

Because all of these human patterns can be reduced to data, they can be studied in conjunction with other city data. Data on lead pipes, housing-code violations, evictions, abandoned buildings, public transportation, economic investment, traffic patterns, streetlight brightness, recreational space, library use, health care, or school attendance levels can also be mapped and tracked. Comparing patterns of social activity and community dysfunction (or vibrancy) can reveal new insights about correlations that undermine economic and social development. Perhaps a correlation between libraries and reducing youth violence could be discovered, or one between parks and improving mental health. By studying and tracking this bright data, the entire city (not just law enforcement) can get a better sense of places of risk and patterns of healthy and lawful behavior to help drive future planning.

Bright Data and Persons

Innovations like Chicago's heat list provide the best example of the conflation of risk and remedy.[11] By design, the heat list predicts both potential victims and potential offenders, meaning that innocent victims have been identified because of a network of associations or prior criminal contacts. Reaching these young people to warn them makes infinite sense. Developing algorithms to spot risk factors captures the essence of bright data. But the remedy of having a police officer knock on the door with a custom notification letter (even accompanied by a social worker) does not necessarily follow from the risk identification. Police involvement is not required to tell a young person to turn his or her life around. Such interventions have been done (more or less successfully) throughout history without police involvement. After all, society does not task police officers to intervene and explain other public health risks to citizens (like the dangers of lead paint, smoking, or drinking). So why do we do so for the public health risk of violence?

The answer, plainly, involves the fact that the technology remains largely initiated by police, funded by police, and of interest to police seeking to maintain connections and social control over at-risk populations. But why not take the police out of it? Why not create a true public health heat list? Putting aside the obvious privacy issues, a "social-need heat list" could precisely target those individuals most in need of social assistance. Young men and women could be equally targeted for educational, financial, and health services. Using big data and well-designed algorithmic techniques, any big city could create a list of the 1,400 children most in need of assistance (mirroring the number of people on the heat list). You could match those at-risk youth with jobs, mentors, services, or counselors. You could track progress. You could reweigh risk factors if some of the underlying concerns were ameliorated.

Going one step further, you could integrate social-service contacts into the existing Palantir-like tracking system.[12] Instead of high-risk offenders getting points for each contact through field interview cards, high-need clients could be scored for the services being provided to them. Every time a social worker helps a child, the data would go in the citywide system. Every counseling session would go in the system. If no contacts are made, an automated alert could go out to signal that the individual is being neglected. Social network technologies could identify at-risk family members who may be the next generation of young people in need of services. Networks of neglect could be tracked instead of networks of criminal associates. In essence, the entire surveillance architecture, currently created for social control, could be restructured for social betterment.

In a bright data world, violence could actually be treated as a public health concern. If you want to remove the toxins poisoning a society, you cannot simply arrest the polluters. You also have to clean up the poison. Informing citizens that they are living in a toxic environment is not enough without resources to allow families to move, young men to escape gangs, or economic support to avoid the sickness of the drug game.

The failure has always been finding a cure for these bigger social ills. Tasking a detective to play the role of doctor (informing patients of their illness with a custom notification letter) fails to understand the optimal role of police. Police are not the doctors in the public health metaphor but more like EMTs, responding from emergency to emergency, bringing the afflicted to the front door of the emergency room. Tasked with delivering the cure are city governments. To find a cure for the public health emergency of violence, cities must address the root cause of those environmental risks. And a cure—like any effective medicine—costs money. Resources are needed to address job training, failing schools, safety issues, and underlying issues of poverty, mental illness, and addiction. In parts of Chicago, Kansas City, Baltimore, and New York City, these environmental risks have not been remedied for generations, so asking police to triage care—even with those who are identified as the greatest risk—will not solve the underlying social problems. But, so far, this is where the money has gone. Predictive policing programs invest in identifying risk without similar investment in remedying that risk.

But investing in social-service remedies has been hard—or at least harder than investing in police. Without that money, cities have instead doubled down on more law-and-order-centered remedies. Because the cure is so difficult, strategies like intelligence-driven prosecution begin to appear more attractive.[13] After all, removing the target from society reduces the spread of violence (at least in the short term). Like quarantining the contagious or, as in ancient times, banishing the afflicted, this type of incapacitation-focused solution might be easier than finding a cure.

But the rise of bright data offers an argument for non-punitive methods to address the same social problems. The risk-identification systems are the same, and the targeted individuals are the same. The only difference is the chosen remedy for the identified risk. Bright data opens the door for non-police-centered big data strategies. But city governments must want to enter that door and go forward into the future. Just as with blue data policing, tweaking the lens of existing big data capabilities can offer new insights and new approaches to the same underlying social problems. Big data, blue data, and bright data all involve identifying risk from vast streams of disparate data sources. The difficult part remains doing something constructive with the information.

A separate difficulty arises when those data streams weaken or do not exist. In a big data world, the places and spaces without data can become neglected. The next chapter examines the problem of "data holes," where the lack of data creates its own distortions.

10

No Data

Filling Data Holes

Data Holes

At age 18, John had lived more than a hard life.[1] In and out of residential homes for juvenile delinquents, a child of the neglect system, essentially abandoned by his mother, with a high school degree and no stable home, John was sleeping on a girlfriend's couch, pondering a bleak future. Anyone assessing the risk factors for involvement in the criminal justice system could see that he was at risk. And, sadly, such an assessment would prove prescient, as he ended up facing cocaine-distribution charges within the year. John's case and thousands like it feed the criminal courts in most cities and populate the criminal justice data systems.

Across town, Charlie, another 18-year-old, was heading off to college. From an affluent home, he was packing up his treasured possessions: iPad, smartphone, laptop, Xbox, Bluetooth speakers, Fitbit, headphones, some clean clothes, and a few vials of cocaine. As a product of the information age, Charlie lived, worked, and played in the digital world. As a child of relative wealth, he consumed media, music, and styles in age-appropriate ways. As an affluent drug dealer, he had never been caught, and he had no profile in any criminal justice system.

Reduced to data, John and Charlie present very different profiles. Consumer data brokers might well ignore people like John with little money, no stable address, and a depressed economic future. A data hole exists because there is little economic incentive to track someone for consumer purposes who will not be a strong consumer. Big data marketing companies just do not care enough about John to figure out his preferences. Charlie, on the other hand, presents the perfect demographic profile for consumer spending and advertising. Charlie is the present and the future for marketing companies, and he needs to be monitored closely.

Similarly, law enforcement data-collection systems might focus on John more than on Charlie even though at age 18 both have no adult criminal record and both are involved with the distribution of the same illegal drug. Data-driven policing systems will be watching John, not Charlie. John will see police surveillance, accumulate the contacts, and be monitored over time. And a data hole will exist about Charlie, even though he is engaging in repetitive risky behaviors involving selling cocaine. Affluence and environment create a buffer zone against invasive police surveillance.

These data gaps present a problem. The promise of big data policing depends on the size and scale of the data analyzed. But data holes remain because of systemic pressures on what type of data gets collected. As society moves toward a more data-dependent policing system, filling these data holes or, at a minimum, acknowledging their existence can counteract a blind reliance on numerical, probabilistic suspicion. Consumer data undercounts people without significant income. Crime data undercounts certain kinds of crime. This chapter briefly examines two big data holes that should caution against trusting in big data numbers and explains some of the difficulties in getting complete data sets.

Not Worth the Data

Three interrelated financial realities create a consumer data gap for poor people. First, much of the data collected by big data systems involves digital capture through personal electronic devices. No access to personal electronic devices means no data trail. As Jonas Lerman has written, "Big data poses risks also to those persons who are *not* swallowed up by it—whose information is not regularly harvested, farmed, or mined. (Pick your anachronistic metaphor.) Although proponents and skeptics alike tend to view this revolution as totalizing and universal, the reality is that billions of people remain on its margins because they do not routinely engage in activities that big data and advanced analytics are designed to capture."[2] If you do not own a smartphone, shop online, use a credit card, own a car, or even have a home address, you will remain hidden from consumer collection. As Kate Crawford has recognized, "not all data is created or even collected equally," and "there are 'signal problems' in big-data sets—dark zones or shadows where some citizens and communities are overlooked or underrepresented."[3] Big data collection will not count those whom it cannot see.

Second, many of the traditional, nondigital data-collection points also do not apply to those who live on the margins. Basic governmental services like driver's licenses, taxes, and voting all require a mailing address. Professional licenses and employment records require a stable-enough life to engage in those pursuits. Poverty, homelessness, and transience undermine the ability to track individuals, even in the criminal justice system. In addition, as data begins driving government services, this lack of visibility also distorts the government benefits available to this forgotten group: "In a future where big data, and the predictions it makes possible, will fundamentally reorder government and the marketplace, the exclusion of poor and otherwise marginalized people from datasets has troubling implications for economic opportunity, social mobility, and democratic participation. These technologies may create a new kind of voicelessness, where certain groups' preferences and behaviors receive little or no consideration when powerful actors decide how to distribute goods and services and how to reform public and private institutions."[4] This voicelessness may create a negative feedback loop whereby data-driven systems undercount the data disenfranchised, which, in turn, will mean less money and services for those under the data-collection radar. Those invisible to big data may be forgotten by a system dependent on it.

Third, from an economic perspective, consumer data brokers simply do not have a strong financial incentive to get the data correct.[5] Consumer data brokers prosper by selling information to companies. People on the margins of the economic system do not merit the time and energy needed to capture good data.[6] This does not mean that the companies might not have some information on every home address or person, but the level of detail and thus accuracy might be less. If police begin depending on commercial systems to inform their risk assessments (as in the Beware system), then such inaccuracy in poor neighborhoods could have unpleasant or even deadly results.

This data gap also holds a warning for police systems growing dependent on outside data collectors. Some of those individuals most at risk for criminal activity will not be picked up by the data collectors. John and his unemployed high school girlfriend whose apartment he shares are not good consumer targets and thus not in the big data systems. Those who are most at risk of criminal activity will not be observable to consumer big data systems. Ironically, the data gap might be a benefit for criminal actors seeking to hide from government surveillance, since overdependence on consumer big data might omit them. But, as has been discussed, other police-centered data surveillance systems exist and will likely capture John in their net.

Rich Data, Poor Data

Law enforcement data-collection systems create the inverse problem of consumer data systems. Large portions of the population do not get tracked or surveilled even though they might be involved in criminal activity.

Class—and the policing decisions impacted by class—protects many people who break the law.[7] Most of the targeted individuals on Chicago's heat list are young men between the ages of 18 and 25. This is the same age as many young people pursuing college or graduate degrees at universities. In both urban Chicago and Ivy League campuses, drug use, drug dealing, thefts, threats, assaults, and sexual assaults are unfortunately common.[8] Young people of all economic backgrounds do foolish, dangerous, and impulsive things—many times under the influence of drugs or alcohol—yet criminal prosecutions are not equally consistent. After a drunken brawl or a theft or a threat or even a rape, a call to campus security leads to a university disciplinary investigation, while a call to the police leads to a criminal prosecution. Only the latter ends up in the city's criminal justice database and as a part of the suspect's permanent criminal record.

A host of other class-based protections exist to keep people with money hidden from law enforcement's big data collection systems. Physical barriers involving private property keep surveillance away from activities that take place behind the walls,[9] and economic mobility allows travel away from high-surveillance, high-crime areas. Social status influences police discretion about whether to stop, search, or arrest.[10] If affluent Charlie should be pulled over on the way to college, the ALPR would reveal no warrants, the computer system would show no contacts, and the data trail would be nonexistent. A presumption of data-driven innocence would shape the police interaction (despite Charlie's possession of illegal narcotics).

Apart from class discrepancies, police data is also quite fragmented. As Ronald Wright has explained, "There are 17,876 state and local law enforcement agencies operating in the United States. Only 6.1% of those agencies employ 100 or more full-time sworn officers. Seventy-four percent of the agencies employ fewer than twenty-four officers."[11] These smaller entities cannot do the data quality control or collection required for most big data systems. The result is that local police data sets are both incomplete and too small to create useful criminal databases.[12] This fragmentation creates further data holes.

Equally problematic, the current criminal justice system does a notoriously poor job of collecting complete crime data. Certain crimes regularly go unreported.[13] Interfamily physical and sexual abuse does not get reported because of the personal relationships involved.[14] Sexual assault remains underreported due to the social stigma and legal difficulties of reporting.[15] Gang violence results in extrajudicial responses rather than police reports. Most drug users do not self-report. Most people illegally possessing firearms do not turn themselves in. White-collar theft remains hard to investigate. Some communities, frustrated with biased policing practices or concerned that contact with the police could have negative consequences, simply decline to report crimes. Even violent crime does not always make it into the data systems.[16] The Bureau of Justice Statistics found that nearly half of violent crimes (3.4 million incidents a year) went unreported.[17] Paralleling the other reasons, the BJS study found that victims of violent crime did not report because they were too afraid or knew the perpetrator or chose some other method to handle the situation.[18]

The combination of class-based and crime-based gaps means that any big data policing system—*at best*—works on only half the crime data available. Such a distortion signifies a huge limitation of data-driven systems, and on a very basic level, the distortion challenges the reliability of the results from data-driven strategies. Police resources and technological investment go into fighting the crime we can see, not necessarily the crime that exists. For victims of sexual abuse, trafficking, drug addiction, and other less reported and, thus, less measurable crimes, this neglect can have real impact, because a data-driven policing system without complete data may give a false vision of success.

At another level, these data holes distort future data analytics. Data-driven systems trained on incomplete data can lead to inaccurate outcomes.[19] Outlying data from a minority community can be seen by a computer as an error and be ignored in later algorithms.[20] This means that a data hole can create further data holes if the algorithm chooses to minimize certain data that does not fit its model.

That said, the omissions do not hold for all crimes. As discussed, certain crimes like homicides, stranger sexual assaults, property crimes connected to insurance (such as car thefts and burglary), and other assaults with serious injuries tend to be reported fairly accurately.[21] In these cases, police reliance on data-driven systems makes sense. Data holes are not everywhere, but they do offer spaces of darkness that must be recognized, even if they cannot be illuminated.

Costly Collection

Data holes also exist for the very simple reason that all big data technology costs money. Lots of money. Money that many police districts simply do not have to spend. Basic hardware for fixed video surveillance cameras costs about $25,000 per camera.[22] Add automated license-plate readers, and it might cost $100,000.[23] The cost of ALPR varies depending on the company and the capabilities,[24] but car-mounted cameras can cost around $24,000 each, plus annual maintenance fees. Police body cameras run about $1,000, but the storage capacity for the thousands of hours of digital storage can run into the millions (a year).[25] It all adds up.

Fancy predictive programs like HunchLab and PredPol can range from $30,000 to $200,000 depending on the size of the jurisdiction, again with annual fees to be paid.[26] The Beware system reportedly costs around $20,000 a year,[27] and a single stingray device can set police back $135,000.[28] These all pale in comparison to the New York Domain Awareness System, which reportedly cost between $30 million and $40 million to build, and the LAPD RACR Headquarters, which cost $107 million (including construction of the building).[29] Although costs of technology will come down significantly and new capacities for storage and analysis will grow to meet the need, the fixed costs for purchasing any big data system are prohibitive.

Adding to the expense of physically creating big data technologies is the cost of hiring people to run and maintain them. Crime analysts, data technicians, and a whole host of information technology support people need to be employed. Consultants to ensure data reliability, security, and usefulness need to be budgeted for from time to time. To run a real-time data-driven system, police need full-time support to make sure the system works. To handle emergencies, the system must remain operational 24 hours a day. To protect law enforcement equities, the system must defend against hackers or criminal elements. All of these people and systems cost money that is not being used to hire officers to patrol the streets.

For very good reasons, police administrators reading this bottom line may decline to adopt new technologies for fear of not being able to continue to use them. Dependence on a system that cannot be maintained may not be in a city's interest. After all, some smaller jurisdictions have a hard time buying gas for patrol cars, let alone paying for smartphone plans. Yet that means data holes will develop and further fragment data collection. The inability to capture and maintain data may mean choosing to remain ignorant of certain criminal patterns.

Privacy Fears

Data holes also exist because citizens react to big data surveillance by hiding or protesting pervasive monitoring.[30] Elizabeth Joh, a national expert on big data surveillance, has called this response to police surveillance a "privacy protest."[31]

Technology now exists to blur facial-recognition technology, blind license-plate readers, and hide from electronic surveillance.[32] A company has made a radar-like watch that vibrates to warn of nearby audio-recording devices.[33] Artist Adam Harvey created a clothing line he called "Stealth Wear": "The collection includes an anti-drone hoodie and scarf that are designed to thwart the thermal-imaging technology widely used by [drones]."[34] A company called Domestic Drone Counter-measures even sells "anti-drone defense systems," which would "neutral-ize the ability of a small air-bound drone to capture sound and images through its on-board cameras, video recorders and microphones."[35] As big data surveillance grows, so will these countersurveillance responses to the monitoring.

More importantly for the collection of criminal data, people com-mitted to criminal activity will learn how to outsmart additional police surveillance. If automobiles are monitored through ALPR, criminal ac-tors will stop using their own cars. If cellphones are intercepted, crimi-nal actors will use disposable phones. The cat-and-mouse game of cops and robbers will continue no matter the technology, and this reaction to big data collection will undermine the reliability of the collected data. Data holes will remain from acts of subversion and will need to be filled.

Finally, privacy advocates may organize against data collection in cer-tain areas. Community objections to drone flights in Seattle shut down police use of drones.[36] Community objection to predictive policing in Oakland prevented its initial adoption,[37] and similar concern has arisen in Baltimore about the use of Persistent Surveillance Systems.[38] This pat-tern recurs, but not all communities have the political will to organize and protest. Those areas that do not have the organization or capacity to protest will be less successful in blocking surveillance, and the result may be a patchwork of surveillance that tends to capture more from disempowered communities and less from well-organized communities. Data holes may exist in those more protected areas, further altering the fairness of data collection and use. After all, if police respond only to where the data exists, then police will target those same disempowered communities more. Perhaps it is just coincidence, but Persistent Surveil-lance Systems first tested its aerial cameras on Compton, California, and West Baltimore, Maryland, two of the poorest and most racially segre-gated areas in the country.[39]

Data holes present a problem for big data surveillance's future. Limi-tations on consumer collection and law enforcement monitoring, in addition to issues of fragmentation, cost, and privacy, all conspire to undermine full utilization of the technologies. The challenge for risk-identification technologies dependent on big data is that the data will be incomplete, if not misleading. The remedy at this stage requires recognition of the danger. Data holes will naturally occur, and so systems reliant on data must see these gaps and account for the distortions that arise. As will be discussed in the conclusion, constant questioning of data-driven systems provides one of the only accountability mechanisms in a constantly evolving landscape.

Conclusion

Questions for the Future

More often than one might think, the unstoppable force of cutting-edge technology and the unsolvable conflict of police-citizen tension winds up on the desk of an overworked police administrator.

In that bureaucratic space, surrounded by much more mundane problems like staffing schedules, sick leave, and training manuals, fundamental decisions must be made about the future. Does the police department purchase a high-tech new data-mining tool? Should the department embrace futuristic proactive patrols? Should the police be open to body cameras? Who will pay for it? Who will train the officers? How will the community or the police union react? That single desk usually cannot bear the weight of historical racial discrimination. Nor can it sustain a searching inquiry into the finer points of machine learning or how "the algorithm was trained." The desk is simply too small to hold the overflowing policy and legal ramifications that might arise from any big data change.

But decisions must be made. This book grapples with these big decisions about new technology, policing strategy, and its community impacts. It has raised a largely hidden issue at the core of big data policing—the problem of "black data"—with all the complications of race, accountability, and constitutional law that come along with it. It has also examined how police practice and societal needs can be illuminated by big data technologies.

In this conclusion, I offer the advice I would give to that overworked police administrator. It is the same advice I would give to a concerned community member or activist or judge or legislator wondering what to do when confronted with big data policing. The advice can be boiled down to five principles—foundational questions—that must be satisfactorily answered before green-lighting any purchase or adopting a big data policing strategy. These questions are keyed to concerns about racial bias, error, and accountability, but they also recognize the base-level humanity that is threatened by data-driven policing. I frame them as questions, but really they are answers to the puzzle of black data policing.

1. Can you identify the risks that your big data technology is trying to address?
2. Can you defend the inputs into the system (accuracy of data, soundness of methodology)?
3. Can you defend the outputs of the system (how they will impact policing practice and community relationships)?
4. Can you test the technology (offering accountability and some measure of transparency)?
5. Is police use of the technology respectful of the autonomy of the people it will impact?

These questions require answers but also require a space to discuss those answers. A time, place, and collaborative environment must be created to debate the adoption and use of new big data surveillance technologies. I propose the establishment of local, state, and federal "surveillance summits"—annual meetings to audit, evaluate, and account for the big data police-surveillance technologies being used in a community. These meetings would involve police, community representatives, elected leaders, technology experts, and civil liberties groups engaged in public and open information sessions about future surveillance acquisitions and past usage. At these forums, which would function as formal reviews of the technology, the preceding five questions would be debated and discussed.

1. Risk: Can You Identify the Risks That Your Big Data Technology Is Trying to Address?

Big data policing is risk-based policing. So the first task for any data-driven system is to make sure that risk identification becomes part of the equation. Which of the big data technologies is right for the crime problem you face? Do you need a "predictive system" to identify places or people suspected of crime? Do you need a "surveillance system" to monitor at-risk areas? Do you need a "search system" to mine data for investigative clues or to develop intelligence nets of helpful data for groups or across communities? Not all police departments need all three.

The risk you care about will be localized to the current crime problems in an area. Predictive systems such as PredPol, HunchLab, RTM, or subject-driven predictive technologies (like the heat list) may be fairly adaptable across jurisdictions. Police want to know where and who might commit crime in almost all localities. Extensive video surveillance technologies might be necessary in big cities like Washington, D.C., or New York City but unnecessary in western Montana. The cost of storing surveillance-camera footage from downtown Missoula would be more expensive than placing a police officer at the town's main intersection. Search systems for biometric data mining may make little sense at a local level because of the lack of data but great sense at a national level with access to a shared, aggregated data set.

Choosing the correct big data system is a political decision, not a policing decision. The nature of big data systems tends to hide this truth, but the choice of where to focus police resources remains a political call. Some political decisions are easy. No one wants people shot in one's community, so targeting violence or violent people may be an unobjectionable top political priority. But other decisions are more difficult. Many police chiefs might love the capabilities of a Domain Awareness System or surveillance drone with video playback. After all, getting a time machine to solve crimes will save a lot of investigative effort. But constant surveillance may not be palatable to the community.[1] Other choices are truly hard. From a police safety perspective, the value of an accurate, Beware-like system that provides real-time threat assessments to police before they knock on a suspect's door overshadows the privacy concerns of citizens who would rather not have police categorize them on the basis of a data broker's assessment of their lifestyle.[2] But weighing officer safety versus community privacy presents a challenge. Both choices have costs. One erroneous assumption that leads to an innocent homeowner getting shot could jeopardize the predictive alert system. But not having the information might also endanger officers responding to emergencies.

For this reason, part of the risk-identification process must include the community. Community input into big data policing choices at the front end will minimize many of the black data concerns of these technologies. In proposing an annual surveillance summit, I envision a formal, public meeting where police would present future technology purchases and provide an accounting of past use. Such a public audit and review process will clarify the extent, sources, and expense of current systems and allow public criticism and concern to be aired. In communities of color, such an annual accountability moment will allow concerns about racial bias to be aired and addressed. But more importantly, community input will allow a more contextual identification of risk. Police might follow the data to focus on a certain high-risk block, but the community might prefer to have a heightened police presence around schools or community centers or parks. The community might realize that encouraging school attendance or after-school sports might be better for the ultimate goal of keeping kids away from that risk-generating "hot spot" of crime. The data might well be accurate about the future crime location, but the community might see the importance of addressing the broader risk factors driving that prediction.

Identifying risks alongside the community reduces some of the black data problems coming from modern big data systems. But issues of transparency, racial bias, and fear of nonhuman automation still need to be dispelled by officials. Big questions must be addressed. Will this technology disproportionately impact people of color? Will it target the right people? Would you implement it in affluent neighborhoods? How will we know if it works? Who is accountable for mistakes? Is it better than other alternatives? Can we afford it? Any police chief standing in front of a community room explaining the next new surveillance technology had better be able to answer these foundational questions.

That same police chief must also be able to look in the mirror and answer two more difficult questions. First, "Am I choosing this technology because it actually will assist police officers and the community, or is it just a good answer to the unanswerable (but unavoidable) question of 'what are you going to do to reduce crime?'?" This question becomes even more pointed in cities burdened by racial unrest or police tension. Leaning on the "sound-bite solution" of big data to turn the page from past scandal or current tension without being convinced of the underlying technological effectiveness is shortsighted.

The second question is, "Are police really the optimal institution to address this identified social or environmental risk?" The idea of turning down money flowing into police coffers and turning away actionable intelligence about criminal patterns may make accepting the technology too hard to resist. But many identifiable risks do not require a policing remedy. Big data technologies could be helpful to predict risk, but they do not have to be built through police channels and with police control.

Answering this foundational risk-identification question is the first step toward defending a big data solution. Making this initial determination will control the design, implementation, accountability, and success of any technology adopted.

2. Inputs: Can You Defend the Inputs into the System (Accuracy of Data, Soundness of Methodology)?

The second big question to be addressed involves the inputs that go into the chosen big data system. For predictive models, this might be the criminal justice data. For surveillance systems, this might be the choice of where to place the camera, what information to flag, which automated alerts to set. For search systems, the inputs might be the raw data (biometrics, arrest records, etc.) that goes into the aggregated database. Ensuring the correct inputs is key to the legitimacy, accuracy, and effectiveness of any big data system.

This book has identified recurring issues of data bias, data error, and the incompleteness of data systems. These input concerns potentially undermine the legitimacy and reliability of big data systems. A data-driven system based on bad data is a bad system. To create a quality system, one must be able to answer the following very basic question: can you trust the data?

Building that trust means that police administrators must know where the data comes from, who collects it, who double checks it, and who corrects it. For police collecting crime data, this means developing systems to train, audit, and cleanse the data. In any system that collects thousands of bits of information a day, from hundreds of different officers, error will exist. The goal must be to ensure that the erroneous inputs do not corrupt the entire system. This may be one of the toughest issues facing administrators, because if you cannot trust the incoming data, how can you rely on the outputs? The only answer is to have systems in place to check the mistakes you know will exist. Right now, arrest systems, gang databases, and many criminal justice databases generate too many errors, with too few corrective measures to really trust.[3] Currently, systems do not exist to guarantee accuracy. Intelligence-led systems vacuum up fragmented data without sufficient investment in intelligence analysts to evaluate the data.[4] In the rush toward data-driven policing, a collect-it-all mind-set has dominated, without a corresponding "check-it-all" system in place. Building a check-it-all compliance system must be a top priority for new systems. Every police administrator should be able to announce at a surveillance summit, "Yes, I trust the data, and here are the compliance systems in place that give me trust in that data."

False positives will still occur. False positives involve predictions that erroneously identify a person who should not be identified.[5] In the data-mining context or person-based heat list, false positives will occur because predictions and correlations can be wrong. Policing is not a profession marked by perfection, and adding data to policing does not suddenly change that reality. Judgments made quickly, by humans and with imperfect information, will be mistaken. So, too, big data systems built on those decisions will make mistakes. But the fact that errors cannot be eliminated does not mean that error rates cannot be addressed. Accepting the natural occurrence of error and building systems and redundancies to reduce and correct error is the only way to maintain trust.

For surveillance systems, the inputs should involve design choices to ensure accuracy. An ALPR that misreads license plates does not help police. A facial-recognition system that misreads faces does not help investigators. And an automated surveillance system that alerts on handshakes and not hand-to-hand drug transactions does not help anyone. These systems must be trustworthy to be useful for police acting on the information. Police administrators' interests are aligned with community interests to get this right, because otherwise there will be unnecessary stops resulting in conflict. But someone must promote the value of accuracy so that systems will be designed for accuracy. Before the investigative report showing racial bias or the governmental audit of data error or the lawsuits alleging negligence, communities must address at the front end the foreseeable data problems that will occur at the back end.

Beyond accuracy, the predictive models themselves must be sound and scientifically reliable. The models must be designed with a consciousness of potential racial bias and the structural inequities in the data sets. Models must address data holes and be careful not to overstate results. These requirements are no different from any big data project. Most data sets involve incomplete information, possible bias, and messy real-world variables.[6] Police administrators who are called on to defend the inherent limitations of human-produced data systems must focus on three recurring problems in predictive analytics: (1) internal validity, (2) overgeneralization, and (3) temporal limitations. These problems recur in all big data systems, and technical solutions have been designed to address and correct for them.

"Internal validity" means "the extent to which a methodology can accurately determine cause-effect relationships."[7] Big data almost by definition does not seek to determine causal relationships.[8] Correlations can be identified, but theories of causation do not arise from pure data crunching. So the fact that a predictive policing strategy lowers crime can be celebrated, but it should not be sold as the cause of the crime reduction. This limitation goes beyond semantics. Correlations encourage caution. We do not know why the result occurs, so we watch to make sure the correlation continues. Causation oversells the technology and can lead to a blind data-driven focus. Defending predictive policing systems means defending on the grounds supported by the data and only those supported by the data.

"Overgeneralization" means accepting the findings of one jurisdiction as necessarily applicable to another, different jurisdiction.[9] This is a common error. Predictive policing may work in the sprawling areas of Los Angeles but work less well in the vertically designed architecture of Manhattan. A 500-by-500-square-foot box might encompass precisely one farmer in Kansas but 100 families in the Bronx. Focused-deterrence theories might work well in New Orleans but not in Chicago due to issues completely unrelated to the technology or underlying theory. Just as policing is a localized process, finding the right technology is also localized. This means thinking carefully about whether a technology that was vetted in a major city would also work well in a smaller town. It very well may, but the question of overgeneralization must be asked and answered before adopting a specific technology.

Models offer predictions, but predictions vary in accuracy on the basis of the time frame established by the model. With a long-enough time frame, almost any prediction could come true. "You will die" is an accurate prediction, but the timing of "when" is a critically important variable. For purposes of actionable intelligence for police, time frames must be limited. Place-based predictive policing models specifically recognize that the "near repeat" phenomenon rapidly decays over time.[10] For place-based systems, temporal awareness means encouraging continuous and up-to-date data collection to ensure usable predictions. For suspect-based predictions, temporal awareness means recognizing that suspects or gang members age out or change habits over time. Recognizing the temporal limitations of predictive models must be factored into any big data policing strategy.

Defending the inputs of data and methodology requires understanding the limitations of any data-driven system. The black-box power of the system can be trusted only if the information going into the box and the system working inside the box can be explained and examined. These requirements may necessitate expert assessment and advice, and thus, at any surveillance summit, techno-legal experts should be present. Currently, a few legal-tech consultancies and nonprofit organizations exist that offer such analysis, and these groups could offer needed objective assessment about how these big data technologies work or fail to work. More formal, independent review boards may also be instituted on a local level.

3. Outputs: Can You Defend the Outputs of the System (How They Will Impact Policing Practice and Community Relationships)?

Ask any police chief—or probably any top executive—about their number-one job, and they will all say their role is to provide "vision."[11] Vision involves setting priorities, strategies, and general values to achieve those goals. Big data technologies can be a part of that vision, but they can also create certain blind spots. To avoid blind spots, the key is to ask the question of what outputs you want to achieve within the system you have designed. Do you care about crime rates, police procedures, officer wellness, officer training, community support, citizen trust, or a balanced budget? And if your answer is "all of the above," how do you adopt a policy that supports those sometimes-conflicting goals?

Crime rates regularly top priority outputs in most big cities, so measuring a reduction in crime using data remains a top attraction of big data systems. But big data policing can distort how we measure success. Outputs that are easily measured will be chosen over those that are more difficult to quantify. Crime rates involve hard numbers. Respect of the community does not. Arrests can be counted, criminals ranked, neighborhoods labeled. But none of these outputs necessarily addresses how police interact with the community. In an age of growing tension between police and citizens, big data's outputs may mask deeper trust problems that need to be addressed. Police administrators must ask themselves whether the chosen metrics accurately reflect the issues in their community, because reducing crime while also reducing trust in law enforcement may not in the end be much of a success.

For administrators, managing limited resources has become a top responsibility in an age of reduced budgets.[12] Big data technologies offer efficiencies in scheduling and staffing. But big data policing may distort how police do their jobs. Reliance on predictive boxes changes how police patrol, and whether or not aggressive police attention on particular blocks is effective at reducing crime, it will change the environment of those blocks. Field interview cards change how police interact with citizens,[13] and whether the repeated contacts are good or bad at collecting intelligence, they alter the relationship with targeted citizens. Persistent surveillance cameras capture criminal activity, but in doing so, they also turn citizens into subjects of surveillance. These outcomes, which encourage social-control efforts in certain neighborhoods and against certain populations, will produce backlash, especially when those same tactics are not used in affluent neighborhoods. Those negative sentiments need to be seen—and admitted—as an output of the technological adoption. Police administrators must acknowledge technology's cost in regular public forums and be able to defend its value to the community.

As the DOJ reports on the Ferguson and Baltimore Police Departments demonstrated, certain policing strategies create racially discriminatory outcomes. Empirically and anecdotally, policing systems resulted in documented racial discrimination against poor communities.[14] Big data policing presents similar risks, which is why police administrators adopting big data systems must be able to defend the racial impact to the community. Police administrators must be able to point to concrete steps, tests, and strategies in place to avoid a racially imbalanced application of the technology. The "color of surveillance" cannot remain black.

If community trust dominates as a priority outcome, police administrators may need to embrace blue data systems to identify and help at-risk officers. If a desired output involves improving community-police relationships or saving money from police-misconduct lawsuits, redirecting at-risk officers makes sense. But such worker surveillance may undercut officers' morale and undermine their well-being. Police officers may respond negatively to increased personal surveillance of their professional duties, and administrators will need to defend these changes to police unions, which may resist additional workplace surveillance. At least at a systems level, looking at general policing patterns, administrators have begun seeing the value in blue data, but targeting individual officers will remain difficult. Adopting a blue data system can create a culture of accountability that ultimately could improve community relations, but it will take significant community and professional pressure to implement.

Finally, if police seek to become involved in addressing the underlying environmental risks that encourage crime and to turn themselves into public health officials, big vision questions arise. Bright data can identify the risk, but police may not be the appropriate remedy for those risks. Seeing social problems in need of social-services solutions and not policing solutions may require police to pull back from certain responsibilities. Plainly stated, it may not be the optimal choice to send an armed, relatively untrained police officer to handle the next mental health crisis, especially if a trained social worker could also respond to the 911 call.[15] One report stated that one-third to one-half of the people shot by police in a two-year period had some mental health issue or disability, so one wonders why alternative solutions are not tested.[16] Funding emergency responders who are trained in crisis management of mental illness or disability might be a way to deescalate foreseeable violent confrontations. This change may also improve the lives of police officers. It may change who gets shot. But it also may mean a redirection of financial resources away from police. Depending on the vision set by police administrators, this move away from police-oriented solutions could have a large impact on police budgets and the role of police in a society.

Police administrators regularly must answer hard questions about outcomes; it is part of the "police chief" job description. For much of the recent past, rising or declining crime rates dominated as the measure of success, but in recent years, police chiefs have been fired when racial tensions overwhelmed community trust (despite lower crime rates).[17] Big data may offer another way to shape outcomes. But to do so successfully, each of these different types of outputs must be measured, weighed, and openly defended to the community as part of a vision of big data policing.

4. Testing: Can You Test the Technology (Offering Accountability and Some Measure of Transparency)?

The recurring themes of this book—error, bias, distortion—and the issues of systemic inputs and outputs all lead to one solution: testing. Big data technology used in policing must be tested and retested constantly.

Testing improves accuracy. Testing fosters legitimacy. Testing ensures security. But more importantly, the fact that the technology *can* be tested allows a measure of accountability necessary in a democratic system of government. Political accountability, more than legal or scientific accountability, will be the most important check on these powerful policing systems.

As a practical matter, traditional forms of accountability may be too slow to police the rise of big data technologies. Legal accountability—challenging police practices through the courts—has been a familiar mechanism to address constitutionally threatening technology. Yet litigation takes time, and the technology changes rapidly. The FBI investigation into Antoine Jones began in 2004. The Supreme Court resolved the constitutionality of the search in 2012.[18] Eight years is a lifetime in technology. Scientific testing also takes time. The RAND study examining the effectiveness of Chicago's Strategic Subjects List 1.0 became practically obsolete before it could be published because the police expanded the criteria for the heat list;[19] so the RAND study, in actual fact, critiqued a system that no longer existed. Media headlines deemed the heat list a failure, when really only the first version failed. Academics and scientists may justifiably have larger goals in testing older systems of prediction, but for real-world accountability, the testing process always gets overtaken by the advancing technology. Many predictive models change daily, and testing such a moving target remains quite difficult.

Political accountability focuses on the political present and requires police administrators to "answer for their actions, possible failings, and wrongdoings."[20] Political accountability in the form of annual public forums—publicized and scrutinized—will offer a window into this quickly changing landscape. At surveillance summits, police chiefs should answer the question of how the big data policing system can be tested. This answer is different from "how the system works," "whether it works," or "why it works." Those are important questions, but the question of how to test the system is even more important. Police chiefs may not be in the best position to explain the details of the algorithm or the criminological theory of why it should work, but they should be able to explain the testing process. "Here is how we test it" may be a more comforting and enlightening answer than "here is how it works."

In the past, however, the testing question came after the "how" or "why" questions. We demanded—perhaps unfairly—a police administrator to justify why an untested system should work, rather than ask how to test whether the system worked. The first answer is an educated guess. The second answer can (and should) have concrete reference points about independent audits, metrics, and compliance standards. Holding police officials accountable to meet those standards may provide clarity about the successful use of any new technology. And if those answers can be backed up by expert examiners, in public and with the engagement of the community, all the participants will feel a greater measure of comfort with these new technologies.

5. Autonomy: Is Police Use of the Technology Respectful of the Autonomy of the People It Will Impact?

Big data policing's allure involves its reliance on seemingly objective, nonhuman judgments. The danger, of course, is that the human consequences get subsumed in the quest for technological guidance.

Policing—data driven or not—is human and touches core issues of individual justice and autonomy. As a result, users of any data-driven policing system need to be cognizant of the human dimension.

Human beings commit crime. Human beings investigate crime. While both actions can be reduced to data points, neither can be understood merely as data without missing something significant in the analysis. Specifically, data-driven policing has the potential to ignore the personal, emotional, and even symbolic aspects of the process and thereby undercut principles of individual justice and dignity.

This reliance on data to influence police action fails to recognize the importance of autonomy. As Barbara Underwood has written in the context of prediction and sentencing, "The use of predictive criteria for selection is subject to challenge not only on grounds of accuracy, however, but also on the ground that it conflicts with other important social values, involving respect for individual autonomy. The attempt to predict an individual's behavior seems to reduce him to a predictable object rather than treating him as an autonomous person."[21] In the context of policing, a focus on the statistical value of an arrest undercuts the humanity of the suspect. If, for example, police are rewarded based on the number of arrests or pressured to generate higher arrest statistics, the persons behind the metric of productivity become somewhat secondary. Or systemically, if administrative policing strategies focus on numbers (crime rates and patterns) and not community needs (people and culture), the data-driven focus can overtake the community caretaking function.

Further, the risk of undermining autonomy grows when the predictive elements involve things beyond the suspect's control.[22] Many elements of an actuarial assessment involve factors that suspects are born into, rather than choose, and, of course, even the choices can be impacted by environmental forces.[23] Person-based predictive methods, like all risk-assessment instruments, include potentially discriminatory socioeconomic factors. Awareness of these influences and intentional correctives to avoid unintended discrimination must be a priority. In other words, the actuarial tools chosen must be cautious to avoid discriminatory effects, and the predictive models must guard against implicit or explicit bias.

Finally, as a legal matter, big data policing shifts the focus from the individual person to group suspicion or place-based suspicion in the predictive data set. The shift to generalized suspicion also encourages stereotyping and guilt by association. This, in turn, weakens Fourth Amendment protections by distorting the individualized suspicion standard on the street.[24] An area might be targeted because of the actions of others, or a group might be identified because of the actions of others. Even targeted individuals might be identified only because of their association with a problematic social network. Every boy whose brother is a gang member cannot be assumed to be a gang associate. Every girl born on a high-crime block is not a suspect. Such generalization ignores the individual characteristics of the particular suspect involved.[25] Individualized suspicion is a Fourth Amendment requirement, but it also serves as a reminder that associational suspicion or correlative suspicion should not be enough to justify infringements on liberty. Although predictions may suggest future criminal involvement for certain populations, many individuals within those populations will avoid such involvement and should not be tarred by generalized suspicion.[26] Regardless of the technology chosen, police departments must continue to prioritize systems designed with a focus on autonomy and a commitment to individualized suspicion.

* * *

Black data policing is just big data policing in the real world. The issues in this book reflect traditional problems in policing, albeit with a new technological gloss. The algorithms and data-driven theories are new and, like most innovations, will disrupt the status quo. But police practice could use some change. The movement that arose to protest police treatment after Ferguson did not begin there. Echoes of frustration, resentment, and rage can be traced all the way back through American history and all across the country. Just because the sparks of rage catch fire only occasionally does not mean that the embers are not always hot. Big data policing should not be used to ignore this past. Believing that technological promise can avoid human problems offers a false hope, because no new technology can turn the page on systemic societal problems.

But the influx of big data technologies does offer space for reflection. With data collection comes more information, better tools, and a clearer picture of the crime and social problems in society. Police administrators can visualize risks illuminated on maps, in charts, and in recorded surveillance video. Police administrators can see deeper into the dark.

My hope with this book is to clear a space on every police administrator's desk for reflection: to encourage thoughtful answers and defenses about risk, inputs, outputs, testing, and autonomy; to recognize that the moment of deciding whether to invest in the next big data innovation also provides a moment to think systemically about the future of law enforcement. Big data may be a part of that future, but so might blue data or bright data. In fact, the thought process of defending the next data-driven acquisition in a public surveillance summit may inspire police administrators to reinvest in community policing over more computer power.

These questions and answers are not for police alone. In a democratic system of government, police serve the community. The introduction of big data policing offers community members, criminal justice advocates, and police critics an opportunity to change the future of law enforcement. The architecture of surveillance also needs an architecture of accountability.

And so this book ends with a prediction: big data technologies will improve the risk-identification capacities of police but will not offer clarity about appropriate remedies. Because traditional budgeting systems and federal grants will direct resources to law enforcement, police administrators will make the initial determination of which big data technologies to use and how to implement them. Due to this reality, police chiefs will be required to decide whether expanding big data's lens to include blue data or bright data adds to their vision. Police chiefs will, ultimately, have to be held accountable for these choices (hopefully in newly regularized surveillance summits). Those engaged citizens and legislatures wishing to influence police decisions will need to find methods of democratic accountability to test the systems and educate the public. In the end, the forecast for big data policing depends on how we choose to illuminate the darkness inherent in the data. Black, blue, bright, or something else, big data will change policing for the foreseeable future, and we need to be able to see the path ahead.

NOTES

INTRODUCTION

1. Darwin Bond & Ali Winston, *Forget the NSA, the LAPD Spies on Millions of Innocent Folks*, LA WKLY. (Feb. 27, 2014). While the term "data" is the plural form of "datum," in this book, I use "data" as a singular noun, in conformity with common usage.
2. Will Federman, *Murder in Los Angeles: Big Data and the Decline of Homicide*, NEON TOMMY: ANNENBERG DIGITAL NEWS (Dec. 18, 2013).
3. Palantir, *Palantir at the Los Angeles Police Department* (promotional video, 2013), *available at* www.youtube.com/watch?v=aJ-u7yDwC6g.
4. *Id.*
5. *See* Jane Bambauer, *Is Data Speech?*, 66 STAN. L. REV. 57, 59 n.3 (2014).
6. Palantir, *Palantir Mobile Prototype for Law Enforcement* (promotional video, 2010), *available at* www.youtube.com/watch?v=aRDW_A8eG8g.
7. *Id.*
8. Kalee Thompson, *The Santa Cruz Experiment: Can a City's Crime Be Predicted and Prevented?*, POP. SCI. (Nov. 1, 2011).
9. Andrew Guthrie Ferguson, *Predictive Policing and Reasonable Suspicion*, 62 EMORY L.J. 259, 265–69 (2012).
10. Clare Garvie & Jonathan Frankle, *Facial Recognition Software Might Have a Racial Bias Problem*, ATLANTIC (Apr. 7, 2016), www.theatlantic.com.
11. Cheryl Corley, *When Social Media Fuels Gang Violence*, ALL TECH CONSIDERED (NPR radio broadcast, Oct. 7, 2015), *available at* www.npr.org.
12. Tal Z. Zarsky, *Governmental Data Mining and Its Alternatives*, 116 PENN ST. L. REV. 285, 287 (2011).
13. Steve Lohr, *Amid the Flood, a Catchphrase Is Born*, N.Y. TIMES (Aug. 12, 2012).
14. Viktor Mayer-Schonberger & Kenneth Cukier, BIG DATA: A REVOLUTION THAT WILL TRANSFORM HOW WE LIVE, WORK, AND THINK 2 (2013); Jules J. Berman, PRINCIPLES OF BIG DATA: PREPARING, SHARING, AND ANALYZING COMPLEX INFORMATION 3–4 (2013).
15. "Big data" is used here as a shorthand term for growing data sets and large quantities of digital information. There are many different definitions of big data, and some may contest this overbroad definition used throughout the book. But it represents an imprecise but revealing descriptor of growing data collections that range from large to very large to massive. In the context of law enforcement, the

concept of big data policing encompasses a host of emerging technologies involving predictive analytics, mass surveillance, data mining, and other digital tracking capabilities.

16. This is the subject of chapter 1.

17. Joshua L. Simmons, *Buying You: The Government's Use of Fourth-Parties to Launder Data about "The People*,*"* 2009 COLUM. BUS. L. REV. 950, 951.

18. Richard Lardner, *Your New Facebook "Friend" May Be the FBI*, NBC NEWS (Mar. 16, 2010), www.nbcnews.com.

19. U.S. Dep't of Justice, FUSION CENTER GUIDELINES: DEVELOPING AND SHARING INFORMATION AND INTELLIGENCE IN A NEW ERA 2 (2006), *available at* www.it.ojp.gov.

20. Ellen Huet, *Server and Protect: Predictive Policing Firm PredPol Promises to Map Crime Before It Happens*, FORBES (Mar. 2, 2015).

21. Jeremy Gorner, *Chicago Police Use "Heat List" as Strategy to Prevent Violence*, CHI. TRIB. (Aug. 21, 2013).

22. Andrew Guthrie Ferguson, *Predictive Prosecution*, 51 WAKE FOREST L. REV. 705, 724 (2016).

23. Erin Murphy, *Databases, Doctrine, & Constitutional Criminal Procedure*, 37 FORDHAM URB. L.J. 803, 830 (2010).

24. This is the subject of chapter 7.

25. This is the subject of chapter 2.

26. Office of the President, BIG DATA: A REPORT ON ALGORITHMIC SYSTEMS, OPPORTUNITY, AND CIVIL RIGHTS (May 2016), *available at* www.whitehouse.gov.

27. Ezekiel Edwards, *Predictive Policing Software Is More Accurate at Predicting Policing than Predicting Crime*, HUFFINGTON POST (Aug. 31, 2016), www.huffingtonpost.com.

CHAPTER 1. BIG DATA'S WATCHFUL EYE

1. Sir Arthur Conan Doyle, SHERLOCK HOLMES: THE HOUND OF THE BASKERVILLES 28 (ebook pub. 2016).

2. Robert Epstein, *Google's Gotcha: The Surprising Way Google Can Track Everything You Do Online*, U.S. NEWS AND WORLD REPORT (May 10, 2013); Charles Duhigg, *How Companies Learn Your Secrets*, N.Y. TIMES MAG. (Feb. 16, 2012).

3. James Manyika et al., McKinsey Global Institute, BIG DATA: THE NEXT FRONTIER FOR INNOVATION, COMPETITION, AND PRODUCTIVITY 87 (June 2011).

4. Kevin Rector, *Car Data Draws Privacy Concerns*, BALTIMORE SUN (Aug. 3, 2014).

5. David Bollier, Aspen Inst., THE PROMISE AND PERIL OF BIG DATA 1–2 (2010).

6. Fed. Trade Comm'n, DATA BROKERS: A CALL FOR TRANSPARENCY AND ACCOUNTABILITY i–ii (May 2014), www.ftc.gov.

7. *Id.*

8. Julia Angwin, *The Web's New Gold Mine: Your Secrets*, WALL ST. J. (July 31, 2010), at W1.

9. John Kelly, *Cellphone Data Spying: It's Not Just the NSA*, USA TODAY (Dec. 8, 2013); Nicolas P. Terry, *Protecting Patient Privacy in the Era of Big Data*, 81 UMKC L. REV. 385, 391 (2012).

10. Julie E. Cohen, *What Is Privacy For?*, 126 HARV. L. REV. 1904, 1920–21 (2013).

11. Exec. Office of the President, BIG DATA: SEIZING OPPORTUNITIES, PRE-SERVING VALUES 2 (2014), www.whitehouse.gov.

12. Jules J. Berman, PRINCIPLES OF BIG DATA: PREPARING, SHARING, AND ANALYZING COMPLEX INFORMATION 2 (2013).

13. Steve Lohr, *Amid the Flood, a Catchphrase Is Born*, N.Y. TIMES (Aug. 12, 2012).

14. Marcus Wohlson, *Amazon's Next Big Business Is Selling You*, WIRED (Oct. 16, 2012).

15. Andrew McAfee & Erik Brynjolfsson, *Big Data: The Management Revolution*, HARV. BUS. REV. (Oct. 2012), http://hbr.org.

16. Constance L. Hayes, *What Wal-Mart Knows about Customers' Habits*, N.Y. TIMES (Nov. 14, 2004).

17. Julia Angwin, DRAGNET NATION: A QUEST FOR PRIVACY, SECURITY, AND FREEDOM IN A WORLD OF RELENTLESS SURVEILLANCE 3 (2014).

18. Herb Weisbaum, *Big Data Knows You're Pregnant (and That's Not All)*, CNBC (Apr. 9, 2014), www.cnbc.com.

19. Kenneth Cukier, *Data, Data Everywhere*, ECONOMIST (Feb. 25, 2010).

20. Caleb Garling, *Google Enters Homes with Purchase of Nest*, S.F. CHRONICLE (Jan. 14, 2014); *see also* http://nest.com.

21. Ron Nixon, *U.S. Postal Service Logging All Mail for Law Enforcement*, N.Y. TIMES (July 3, 2013).

22. *See* United States Postal Service, *United States Postal Facts*, http://about.usps.com (accessed Feb. 15, 2017).

23. Lior Jacob Strahilevitz, *Reputation Nation: Law in an Era of Ubiquitous Personal Information*, 102 NW. U. L. REV. 1667, 1720 (2008); Christopher Slobogin, *Transactional Surveillance by the Government*, 75 MISS. L.J. 139, 145 (2005).

24. Omer Tene & Jules Polonetsky, *To Track or "Do Not Track": Advancing Transparency and Individual Control in Online Behavioral Advertising*, 13 MINN. J. L. SCI. & TECH. 281, 282 (2012); Larry Port, *Disconnect from Tech*, 29:6 LEGAL MGMT. 46, 49–50 (Nov./Dec. 2010).

25. Andrew William Bagley, *Don't Be Evil: The Fourth Amendment in the Age of Google, National Security and Digital Papers and Effects*, 21 ALB. L.J. SCI. & TECH. 153, 163 (2011).

26. Alexandra Alter, *Your E-Book Is Reading You*, WALL ST. J. (July 19, 2012).

27. Thomas P. Crocker, *Ubiquitous Privacy*, 66 OKLA. L. REV. 791, 798 (2014).

28. Rodolfo Ramirez, Kelly King, & Lori Ding, *Location! Location! Location! Data Technologies and the Fourth Amendment*, 30:4 CRIM. JUST. 19 (2016).

29. United States v. Jones, 132 S. Ct. 945, 963 (2012) (Alito, J., concurring).
30. Ned Potter, *Privacy Battles: OnStar Says GM Can Record Car's Use, Even If You Cancel Service*, ABC NEWS (Sept. 26, 2011), http://abcnews.go.com.
31. Jim Henry, *Drivers Accept Monitoring Devices to Earn Discounts on Auto Insurance*, FORBES (Sept. 30, 2012).
32. Troy Wolverton, *iSpy: Apple's iPhones Can Track Users' Movements*, SAN JOSE MERCURY NEWS (Apr. 20, 2011); Hayley Tsukayama, *Alarm on Hill over iPhone Location Tracking*, WASH. POST (Apr. 22, 2011).
33. Danielle Keats Citron, *Spying Inc.*, 72 WASH. & LEE L. REV. 1243, 1272 (2015).
34. Tony Bradley, *Study Finds Most Mobile Apps Put Your Security and Privacy at Risk*, PC WORLD (Dec. 5, 2013), www.pcworld.com.
35. Chris Jay Hoofnagle, *Big Brother's Little Helpers: How ChoicePoint and Other Commercial Data Brokers Collect and Package Your Data for Law Enforcement*, 29 N.C. J. INT'L L. & COM. REG. 595, 595–96 (2004).
36. Fed. Trade Comm'n, DATA BROKERS: A CALL FOR TRANSPARENCY AND ACCOUNTABILITY 8 (May 2014).
37. Morgan Hochheiser, *The Truth behind Data Collection and Analysis*, 32 J. MARSHALL J. INFO. TECH. & PRIVACY L. 32, 33 (2015).
38. Eric Lichtblau, *F.B.I.'s Reach into Records Is Set to Grow*, N.Y. TIMES (Nov. 12, 2003); Josh Meyer & Greg Miller, *U.S. Secretly Tracks Global Bank Data*, L.A. TIMES (June 23, 2006).
39. Susanne Craig, *Getting to Know You*, N.Y. TIMES (Sept. 5, 2012); *see also* www.opentable.com.
40. Andrew Guthrie Ferguson, *The Internet of Things and the Fourth Amendment of Effects*, 104 CALIF. L. REV. 805, 806–07 (2016); Scott R. Peppet, *Regulating the Internet of Things: First Steps toward Managing Discrimination, Privacy, Security, and Consent*, 93 TEX. L. REV. 85, 93 (2014).
41. Tony Danova, *Morgan Stanley: 75 Billion Devices Will Be Connected to the Internet of Things by 2020*, BUSINESS INSIDER (Oct. 2, 2013).
42. Lois Beckett, *Everything We Know about What Data Brokers Know about You*, PROPUBLICA (Sept. 13, 2013), www.propublica.org.
43. *See, e.g.*, Daniel J. Solove, *Access and Aggregation: Public Records, Privacy and the Constitution*, 86 MINN. L. REV. 1137 (2002).
44. Fed. Trade Comm'n, DATA BROKERS: A CALL FOR TRANSPARENCY AND ACCOUNTABILITY i–ii (May 2014), *available at* www.ftc.gov.
45. *Id.*
46. Chris Jay Hoofnagle, *Big Brother's Little Helpers: How ChoicePoint and Other Commercial Data Brokers Collect and Package Your Data for Law Enforcement*, 29 N.C. J. INT'L L. & COM. REG. 595, 595–96 (2004).
47. Fed. Trade Comm'n, DATA BROKERS: A CALL FOR TRANSPARENCY AND ACCOUNTABILITY 8 (May 2014).
48. Majority Staff of S. Comm. on Commerce, Sci., & Transp., Office of Oversight & Investigations, A REVIEW OF THE DATA BROKER INDUSTRY: COLLEC-

TION, USE, AND SALE OF CONSUMER DATA FOR MARKETING PURPOSES
5–8 (Dec. 18, 2013), *available at* www.commerce.senate.gov [*hereinafter* A RE-
VIEW OF THE DATA BROKER INDUSTRY].

49. *Id.*
50. *Id.*
51. Omer Tene & Jules Polonetsky, *A Theory of Creepy: Technology, Privacy, and Shift-
ing Social Norms*, 16 YALE J. L. & TECH. 59, 66–68 (2013).
52. A REVIEW OF THE DATA BROKER INDUSTRY at 14.
53. *Id.* at 14–15.
54. Leo Mirani & Max Nisen, *The Nine Companies That Know More about You than
Google or Facebook*, QUARTZ (May 27, 2014), http://qz.com.
55. Fed. Trade Comm'n, DATA BROKERS: A CALL FOR TRANSPARENCY AND
ACCOUNTABILITY 20 (May 2014).
56. *Id.* at 47.
57. 2 Leon Radzinowicz, A HISTORY OF ENGLISH CRIMINAL LAW 46–47 (1956).
58. Wayne A. Logan & Andrew G. Ferguson, *Policing Criminal Justice Data*, 101
MINN. L. REV. 541, 554 (2016).
59. 28 C.F.R. §§ 25.2, 25.4 (2012); US Department of Justice, FBI, Criminal Justice
Information Services Division, CJIS ANNUAL REPORT 4 (2015).
60. US Department of Justice, FBI, Criminal Justice Information Services Division,
CJIS ANNUAL REPORT 4 (2015).
61. Dara Lind, *Turning the No Fly List into the No Gun List Explained*, VOX (June 21,
2016), www.vox.com; Bart Jansen, *America's Terrorist Watchlist Explained*, USA
TODAY (June 14, 2016).
62. K. Babe Howell, *Gang Policing: The Post Stop-and-Frisk Justification for Profile-
Based Policing*, 5 U. DENV. CRIM. L. REV. 1, 15–16 (2015).
63. *See generally* Wayne A. Logan, *Database Infamia: Exit from the Sex Offender Registries*, 2015 WIS. L. REV. 219.
64. Wayne A. Logan, KNOWLEDGE AS POWER: CRIMINAL REGISTRATION AND
COMMUNITY NOTIFICATION LAWS IN AMERICA 178–81 (2009).
65. *See generally* Wayne A. Logan, *Database Infamia: Exit from the Sex Offender Registries*, 2015 WIS. L. REV. 219.
66. Christopher Slobogin, *Transactional Surveillance by the Government*, 75 MISS.
L.J. 139, 145 (2005).
67. Danielle Keats Citron & Frank Pasquale, *Network Accountability for the Domestic
Intelligence Apparatus*, 62 HASTINGS L.J. 1441, 1451 (2011).
68. Robert L. Mitchell, *It's Criminal: Why Data Sharing Lags among Law Enforcement
Agencies*, COMPUTER WORLD (Oct. 24, 2013), www.computerworld.com.
69. N-DEx, PRIVACY IMPACT ASSESSMENT FOR THE NATIONAL DATA EX-
CHANGE (N-DEx) SYSTEM (approved May 9, 2014), *available at* www.fbi.gov.
70. *Id.*
71. Margaret Hu, *Biometric ID Cybersurveillance*, 88 IND. L.J. 1475, 1478 (2013);
Laura K. Donohue, *Technological Leap, Statutory Gap, and Constitutional Abyss:*

Remote Biometric Identification Comes of Age, 97 MINN. L. REV. 407, 435 (2012); Erin Murphy, *The New Forensics: Criminal Justice, False Certainty, and the Second Generation of Scientific Evidence*, 95 CAL. L. REV. 721, 728 (2007).

72. FBI, CODIS NDIS STATISTICS (July 2016), www.fbi.gov.

73. U.S. Dep't of Justice, FBI, Criminal Information Services Division, NEXT GENERATION IDENTIFICATION FACTSHEET (2016), *available at* www.fbi.gov.

74. Andrew Guthrie Ferguson, *Big Data and Predictive Reasonable Suspicion*, 163 U. PA. L. REV. 327, 370 (2015); Elizabeth E. Joh, *Policing by Numbers: Big Data and the Fourth Amendment*, 89 WASH. L. REV. 35, 42 (2014); Andrew Guthrie Ferguson, *Predictive Policing and Reasonable Suspicion*, 62 EMORY L.J. 259, 266 (2012).

75. Alex Chohlas-Wood is the current director of analytics at the Office of Management Analysis and Planning, New York Police Department.

76. Laura Myers, Allen Parrish, & Alexis Williams, *Big Data and the Fourth Amendment: Reducing Overreliance on the Objectivity of Predictive Policing*, 8 FED. CTS. L. REV. 231, 234 (2015).

77. Charlie Beck & Colleen McCue, *Predictive Policing: What Can We Learn from Wal-Mart and Amazon about Fighting Crime in a Recession?*, POLICE CHIEF (Nov. 2009), www.policechiefmagazine.org.

78. 5 U.S.C. § 552a (1994).

79. Pub. L. No. 99–508, 100 Stat. 1848 (codified as amended in sections of 18 U.S.C.); Communications Assistance for Law Enforcement Act, Pub. L. No. 103–414 (1994) at §207(2).

80. 18 U.S.C. §§ 2701–12.

81. 50 U.S.C. §§ 1801–13.

82. 44 U.S.C. §§ 3501–21.

83. 12 U.S.C. §§ 35.

84. 15 U.S.C. § 6801.

85. 12 U.S.C. §§ 1951–59 (2006)

86. 12 U.S.C. §§ 3401–22 (2006); 12 U.S.C. § 3407

87. 15 U.S.C. §1681.

88. 45 C.F.R. 164.512(f)(1)(ii); 45 C.F.R. 164.512(f)(2).

89. 42 U.S.C. §§ 2000ff to 2000ff-11 (2012).

90. 15 U.S.C. §§ 6501–06.

91. 20 U.S.C. § 1232g (2012).

92. 18 U.S.C. § 1039; *but see* 18 U.S.C. §§ 2703(c)(1)(B), 2703(d).

93. 18 U.S.C. § 2710 (1994).

94. Erin Murphy, *The Politics of Privacy in the Criminal Justice System: Information Disclosure, the Fourth Amendment, and Statutory Law Enforcement Exemptions*, 111 MICH. L. REV. 485, 487 n.2 (2013).

95. Megha Rajagopalan, *Cellphone Companies Will Share Your Location Data—Just Not with You*, PROPUBLICA (June 26, 2012), www.propublica.org.

96. Joshua L. Simmons, *Buying You: The Government's Use of Fourth-Parties to Launder Data about "The People,"* 2009 COLUM. BUS. L. REV. 950, 976; Jon D.

Michaels, *All the President's Spies: Private-Public Intelligence Partnerships in the War on Terror*, 96 CAL. L. REV. 901, 902 (2008).

97. Bob Sullivan, *Who's Buying Cell Phone Records Online? Cops*, MSNBC (June 20, 2006), www.msnbc.msn.com; Robert Block, *Requests for Corporate Data Multiply: Businesses Juggle Law-Enforcement Demands for Information about Customers, Suppliers*, WALL ST. J. (May 20, 2006), at A4.

98. Megha Rajagopalan, *Cellphone Companies Will Share Your Location Data—Just Not with You*, PROPUBLICA (June 26, 2012), www.propublica.org.

99. Matt Apuzzo, David E. Sanger, & Michael S. Schmidt, *Apple and Other Companies Tangle with U.S. over Data Access*, N.Y. TIMES (Sept. 7, 2015), www.nytimes.com; Cory Bennett, *Apple Couldn't Comply with Warrant Because of Encryption*, HILL (Sept. 8, 2015), http://thehill.com.

100. Viktor Mayer-Schonberger & Kenneth Cukier, BIG DATA: A REVOLUTION THAT WILL TRANSFORM HOW WE LIVE, WORK, AND THINK 2 (2013); Kate Crawford & Jason Schultz, *Big Data and Due Process: Toward a Framework to Redress Predictive Privacy Harms*, 55 B.C. L. REV. 93, 96 (2014); Neil M. Richards & Jonathan H. King, *Big Data Ethics*, 49 WAKE FOREST L. REV. 393, 394 (2014).

101. Jonas Lerman, *Big Data and Its Exclusions*, 66 STAN. L. REV. ONLINE 55, 57 (2013); Exec. Office of the President, BIG DATA: SEIZING OPPORTUNITIES, PRESERVING VALUES 2 (2014), *available at* www.whitehouse.gov.

102. Charles Duhigg, *How Companies Learn Your Secrets*, N.Y. TIMES MAG. (Feb. 16, 2012), www.nytimes.com.

103. *Id.*

104. Cathy O'Neil, WEAPONS OF MATH DESTRUCTION: HOW BIG DATA INCREASES INEQUALITY AND THREATENS DEMOCRACY 98 (2016).

105. *See* chapter 2.

106. *Id.*

CHAPTER 2. DATA IS THE NEW BLACK

1. David Black, *Predictive Policing Is Here Now, but at What Cost?*, DALLAS MORNING NEWS (Feb. 26, 2016).

2. Andrew Guthrie Ferguson, *Crime Mapping and the Fourth Amendment: Redrawing High Crime Areas*, 63 HASTINGS L.J. 179, 223–25 (2011).

3. U.S. Dep't of Justice, Community Oriented Policing Services (COPS), THE IMPACT OF THE ECONOMIC DOWNTURN ON POLICE AGENCIES 2–5 (2011), *available at* www.smartpolicinginitiative.com; Police Executive Research Forum, POLICING AND THE ECONOMIC DOWNTURN: STRIVING FOR EFFICIENCY IS THE NEW NORMAL 1–3 (Feb. 2013).

4. *Id.*

5. *Id.*

6. Vera Institute, THE IMPACT OF FEDERAL BUDGET CUTS FROM FY10–FY13 ON STATE AND LOCAL PUBLIC SAFETY: RESULTS FROM A SURVEY OF CRIMINAL JUSTICE PRACTITIONERS 1–4 (2013), *available at* www.vera.org.

7. *Id.*

8. Monica Davey & Julie Bosman, *Protests Flare after Ferguson Police Officer Is Not Indicted*, N.Y. TIMES (Nov. 24, 2014); Dana Ford, Greg Botelho, & Ben Brumfield, *Protests Erupt in Wake of Chokehold Death Decision*, CNN (Dec. 8, 2014), www.cnn.com.

9. *Reactions to the Shooting in Ferguson, Mo., Have Sharp Racial Divides*, N.Y. TIMES (Aug. 21, 2014); Yamiche Alcindor, Aamer Madhani, & Doug Stanglin, *Hundreds of Peaceful Protesters March in Ferguson*, USA TODAY (Aug. 19, 2014).

10. Roger Parloff, *Two Deaths: The Crucial Difference between Eric Garner's Case and Michael Brown's*, FORTUNE (Dec. 5, 2014); Shaila Dewan & Richard A. Oppel Jr., *In Tamir Rice Case, Many Errors by Cleveland Police, Then a Fatal One*, N.Y. TIMES (Jan. 22, 2015); Alan Blinder, *Walter Scott Shooting Seen as Opening for Civil Suits against North Charleston's Police Dept.*, N.Y. TIMES (Apr. 13, 2015).

11. Osagie K. Obasogie & Zachary Newman, *Black Lives Matter and Respectability Politics in Local News Accounts of Officer-Involved Civilian Deaths: An Early Empirical Assessment*, 2016 WIS. L. REV. 541, 544.

12. *Ferguson Unrest: From Shooting to Nationwide Protests*, BBC NEWS (Aug. 10, 2015), www.bbc.com.

13. Andrew E. Taslitz, *Stories of Fourth Amendment Disrespect: From Elian to the Internment*, 70 FORDHAM L. REV. 2257, 2358–59 (2002); Andrew E. Taslitz, RECONSTRUCTING THE FOURTH AMENDMENT: A HISTORY OF SEARCH AND SEIZURE 1789–1868, 91–121 (2006).

14. James B. Comey, *Hard Truths: Law Enforcement and Race*, Remarks at Georgetown University (Feb. 12, 2105), *available at* www.fbi.gov.

15. *Id.*

16. Statement by IACP president Terrence M. Cunningham on the law enforcement profession and historical injustices, Remarks Made at the 2016 IACP Annual Conference, San Diego (Oct. 17, 2016), *available at* www.iacp.org.

17. U.S. Dep't of Justice, Civil Rights Div., INVESTIGATION OF THE FERGUSON POLICE DEPARTMENT 5–8 (2015), *available at* www.justice.gov.

18. *Id.* at 4.

19. *Id.* at 5.

20. *Id.* at 4.

21. *Id.* at 72–73.

22. *Id.* 9–15.

23. *Id.* at 2.

24. *Id.* at 15–41, 88.

25. *Id.* at 2.

26. Floyd v. City of New York, 959 F. Supp. 2d 540, 625 (S.D.N.Y. Aug. 12, 2013), *appeal dismissed* (Sept. 25, 2013); *see also* Daniels v. City of New York, 198 F.R.D. 409 (S.D.N.Y. 2001); Ligon v. City of New York, 736 F.3d 118, 129 (2d Cir. 2013), *vacated in part*, 743 F.3d 362 (2d Cir. 2014).

27. *Floyd*, 959 F. Supp. 2d at 562.

28. *Id.* at 603.
29. *Id.* at 573–76.
30. *Id.*
31. *Id.*
32. *Id.*
33. Chip Mitchell, *Police Data Cast Doubt on Chicago-Style Stop-and-Frisk*, WBEZ NEWS (May 4, 2016), *available at* www.wbez.org.
34. Center for Constitutional Rights, STOP AND FRISK: THE HUMAN IMPACT 3–4 (July 2012).
35. *Id.* at 17.
36. *Id.* at 15.
37. Sarah Childress, *Fixing the Force*, FRONTLINE (Dec. 14, 2016), www.pbs.org.
38. *Id.*
39. Kimbriell Kelly, Sarah Childress, & Steven Rich, *Forced Reforms, Mixed Results*, WASH. POST (Nov. 13, 2015).
40. David Rudovsky, *Litigating Civil Rights Cases to Reform Racially Biased Criminal Justice Practices*, 39 COLUM. HUM. RTS. L. REV. 97, 103 (2007); David A. Harris, *Across the Hudson: Taking the Stop and Frisk Debate beyond New York City*, 16 N.Y.U. J. LEGIS. & PUB. POL'Y 853, 871–72 (2013) (citing Settlement Agreement, Class Certification, & Consent Decree, *Bailey v. City of Philadelphia*, No. 10–5952 (E.D. Pa. June 21, 2011)).
41. U.S. Dep't of Justice, INVESTIGATION INTO THE BALTIMORE CITY POLICE DEPARTMENT 21–121 (Aug. 10, 2016), *available at* www.justice.gov.
42. *Id.*
43. Heather Mac Donald, *An Urgent Desire for More Policing*, WASH. POST: VOLOKH CONSPIRACY (July 22, 2016), www.washingtonpost.com.
44. Jelani Cobb, *Honoring the Police and Their Victims*, NEW YORKER (July 25, 2016); Jennifer Emily & Elizabeth Djinis, *Slayings of Baton Rouge Officers Compound Dallas' Grief but Don't Lessen City's Resolve*, DALLAS MORNING NEWS (July 17, 2016); J. B. Wogan, *In Wake of Dallas and Baton Rouge, Police around U.S. Take Extra Safety Precautions*, GOVERNING (July 19, 2016).
45. Simone Weichselbaum, *The "Chicago Model" of Policing Hasn't Saved Chicago*, MARSHALL PROJECT (Apr. 19, 2016), www.themarshallproject.org.
46. *Chicago Experiences Most Violent Month in Nearly 20 Years*, ALL THINGS CONSIDERED (NPR radio broadcast, Aug. 31, 2016), *available at* www.npr.org.
47. Simone Weichselbaum, *The "Chicago Model" of Policing Hasn't Saved Chicago*, MARSHALL PROJECT (Apr. 19, 2016), www.themarshallproject.org.
48. *Id.*; Andrew Fan, *The Most Dangerous Neighborhood, the Most Inexperienced Cops*, MARSHALL PROJECT (Sept. 20, 2016), www.themarshallproject.org.
49. Jess Bidgood, *The Numbers behind Baltimore's Record Year in Homicides*, N.Y. TIMES (Jan. 15, 2016).
50. Justin Fenton & Justin George, *Violence Surges as Baltimore Police Officers Feel Hesitant*, BALTIMORE SUN (May 8, 2015).

51. *Id.*
52. John M. Violanti & Anne Gehrke, *Police Trauma Encounters: Precursors of Compassion Fatigue*, 6:2 INT'L J. OF EMERGENCY MENTAL HEALTH 75–80 (2004); Mélissa Martin, André Marchand, & Richard Boyer, *Traumatic Events in the Workplace: Impact of Psychopathology and Healthcare Use of Police Officers*, 11:3 INT'L J. OF EMERGENCY MENTAL HEALTH 165–76 (2009); Allen R. Kates, COPSHOCK: SURVIVING POSTTRAUMATIC STRESS DISORDER (2nd ed. 2008).
53. Pamela Kulbarsh, *2015 Police Suicide Statistics*, OFFICER.COM (Jan. 13, 2016).
54. Thomas R. O'Connor, *Intelligence-Led Policing and Transnational Justice*, 6 J. INST. JUST. & INT'L STUD. 233, 233 (2006) (citing Jerry H. Ratcliffe, *Intelligence-Led Policing*, TRENDS & ISSUES CRIME & CRIM. JUST. 1 (Apr. 2003)); Nina Cope, *Intelligence Led Policing or Policing Led Intelligence?*, 44 BRIT. J. CRIMINOL. 188, 191 (2004); Olivier Ribaux et al., *Forensic Intelligence and Crime Analysis*, 2 L. PROBABILITY & RISK 47, 48, 54 (2003).
55. James J. Willis, Stephen D. Mastrofski, & David Weisburd, *Making Sense of Compstat: A Theory-Based Analysis of Organizational Change in Three Police Departments*, 41 LAW & SOC'Y REV. 147, 148 (2007); James J. Willis, Stephen D. Mastrofski, & David Weisburd, Police Foundation, COMPSTAT IN PRACTICE: AN IN-DEPTH ANALYSIS OF THREE CITIES (1999), www.policefoundation. org; Jack Maple, THE CRIME FIGHTER: HOW YOU CAN MAKE YOUR COMMUNITY CRIME-FREE 93–96 (1999).
56. Stephen Rushin, *Structural Reform Litigation in American Police Departments*, 99 MINN. L. REV. 1343, 1400 (2015).
57. Andrew Guthrie Ferguson, *Policing "Stop and Frisk" with "Stop and Track" Policing*, HUFFINGTON POST (Aug. 17, 2014), www.huffingtonpost.com.
58. Selwyn Robb, *New York's Police Allow Corruption, Mollen Panel Says*, N.Y. TIMES (Dec. 29, 1993).
59. *Id.*
60. William J. Bratton & Sean W. Malinowski, *Police Performance Management in Practice: Taking COMPSTAT to the Next Level*, 2:3 POLICING 259, 262 (2008).
61. Tina Daunt, *Consent Decree Gets Federal Judge's OK*, L.A. TIMES (June 16, 2001); Rick Orlov, *LAPD Consent Decree Wins Council OK*, L.A. DAILY NEWS (Nov. 3, 2000); Consent Decree, United States v. Los Angeles, No. 00–11769 GAF (C.D. Cal. June 15, 2001), *available at* www.lapdonline.org.
62. William J. Bratton & Sean W. Malinowski, *Police Performance Management in Practice: Taking COMPSTAT to the Next Level*, 2:3 POLICING 259, 262 (2008).
63. *Id.*
64. Anna Sanders, *NYPD Going Mobile with 41,000 Tablets and Handheld Devices for Cops*, SILIVE.COM (Oct. 23, 2014).
65. *See, e.g.*, Tracey Meares, Andrew V. Papachristos, & Jeffrey Fagan, Project Safe Neighborhoods in Chicago, *Homicide and Gun Violence in Chicago: Evaluation*

and Summary of the Project Safe Neighborhoods Program (Jan. 2009); Michael
Sierra-Arevalo, *How Targeted Deterrence Helps Police Reduce Gun Deaths*,
SCHOLARS STRATEGY NETWORK (June 3, 2013), http://thesocietypages.org;
Tracey Meares, Andrew V. Papachristos, & Jeffrey Fagan, ATTENTION FELONS:
EVALUATING PROJECT SAFE NEIGHBORHOOD IN CHICAGO (Nov. 2005),
available at www.law.uchicago.edu.

66. David M. Kennedy, Anne M. Diehl, & Anthony A. Braga, *Youth Violence in Bos-
ton: Gun Markets, Serious Youth Offenders, and a Use-Reduction Strategy*, 59 LAW
& CONTEMP. PROBS. 147 (Winter 1996); David M. Kennedy, *Pulling Levers:
Chronic Offenders, High-Crime Settings, and a Theory of Prevention*, 31 VAL. U. L.
REV. 449 (1997); Andrew V. Papachristos, Tracy L. Meares, & Jeffrey Fagan, *Why
Do Criminals Obey the Law? The Influence of Legitimacy and Social Networks on
Active Gun Offenders*, 102 J. CRIM. L. & CRIMINOL. 397, 436 (2012).

67. Paul J. Brantingham & Patricia L. Brantingham (eds.), ENVIRONMENTAL
CRIMINOL. (1981); Luc Anselin et al., *Spatial Analyses of Crime, in* 4 CRIMINAL
JUSTICE 2000: MEASUREMENT AND ANALYSIS OF CRIME AND JUS-
TICE 215 (2000); Ralph B. Taylor, *Crime and Small-Scale Places: What We Know,
What We Can Prevent, and What Else We Need to Know*, CRIME AND PLACE:
PLENARY PAPERS OF THE 1997 CONFERENCE ON CRIMINAL JUSTICE
RESEARCH AND EVALUATION 2 (National Institute of Justice, 1998); Anthony
A. Braga, *Pulling Levers: Focused Deterrence Strategies and Prevention of Gun
Homicide*, 36:4 J. CRIM. JUST. 332–343 (2008); Daniel J. Steinbock, *Data Mining,
Data Matching and Due Process*, 40 GA. L. REV. 1, 4 (2005).

68. These partnerships are discussed in chapters 3 and 4.

69. *See, e.g.*, Kate J. Bowers & Shane D. Johnson, *Who Commits Near Repeats? A Test
of the Boost Explanation*, 5 W. CRIMINOL. REV. 12, 21 (2004); Shane D. Johnson
et al., *Space-Time Patterns of Risk: A Cross National Assessment of Residential
Burglary Victimization*, 23 J. QUANT. CRIMINOL. 201, 203–04 (2007); Wim
Bernasco, *Them Again? Same-Offender Involvement in Repeat and Near Repeat
Burglaries*, 5 EUR. J. CRIMINOL. 411, 412 (2008); Lawrence W. Sherman, Patrick
R. Gartin, & Michael E. Buerger, *Hot Spots of Predatory Crime: Routine Activities
and the Criminology of Place*, 27 CRIMINOL. 27, 37 (1989).

70. David Alan Sklansky, THE PERSISTENT PULL OF POLICE PROFESSIONAL-
ISM 8–9 (2011); O. Ribaux et al., *Forensic Intelligence and Crime Analysis*, 2 L.
PROBABILITY & RISK 47, 48 (2003).

71. Christopher Beam, *Time Cops: Can Police Really Predict Crime before It Happens?*,
SLATE (Jan. 24, 2011), www.slate.com.

72. *See* National Institutes of Justice, Predictive Policing Research website, www.nij.
gov.

73. *Id.*

74. Additional discussion of the rise of biometric databases is discussed in chapter 6.

75. MINORITY REPORT (DreamWorks 2002).

CHAPTER 3. WHOM WE POLICE

1. Robert L. Mitchell, *Predictive Policing Gets Personal*, COMPUTERWORLD (Oct. 24, 2013).
2. Monica Davey, *Chicago Tactics Put Major Dent in Killing Trend*, N.Y. TIMES (June 11, 2013); Bryan Llenas, *The New World of "Predictive Policing" Belies Specter of High-Tech Racial Profiling*, FOX NEWS LATINO (Feb. 25, 2014), http://latino.foxnews.com.
3. Jeremy Gorner, *The Heat List*, CHI. TRIB. (Aug. 21, 2013); Jack Smith IV, *"Minority Report" Is Real—and It's Really Reporting Minorities*, MIC (Nov. 9, 2015), http://mic.com.
4. Nissa Rhee, *Can Police Big Data Stop Chicago's Spike in Crime?*, CHRISTIAN SCI. MONITOR (June 2, 2016); Monica Davey, *Chicago Police Try to Predict Who May Shoot or Be Shot*, N.Y. TIMES (May 23, 2016).
5. *See* Chi. Police Dep't, CUSTOM NOTIFICATIONS IN CHICAGO, SPECIAL ORDER S10–05 IV.B (Oct. 6, 2015), *available at* http://directives.chicagopolice.org.
6. Palantir, NOLA MURDER REDUCTION: TECHNOLOGY TO POWER DATA-DRIVEN PUBLIC HEALTH STRATEGIES 7 (white paper, 2014).
7. Matt Stroud, *Should Los Angeles County Predict Which Children Will Become Criminals?*, PACIFIC STANDARD (Jan. 27, 2016), http://psmag.com; Maya Rao, *Rochester Hopes Predictive Policing Can Steer Juveniles Away from Crime*, STAR-TRIBUNE (Oct. 24, 2014).
8. Anthony A. Braga, *Pulling Levers: Focused Deterrence Strategies and the Prevention of Gun Homicide*, 36 J. CRIM. JUST. 332, 332–34 (2008).
9. Andrew V. Papachristos & David S. Kirk, *Changing the Street Dynamic: Evaluating Chicago's Group Violence Reduction Strategy*, 14 CRIMINOL. & PUB. POL'Y 3, 9 (2015).
10. Anthony A. Braga et al., SMART APPROACHES TO REDUCING GUN VIOLENCE 12–13 (2014), *available at* www.smartpolicinginitiative.com.
11. *Id.*
12. *Id.* at 18.
13. *Id.* at 13.
14. *Id.*
15. K. J. Novak, A. M. Fox, & C. N. Carr, KANSAS CITY'S SMART POLICING INITIATIVE: FROM FOOT PATROL TO FOCUSED DETERRENCE ii (Dec. 2015), *available at* www.smartpolicinginitiative.com.
16. *Id.* at ii, 9.
17. *Id.* at ii.
18. *Id.*
19. John Eligon & Timothy Williams, *On Police Radar for Crimes They Might Commit*, N.Y. TIMES (Sept. 25, 2015).
20. *Id.*
21. *Id.*

22. *Id.*
23. *Id.*
24. Tony Rizzo, *Amid A Crackdown on Violent Criminals, Kansas City Homicides Sharply Decline*, KANSAS CITY STAR (Jan. 1, 2015).
25. Glen Rice & Tony Rizzo, *2015 Was Kansas City's Deadliest Year for Homicides since 2011*, KANSAS CITY STAR (Dec. 31, 2015).
26. Mark Guarnio, *Can Math Stop Murder?*, CHRISTIAN SCI. MONITOR (July 20, 2014).
27. Nissa Rhee, *Can Police Big Data Stop Chicago's Spike in Crime?*, CHRISTIAN SCI. MONITOR (June 2, 2016).
28. Editorial, *Who Will Kill or Be Killed in Violence-Plagued Chicago? The Algorithm Knows*, CHI. TRIB. (May 10, 2016).
29. Andrew V. Papachristos, *Commentary: CPD's Crucial Choice: Treat Its List as Offenders or as Potential Victims?*, CHI. TRIB. (July 29, 2016).
30. Chi. Police Dep't, CUSTOM NOTIFICATIONS IN CHICAGO, SPECIAL ORDER S10–05 III.C (Oct. 6, 2015), *available at* http://directives.chicagopolice.org.
31. *Id.*
32. Chi. Police Dep't, CUSTOM NOTIFICATIONS IN CHICAGO, SPECIAL ORDER S10–05 IV.A, IV.D, V.C (Oct. 6, 2015), *available at* http://directives.chicagopolice.org.
33. Jeremy Gorner, *The Heat List*, CHI. TRIB. (Aug. 21, 2013).
34. Chi. Police Dep't, CUSTOM NOTIFICATIONS IN CHICAGO, SPECIAL ORDER S10–05 IV.D (Oct. 6, 2015), *available at* http://directives.chicagopolice.org.
35. Jeremy Gorner, *The Heat List*, CHI. TRIB. (Aug. 21, 2013).
36. *Id.*
37. Monica Davey, *Chicago Police Try to Predict Who May Shoot or Be Shot*, N.Y. TIMES (May 23, 2016).
38. *Id.*
39. Matt Stroud, *The Minority Report, Chicago's New Police Computer Predicts Crimes, but Is It Racist?* VERGE (Feb. 19, 2014), www.theverge.com.
40. Monica Davey, *Chicago Has Its Deadliest Month in About Two Decades*, N.Y. TIMES (Sept. 1, 2016).
41. Jennifer Saunders, Priscilla Hunt, & John S. Hollywood, *Predictions Put into Practice: A Quasi-Experimental Evaluation of Chicago's Predictive Policing Pilot*, 12 J. EXPERIMENTAL CRIMINOL. 347, 355–64 (2016).
42. *Id.* at 363.
43. *Id.* at 364.
44. Andrew V. Papachristos, *Commentary: CPD's Crucial Choice: Treat Its List as Offenders or as Potential Victims?*, CHI. TRIB. (July 29, 2016).
45. *Id.*; *see also* Monica Davey, *Chicago Police Try to Predict Who May Shoot or Be Shot*, N.Y. TIMES (May 23, 2016).
46. Nissa Rhee, *Study Casts Doubt on Chicago Police's Secretive "Heat List,"* CHI. MAG. (Aug. 17, 2016).

47. Monica Davey, *Chicago Police Try to Predict Who May Shoot or Be Shot*, N.Y. TIMES (May 23, 2016).

48. Jeffrey Goldberg, *A Matter of Black Lives*, ATLANTIC (Sept. 2015).

49. Jason Sheuh, *New Orleans Cuts Murder Rate Using Data Analytics*, GOVTECH. COM (Oct. 22, 2014); City of New Orleans, NOLA FOR LIFE: COMPREHENSIVE MURDER REDUCTION STRATEGY, *available at* www.nolaforlife.org.

50. Palantir, PHILANTHROPY ENGINEERING 2015 ANNUAL IMPACT REPORT, *available at* www.palantir.com (quoting Sarah Schirmer, Criminal Justice Policy Advisor, Mayor's Office of Criminal Justice Coordination: "Since 2012, Mayor Mitch Landrieu has committed significant resources and effort to reducing murder in New Orleans, and has asked every partner and stakeholder in the city to play a role. Palantir has made it possible for our intelligence analysts to question preconceived ideas about murder victims and suspects. The analysis has strengthened our ability to prevent and intervene in violent conflicts, and connect at-risk individuals to services.").

51. Palantir, NOLA MURDER REDUCTION: TECHNOLOGY TO POWER DATA-DRIVEN PUBLIC HEALTH STRATEGIES 1–5 (white paper, 2014); City of New Orleans, NOLA FOR LIFE: COMPREHENSIVE MURDER REDUCTION STRATEGY 33, *available at* www.nolaforlife.org.

52. Palantir, NOLA MURDER REDUCTION: TECHNOLOGY TO POWER DATA-DRIVEN PUBLIC HEALTH STRATEGIES 5 (white paper, 2014).

53. *Id.* at 1.

54. *Id.* at 7.

55. *Id.* at 8.

56. *Id.* at 4.

57. *Id.*

58. City of New Orleans, NOLA FOR LIFE: COMPREHENSIVE MURDER REDUCTION STRATEGY 2, *available at* www.nolaforlife.org.

59. *Id.*

60. Palantir, NOLA MURDER REDUCTION: TECHNOLOGY TO POWER DATA-DRIVEN PUBLIC HEALTH STRATEGIES 9 (white paper, 2014).

61. City of New Orleans, NOLA FOR LIFE: COMPREHENSIVE MURDER REDUCTION STRATEGY 3, *available at* www.nolaforlife.org.

62. Heather Mac Donald, *Prosecution Gets Smart*, CITY J. (Summer 2014), www. city-journal.org; John Eligon, *Top Prosecutor Creates a Unit on Crime Trends*, N.Y. TIMES (May 25, 2010), at A22.

63. Chip Brown, *The Data D.A.*, N.Y. TIMES MAG. (Dec. 7, 2014), at 22, 24–25.

64. New York District Attorney's Office, INTELLIGENCE-DRIVEN PROSECUTION: AN IMPLEMENTATION GUIDE 10 (symposium materials, 2015).

65. *Id.* at 13.

66. *Id.* at 8.

67. *Id.*; Heather Mac Donald, *Prosecution Gets Smart*, CITY J. (Summer 2014), www. city-journal.org.

68. New York District Attorney's Office, INTELLIGENCE-DRIVEN PROSECUTION: AN IMPLEMENTATION GUIDE 11, 16 (symposium materials, 2015).

69. Heather Mac Donald, *A Smarter Way to Prosecute*, L.A. TIMES (Aug. 10, 2014), at A24.

70. Chip Brown, *The Data D.A.*, N.Y. TIMES MAG. (Dec. 7, 2014), at 22, 24–25.

71. New York District Attorney's Office, INTELLIGENCE-DRIVEN PROSECUTION: AN IMPLEMENTATION GUIDE 2–3 (symposium materials, 2015).

72. Chip Brown, *The Data D.A.*, N.Y. TIMES MAG. (Dec. 7, 2014), at 22, 24–25.

73. James C. McKinley Jr., *In Unusual Collaboration, Police and Prosecutors Team Up to Reduce Crime*, N.Y. TIMES (June 5, 2014), at A25.

74. *To Stem Gun Crime, "Moneyball,"* ST. LOUIS POST-DISPATCH (June 28, 2015), at A20.

75. Heather Mac Donald, *Prosecution Gets Smart*, CITY J. (Summer 2014), www.city-journal.org.

76. *Id.*

77. Heather Mac Donald, *First Came Data-Driven Policing. Now Comes Data-Driven Prosecutions*, L.A. TIMES (Aug. 8, 2014).

78. David M. Kennedy, Anne M. Diehl, & Anthony A. Braga, *Youth Violence in Boston: Gun Markets, Serious Youth Offenders, and a Use-Reduction Strategy*, 59 LAW & CONTEMP. PROBS. 147, 147–49, 156 (1996); Anthony A. Braga et al., *Problem-Oriented Policing, Deterrence, and Youth Violence: An Evaluation of Boston's Operation Ceasefire*, 38 J. RES. CRIME & DELINQ. 195, 195–200 (2001); Andrew V. Papachristos & David S. Kirk, *Changing the Street Dynamic: Evaluating Chicago's Group Violence Reduction Strategy*, 14 CRIMINOL. & PUB. POL'Y 525, 533 (2015).

79. Andrew V. Papachristos, *Social Networks Can Help Predict Gun Violence*, WASH. POST (Dec. 19, 2013) (*citing* Andrew V. Papachristos & Christopher Wildeman, *Network Exposure and Homicide Victimization in an African American Community*, 104:1 AM. J. PUB. HEALTH 143 (2014)).

80. Andrew V. Papachristos, David M. Hureau, & Anthony A. Braga, *The Corner and the Crew: The Influence of Geography and Social Networks on Gang Violence*, 78:3 AM. SOC. REV. 417–47 (2013).

81. *Id.* at 419–23.

82. Andrew V. Papachristos, Anthony A. Braga, & David M. Hureau, *Social Networks and the Risk of Gunshot Injury*, 89:6 J. URB. HEALTH 992–1003 (2012).

83. Andrew V. Papachristos & David S. Kirk, *Changing the Street Dynamic: Evaluating Chicago's Group Violence Reduction Strategy*, 14 CRIMINOL. & PUB. POL'Y 525, 533 (2015).

84. Matt Stroud, *Chicago's Predictive Policing Tool Just Failed a Major Test*, VERGE (Aug. 19, 2016), www.theverge.com.

85. Nate Silver, *Black Americans Are Killed at 12 Times the Rate of People in Other Developed Countries*, FIVETHIRTYEIGHT (June 18, 2015), http://fivethirtyeight.com ("Black Americans are almost eight times as likely as white ones to be homicide victims.").

86. Kenneth B. Nunn, *Race, Crime and the Pool of Surplus Criminality: Or Why the "War on Drugs" Was a "War on Blacks,"* 6 J. GENDER, RACE, & JUST. 381, 391–412 (2002); David Rudovsky, *Law Enforcement by Stereotypes and Serendipity: Racial Profiling and Stops and Searches without Cause*, 3 U. PA. J. CONST. L. 296, 311 (2001); Jeffrey Fagan & Garth Davies, *Street Stops and Broken Windows: Terry, Race, and Disorder in New York City*, 28 FORDHAM URB. L.J. 457, 482 (2000).

87. Bryan Llenas, *Brave New World of "Predictive Policing" Raises Specter of High-Tech Racial Profiling*, FOX NEWS LATINO, Feb. 25, 2014, http://latino.foxnews.com.

88. ACLU, THE WAR ON MARIJUANA IN BLACK AND WHITE 47 (2013), *available at* www.aclu.org.

89. *Id.* at 18.

90. *Id.* at 18–20.

91. Vera Institute of Justice, RACIAL DISPARITY IN MARIJUANA POLICING IN NEW ORLEANS 9–10 (July 2016), *available at* www.vera.org.

92. The Sentencing Project, THE COLOR OF JUSTICE: RACIAL AND ETHNIC DISPARITY IN STATE PRISONS 3 (2016) *available at* www.sentencingproject.org.

93. Stephen M. Haas, Erica Turley, & Monika Sterling, CRIMINAL JUSTICE STATISTICAL ANALYSIS CENTER, WEST VIRGINIA TRAFFIC STOP STUDY: FINAL REPORT (2009), *available at* www.legis.state.wv.us; ACLU and Rights Working Group, THE PERSISTENCE OF RACIAL AND ETHNIC PROFILING IN THE UNITED STATES 56 (Aug. 2009); Sylvia Moreno, *Race a Factor in Texas Stops: Study Finds Police More Likely to Pull over Blacks, Latinos*, WASH. POST (Feb. 25, 2005); James Kimberly, *Minorities Stopped at Higher Rate in DuPage*, CHI. TRIB. (April 29, 2006).

94. Leadership Conference on Civil and Human Rights, RESTORING A NATIONAL CONSENSUS: THE NEED TO END RACIAL PROFILING IN AMERICA 9–12 (2011), *available at* www.civilrights.org.

95. Univ. of Minn. Inst. on Race & Poverty, MINNESOTA STATEWIDE RACIAL PROFILING REPORT 36 (2003), *available at* www1.umn.edu.

96. W. Va. Division Just. & Community Services, WEST VIRGINIA TRAFFIC STOP STUDY: 2009 FINAL REPORT (2009), *available at* www.djcs.wv.gov.

97. L. Song Richardson, *Police Efficiency and the Fourth Amendment*, 87 IND. L.J. 1143, 1170 (2012); L. Song Richardson, *Arrest Efficiency and the Fourth Amendment*, 95 MINN. L. REV. 2035, 2061–63 (2011).

98. L. Song Richardson, *Police Efficiency and the Fourth Amendment*, 87 IND. L.J. 1143, 1170 (2012); L. Song Richardson, *Arrest Efficiency and the Fourth Amendment*, 95 MINN. L. REV. 2035, 2061–63 (2011).

99. Chip Mitchell, *Police Data Cast Doubt on Chicago-Style Stop and Frisk*, WBEZ NEWS (May 4, 2016), *available at* www.wbez.org.

100. Calf. State Auditor, THE CALGANG CRIMINAL INTELLIGENCE SYSTEM, REPORT 2015–130 3 (2016), *available at* www.voiceofsandiego.org.

101. *Id.*
102. Julia Angwin et al., *Machine Bias*, PROPUBLICA (May 23, 2016), www.propublica.org.
103. *Id.*
104. *Id.*
105. *Id.*
106. *Id.*
107. *Id.*
108. *Id.*
109. Anthony W. Flores, Christopher T. Lowenkamp, & Kristin Bechtel, *False Positives, False Negatives, and False Analyses: A Rejoinder to "Machine Bias": There's Software Used across the Country to Predict Future Criminals. And It's Biased against Blacks* 2 (unpublished paper, 2016).
110. *Id.* at 10–12.
111. *Id.* at 21–22.
112. Max Ehrenfreund, *The Machines That Could Rid Courtrooms of Racism*, WASH. POST (Aug. 18, 2016).
113. Sonja B. Starr, *Evidence-Based Sentencing and the Scientific Rationalization of Discrimination*, 66 STAN. L. REV. 803, 806 (2014).
114. *Id.*
115. Andrew Guthrie Ferguson, *Big Data and Predictive Reasonable Suspicion*, 163 U. PA. L. REV. 327, 398–400 (2015).
116. *See generally* Wayne A. Logan & Andrew Guthrie Ferguson, *Policing Criminal Justice Data*, 101 MINN. L. REV. 541 (2016).
117. U.S. Dep't of Justice, Office of the Attorney General, THE ATTORNEY GENERAL'S REPORT ON CRIMINAL HISTORY BACKGROUND CHECKS 3 (2006); U.S. Gov't Accountability Office, REPORT TO CONGRESSIONAL REQUESTERS: CRIMINAL HISTORY RECORDS: ADDITIONAL ACTIONS COULD ENHANCE THE COMPLETENESS OF RECORDS USED FOR EMPLOYMENT-RELATED BACKGROUND CHECKS 20 (Feb. 2015).
118. Herring v. United States, 555 U.S. 135, 155 (2009) (Ginsburg, J., dissenting).
119. Amy Myrick, *Facing Your Criminal Record: Expungement and the Collateral Problem of Wrongfully Represented Self*, 47 LAW & SOC'Y REV. 73 (2013); Gary Fields & John R. Emshwiller, *As Arrest Records Rise, Americans Find Consequences Can Last a Lifetime*, WALL. ST. J. (Aug. 18, 2014).
120. U.S. CONST. AMEND. V ("No person shall be . . . deprived of life, liberty, or property, without due process of law."); U.S. CONST. AMEND. XIV, § 1 ("Nor shall any State deprive any person of life, liberty, or property, without due process of law.").
121. Jennifer C. Daskal, *Pre-Crime Restraints: The Explosion of Targeted, Noncustodial Prevention*, 99 CORNELL L. REV. 327, 344–45 (2014).
122. Margaret Hu, *Big Data Blacklisting*, 67 FLA. L. REV. 1735, 1747–49 (2015).

123. Ramzi Kassem, *I Help Innocent People Get of Terrorism Watch Lists. As a Gun Control Tool, They're Useless,* WASH. POST (June 28, 2016).

124. Andrew Guthrie Ferguson, *Big Data and Predictive Reasonable Suspicion,* 163 U. PA. L. REV. 327, 327 (2015).

125. Terry v. Ohio, 392 U.S. 1, 21–22 (1968).

126. United States v. Sokolow, 490 U.S. 1, 7 (1989)

127. Illinois v. Gates, 462 U.S. 213, 238 (1983).

128. Andrew Guthrie Ferguson, *Big Data and Predictive Reasonable Suspicion,* 163 U. PA. L. REV. 327, 337–38 (2015).

129. *Terry,* 392 U.S. at 6–8.

130. *Id.* at 8.

131. *Id.* at 7.

132. *Id.* at 8.

133. *Id.* at 30.

134. Andrew Guthrie Ferguson, *Big Data and Predictive Reasonable Suspicion,* 163 U. PA. L. REV. 327, 376 (2015).

135. *Id.*

136. *Id.* at 401.

137. *Id.* at 389.

138. *Id.*

139. *Id.* at 393–94.

140. Andrew Guthrie Ferguson, *Predictive Prosecution,* 51 WAKE FOREST L. REV. 705, 722 (2016).

141. David O'Keefe, head of the Manhattan District Attorney's Crime Strategies Unit, interview by Aubrey Fox, CTR. FOR COURT INNOVATION (May 29, 2013), www.courtinnovation.org.

142. Madhumita Venkataramanan, *A Plague of Violence: Shootings Are Infectious and Spread like a Disease,* NEW SCIENTIST (May, 18, 2014) (interviewing Gary Slutkin, professor at the University of Illinois).

143. Andrew Guthrie Ferguson, *Predictive Prosecution,* 51 WAKE FOREST L. REV. 705, 726–27 (2016).

144. Micah Zenko, *Inside the CIA Red Cell,* FOREIGN POLICY (Oct. 30, 2015).

145. *See generally* Ellen S. Podgor, *The Ethics and Professionalism of Prosecutors in Discretionary Decisions,* 68 FORDHAM L. REV. 1511 (2000).

146. A similar story (or perhaps the same story) is recounted in Heather Mac Donald, *Prosecution Gets Smart,* CITY J. (Summer 2014), www.city-journal.org ("In 2012, police arrested a leading gang member in East Harlem for running toward people in a brawl brandishing a metal lock tied into a bandanna. The defendant had been shot in the past and had also likely witnessed a homicide, without cooperating with police after either crime. The attempted assault would ordinarily have gone nowhere, had the CSU not closely tracked the assailant. Instead, the prosecutor indicted him for criminal possession of a weapon in the third degree—a felony charge.").

CHAPTER 4. WHERE WE POLICE

1. Nate Berg, *Predicting Crime, LAPD-Style: Cutting-Edge Data-Driven Analysis Directs Los Angeles Patrol Officers to Likely Future Crime Scenes*, GUARDIAN (June 25, 2014).

2. Guy Adams, *The Sci-Fi Solution to Real Crime*, INDEPENDENT (London) (Jan. 11, 2012), at 32; Joel Rubin, *Stopping Crime before It Starts*, L.A. TIMES (Aug. 21, 2010).

3. Kalee Thompson, *The Santa Cruz Experiment*, POPULAR SCI. (Nov. 2011), at 38, 40.

4. Martin Kaste, *Can Software That Predicts Crime Pass Constitutional Muster?*, ALL THINGS CONSIDERED (NPR radio broadcast, July 26, 2013), *available at* www.npr.org; Timothy B. Clark, *How Predictive Policing Is Using Algorithms to Deliver Crime-Reduction Results for Cities*, GOV. EXEC. (Mar. 9, 2015); David Smiley, *Not Science Fiction: Miami Wants to Predict When and Where Crime Will Occur*, MIAMI HERALD (Mar. 30, 2015).

5. Andrew Guthrie Ferguson, *Predictive Policing and Reasonable Suspicion*, 62 EMORY L.J. 259, 265–69 (2012).

6. Juliana Reyes, *Philly Police Will Be First Big City Cops to Use Azavea's Crime Predicting Software*, TECHNICALLY MEDIA INC. (Nov. 7, 2013), http://technical.ly.

7. HunchLab, UNDER THE HOOD (white paper, 2015) (on file with author).

8. Maurice Chammah, *Policing the Future*, MARSHALL PROJECT (Feb. 3, 2016), www.themarshallproject.org.

9. *Id.*

10. *Id.*

11. *Id.*

12. *See* P. Jeffrey Brantingham's publications listed on his university website, http://paleo.sscnet.ucla.edu.

13. Sam Hoff, *Professor Helps Develop Predictive Policing by Using Trends to Predict, Prevent Crimes*, DAILY BRUIN (Apr. 26, 2013), http://dailybruin.com.

14. Leslie A. Gordon, *Predictive Policing May Help Bag Burglars—but It May Also Be a Constitutional Problem*, A.B.A. J. (Sept. 1, 2013), www.abajournal.com; Ronald Bailey, *Stopping Crime before It Starts*, REASON (July 10, 2012), http://reason.com.

15. G. O. Mohler et al., *Randomized Controlled Field Trials of Predictive Policing*, 110 J. AM. STATISTICAL ASSOC. 1399 (2015).

16. Joel Rubin, *Stopping Crime before It Starts*, L.A. TIMES (Aug. 21, 2010).

17. *See, e.g.*, Spencer Chainey, Lisa Tompson, & Sebastian Uhlig, *The Utility of Hotspot Mapping for Predicting Spatial Patterns of Crime*, 21 SECURITY J. 4, 5 (2008); Anthony A. Braga, David M. Hureau, & Andrew V. Papachristos, *The Relevance of Micro Places to Citywide Robbery Trends: A Longitudinal Analysis of Robbery Incidents at Street Corners and Block Faces in Boston*, 48 J. RES. CRIME & DELINQ. 7, 9 (2011).

18. Shane D. Johnson, Lucia Summers, & Ken Pease, *Offender as Forager? A Direct Test of the Boost Account of Victimization*, 25 J. QUANT. CRIMINOL. 181, 184 (2009).

19. Wim Bernasco, *Them Again? Same-Offender Involvement in Repeat and Near Repeat Burglaries*, 5 EUR. J. CRIMINOL. 411, 412 (2008); Andrew Guthrie Ferguson, *Predictive Policing and Reasonable Suspicion*, 62 EMORY L.J. 259, 274–76 (2012).

20. Shane D. Johnson, Lucia Summers, & Ken Pease, *Offender as Forager? A Direct Test of the Boost Account of Victimization*, 25 J. QUANT. CRIMINOL. 181, 184 (2009).

21. Shane D. Johnson et al., *Space-Time Patterns of Risk: A Cross National Assessment of Residential Burglary Victimization*, 23 J. QUANT. CRIMINOL. 201, 203–04 (2007).

22. *Id.* at 204.

23. Spencer Chainey & Jerry Ratcliffe, GIS AND CRIME MAPPING 8 (2005); Keith Harries, Nat'l Inst. of Justice, MAPPING CRIME: PRINCIPLE AND PRACTICE 92–94 (1999); Derek J. Paulsen & Matthew B. Robinson, CRIME MAPPING AND SPATIAL ASPECTS OF CRIME 154 (2d ed. 2009); Luc Anselin et al., *Spatial Analyses of Crime*, in 4 CRIMINAL JUSTICE 2000: MEASUREMENT AND ANALYSIS OF CRIME AND JUSTICE 213, 215 (2000).

24. Vince Beiser, *Forecasting Felonies: Can Computers Predict Crimes of the Future?*, PACIFIC STANDARD (July/Aug. 2011), at 20, http://psmag.com; Joel Rubin, *Stopping Crime before It Starts*, L.A. TIMES (Aug. 21, 2010); Christopher Beam, *Time Cops: Can Police Really Predict Crime before It Happens?*, SLATE (Jan. 24, 2011), www.slate.com.

25. Aaron Mendelson, *Can LAPD Anticipate Crime with Predictive Policing?*, CALIF. REP. (Sept. 6, 2013), http://audio.californiareport.org.

26. David Talbot, *L.A. Cops Embrace Crime Predicting Algorithm*, MIT TECH. REV. (July 2, 2012).

27. Lev Grossman et al., *The 50 Best Inventions of the Year*, TIME (Nov. 28, 2011), at 55, 82.

28. Vince Beiser, *Forecasting Felonies: Can Computers Predict Crimes of the Future?*, PACIFIC STANDARD (July/Aug. 2011), at 20, http://psmag.com.

29. Tessa Stuart, *The Policemen's Secret Crystal Ball*, SANTA CRUZ WKLY. (Feb. 15, 2012), at 9.

30. Will Frampton, *With New Software, Norcross Police Practice Predictive Policing*, CBS ATLANTA (Aug. 19, 2013), www.cbsatlanta.com.

31. Erica Goode, *Sending the Police before There's a Crime*, N.Y. TIMES (Aug. 16, 2011); *Predictive Policing: Don't Even Think about It*, ECONOMIST (July 20, 2013), at 24, 26.

32. Upturn, STUCK IN A PATTERN: EARLY EVIDENCE OF "PREDICTIVE POLICING" AND CIVIL RIGHTS 3–5 (Aug. 2016).

33. Tessa Stuart, *The Policemen's Secret Crystal Ball*, SANTA CRUZ WKLY. (Feb. 15, 2012), at 9.

34. Joel Caplan & Leslie Kennedy (eds.), Rutgers Center on Public Security, RISK TERRAIN MODELING COMPENDIUM Ch. 18 (2011).

35. As a disclosure, I have worked in a very limited capacity as an unpaid consultant with Joel Caplan, Leslie Kennedy, and Eric Piza as part of a National Institute of

Justice grant for a study titled "A Multi-Jurisdictional Test of Risk Terrain Modeling and a Place-Based Evaluation of Environmental Risk-Based Patrol Deployment Strategies." My contribution has been limited to a handful of brief consultations with no financial compensation, and I have had no role in the development of the RTM technology or the research studies.

36. Leslie Kennedy, Joel Caplan, & Eric Piza, RESULTS EXECUTIVE SUMMARY: A MULTI-JURISDICTIONAL TEST OF RISK TERRAIN MODELING AND A PLACE-BASED EVALUATION OF ENVIRONMENTAL RISK-BASED PATROL DEPLOYMENT STRATEGIES 4–6 (2015), *available at* www.rutgerscps.org.

37. *Id.*

38. *Id.*

39. *Id.* at 6–9.

40. *Id.*

41. *Id.*

42. *Id.*

43. *Id.* at 10–11, 13–14, 17.

44. Jie Xu, Leslie W. Kennedy, & Joel M. Caplan, *Crime Generators for Shootings in Urban Areas: A Test Using Conditional Locational Interdependence as an Extension of Risk Terrain Modeling*, RUTGERS CENTER ON PUBLIC SECURITY BRIEF 1 (Oct. 2010).

45. This figure comes from a Los Angeles Police Department media report promoted by PredPol on its website. PredPol, MANAGEMENT TEAM, www.predpol.com (last visited Feb. 15, 2017).

46. Ben Poston, *Crime in Los Angeles Rose in All Categories in 2015, LAPD Says*, L.A. TIMES (Dec. 30, 2015).

47. Zen Vuong, *Alhambra Police Chief Says Predictive Policing Has Been Successful*, PASADENA STAR-NEWS (Feb. 11, 2014); Rosalio Ahumada, *Modesto Sees Double-Digit Drop in Property Crimes—Lowest in Three Years*, MODESTO BEE (Nov. 11, 2014).

48. Mike Aldax, *Richmond Police Chief Says Department Plans to Discontinue "Predictive Policing" Software*, RICHMOND STANDARD (June 24, 2015).

49. G. O. Mohler et al., *Randomized Controlled Field Trials of Predictive Policing*, 110 J. AM. STAT. ASSOC. 1399 (2015).

50. *Id.* at 1402.

51. *Id.*

52. *Id.*

53. *Id.*

54. Priscilla Hunt, Jessica Saunders, & John S. Hollywood, Rand Corp., EVALUATION OF THE SHREVEPORT PREDICTIVE POLICING EXPERIMENT (2014), *available at* www.rand.org.

55. *Id.* at 4.

56. *Id.* at 10.

57. *Id.* at 33.

58. Andrew Papachristos, Anthony A. Braga, & David M. Hureau, *Social Networks and the Risk of Gunshot Injury*, 89:6 J. URB. HEALTH 992 (2012).

59. *Id.*

60. Leslie Brokaw, *Predictive Policing: Working the Odds to Prevent Future Crimes*, MIT SLOAN MANAGEMENT REV. (Sept. 12, 2011), *available at* http://sloanreview.mit.edu.

61. Laura M. Smith et al., *Adaption of an Ecological Territorial Model to Street Gang Spatial Patterns in Los Angeles*, 32:9 DISCRETE & CONTINUOUS DYNAMICAL SYS. 3223 (2012); *see also* interview with George Mohler, DATA SCI. WKLY. (undated), *available at* www.datascienceweekly.org.

62. Press Release, Bureau of Justice Statistics, U.S. Dep't of Justice, Office of Justice Programs, Nearly 3.4 Million Violent Crimes per Year Went Unreported to Police from 2006 to 2010 (Aug. 9, 2012), *available at* www.bjs.gov.

63. David N. Kelly & Sharon L. McCarthy, *The Report of the Crime Reporting Review Committee to Commissioner Raymond W. Kelly Concerning CompStat Auditing*, NYPD REPORTS 5 (2013), *available at* www.nyc.gov; Graham Rayman, *The NYPD Police Tapes: Inside Bed-Stuy's 81st Precinct*, VILLAGE VOICE (May 5, 2010), at 12, 14, 15; Jeff Morganteen, *What the CompStat Audit Reveals about the NYPD*, N.Y. WORLD (July 12, 2013).

64. Graham Rayman, *The NYPD Police Tapes: Inside Bed-Stuy's 81st Precinct*, VILLAGE VOICE (May 5, 2010), at 12, 14, 15.

65. Jeff Morganteen, *What the CompStat Audit Reveals about the NYPD*, N.Y. WORLD (July 12, 2013).

66. Amos Maki, *Crimes Lurk in Police Memos*, COM. APPEAL (Memphis) (Jan. 25, 2012); Mike Matthews, *MPD Memos Predicted to Drastically Increase Crime Stats*, ABC24 (Jan. 25, 2012), www.abc24.com; Chip Mitchell, *Police Data Cast Doubt on Chicago-Style Stop and Frisk*, WBEZ NEWS (May 4, 2016), *available at* www.wbez.org.

67. Ezekiel Edwards, *Predictive Policing Software Is More Accurate at Predicting Policing than Predicting Crime*, HUFFINGTON POST (Aug. 31, 2016), www.huffingtonpost.com.

68. Ingrid Burrington, *What Amazon Taught the Cops*, NATION (May 27, 2015).

69. Sean Malinowski, Captain, LAPD, email to author (Feb. 9, 2012).

70. Ruth D. Peterson & Lauren J. Krivo, *Race, Residence, and Violent Crime: A Structure of Inequality*, 57 U. KAN. L. REV. 903, 908 (2009).

71. Illinois v. Wardlow, 528 U.S. 119, 124 (2000).

72. Andrew Guthrie Ferguson, *Predictive Policing and Reasonable Suspicion*, 62 EMORY L.J. 259, 312–13 (2012).

73. Tessa Stuart, *The Policemen's Secret Crystal Ball*, SANTA CRUZ WKLY. (Feb. 15, 2012), at 9.

74. Andrew Guthrie Ferguson & Damien Bernache, *The "High-Crime Area" Question: Requiring Verifiable and Quantifiable Evidence for Fourth Amendment Reasonable Suspicion Analysis*, 57 AM. U. L. REV. 1587, 1627 (2008).

75. Andrew Guthrie Ferguson, *Predictive Policing and Reasonable Suspicion*, 62 EMORY L.J. 259, 305–11 (2012).

76. *Stop LAPD Spying Coalition Visits the Regional Fusion Center*, PRIVACY SOS (Dec. 17, 2012), www.privacysos.org.

77. Hamid Kahn, Executive Director, Stop LAPD Spying Coalition, email to author (Aug. 18, 2016).

78. United States v. Montero-Camargo, 208 F.3d 1122, 1143 (9th Cir. 2000) (*en banc*) (Kozinski, J., concurring).

79. Darwin Bond-Graham & Ali Winston, *All Tomorrow's Crimes: The Future of Policing Looks a Lot like Good Branding*, S.F. WKLY. (Oct. 30, 2013), www.sfweekly.com.

80. *Id.*

81. Priscilla Hunt, Jessica Saunders, & John S. Hollywood, Rand Corp., EVALUATION OF THE SHREVEPORT PREDICTIVE POLICING EXPERIMENT 12 (2014), *available at* www.rand.org.

82. *Id.* at 12–13.

83. Emily Thomas, *Why Oakland Police Turned Down Predictive Policing*, VICE MOTHERBOARD (Dec. 28, 2016), http://motherboard.vice.com.

84. *See, e.g.,* Danielle Keats Citron, *Technological Due Process*, 85 WASH. U. L. REV. 1249, 1271–72 (2008); Kenneth A. Bamberger, *Technologies of Compliance: Risk and Regulation in a Digital Age*, 88 TEX. L. REV. 669, 711–12 (2010).

85. Joel Caplan & Les Kennedy, RISK TERRAIN MODELING: CRIME PREDICTION AND RISK REDUCTION 106 (2016).

86. Kat Mather & Richard Winton, *LAPD Uses Its Helicopters to Stop Crimes before They Start*, L.A. TIMES (Mar. 7, 2015); Geoff Manaughmarch, *How Aerial Surveillance Has Changed Policing—and Crime—in Los Angeles*, N.Y. TIMES MAG. (Mar. 23, 2015).

87. Kat Mather & Richard Winton, *LAPD Uses Its Helicopters to Stop Crimes before They Start*, L.A. TIMES (Mar. 7, 2015); Geoff Manaughmarch, *How Aerial Surveillance Has Changed Policing—and Crime—in Los Angeles*, N.Y. TIMES MAG. (Mar. 23, 2015).

88. Upturn, STUCK IN A PATTERN: EARLY EVIDENCE OF "PREDICTIVE POLICING" AND CIVIL RIGHTS 3–5 (Aug. 2016).

89. Christopher Bruce, *Districting and Resource Allocation: A Question of Balance*, 1:4 GEOGRAPHY & PUB. SAFETY 1, 1 (2009).

CHAPTER 5. WHEN WE POLICE

1. Justin Jouvenal, *The New Way Police Are Surveilling You: Calculating Your Threat "Score,"* WASH. POST (Jan. 10, 2016); Brent Skorup, *Cops Scan Social Media to Help Assess Your "Threat Rating,"* REUTERS (Dec. 12, 2014).

2. Justin Jouvenal, *The New Way Police Are Surveilling You: Calculating Your Threat "Score,"* WASH. POST (Jan. 10, 2016).

3. *Id.*

4. *Id.*

5. David Robinson, *Buyer Beware: A Hard Look at Police "Threat Scores,"* EQUALFU-TURE (Jan. 16, 2016), *available at* www.equalfuture.us.

6. *Id.*

7. Justin Jouvenal, *The New Way Police Are Surveilling You: Calculating Your Threat "Score,"* WASH. POST (Jan. 10, 2016).

8. Thomas H. Davenport, *How Big Data Is Helping the NYPD Solve Crimes Faster,* FORTUNE (July 17, 2016).

9. *Id.*

10. *Manhunt—Boston Bombers,* NOVA (June 7, 2013), *excerpt available at* www.youtube.com/watch?v=ozUHOHAAhzg.

11. *Id.*

12. Tim Fleischer, *Officers Embrace New Smartphones as Crime Fighting Tools,* ABC7NY (Aug. 13, 2015), http://abc7ny.com.

13. Justin Jouvenal, *The New Way Police Are Surveilling You: Calculating Your Threat "Score,"* WASH. POST (Jan. 10, 2016).

14. Michael L. Rich, *Machine Learning, Automated Suspicion Algorithms, and the Fourth Amendment,* 164 U. PA. L. REV. 871, 880 (2016).

15. AOL Digital Justice, *Digisensory Technologies Avista Smart Sensors* (Sept. 14, 2012), *available at* www.youtube.com/watch?v=JamGobiS5wg; Associated Press, *NJ City Leading Way in Crime-Fighting Tech,* CBS NEWS (June 19, 2010), *available at* www.cbsnews.com.

16. Halley Bondy, *East Orange Installs Surveillance Cameras That Sense Criminal Activities, Alerts Police,* STAR-LEDGER (Newark) (Mar. 18, 2010), www.nj.com.

17. Ethan Watters, *ShotSpotter,* WIRED (Apr. 2007), at 146–52; Colin Neagle, *How the Internet of Things Is Transforming Law Enforcement,* NETWORK WORLD (Nov. 3, 2014).

18. Tatiana Schlossbergmarch, *New York Police Begin Using ShotSpotter System to Detect Gunshots,* N.Y. TIMES (Mar. 16, 2015).

19. Linda Merola & Cynthia Lum, *Emerging Surveillance Technologies: Privacy and the Case of License Plate Recognition (LPR) Technology,* 96:3 JUDICATURE 119–21 (2012).

20. Stephen Rushin, *The Judicial Response to Mass Police Surveillance,* 2011 U. ILL. J. L. TECH. & POL'Y 281, 285–86.

21. Margot E. Kaminski, *Regulating Real-World Surveillance,* 90 WASH. L. REV. 1113, 1153 (2015).

22. Michael Martinez, *Policing Advocates Defend Use of High-Tech License Plate Readers,* CNN (July 18, 2013), *available at* www.cnn.com.

23. Simone Wilson, *L.A. Sheriff's Creepy New Facial-Recognition Software Matches Surveillance Video with Mug Shot Database,* L.A. WKLY. (Jan. 27, 2012).

24. Clare Garvie & Jonathan Frankle, *Facial-Recognition Software Might Have a Racial Bias Problem,* ATLANTIC (Apr. 7, 2016).

25. General Accounting Office, FACE RECOGNITION TECHNOLOGY, FBI SHOULD BETTER ENSURE PRIVACY AND ACCURACY 10 (report to the Ranking Member, Subcommittee on Privacy, Technology, and the Law, Committee on the Judiciary, U.S. Senate, May 2016).

26. *Id.* at 15–18.

27. Clare Garvie, Alvaro Bedoya, & Jonathan Frankle, Georgetown Law Center on Privacy & Tech., THE PERPETUAL LINE-UP: UNREGULATED POLICE FACIAL RECOGNITION IN AMERICA (Oct. 18, 2016), *available at* www.perpetuallineup.org.

28. *Id.* at 17.

29. Cyrus Farivar, *Meet Visual Labs, a Body Camera Startup That Doesn't Sell Body Cameras*, ARS TECHNICA (Sept. 3, 2016), http://arstechnica.com.

30. Elizabeth E. Joh, *The New Surveillance Discretion: Automated Suspicion, Big Data, and Policing*, 10 HARV. L. & POL'Y REV. 15, 15 (2016).

31. Karen Weise, *Will a Camera on Every Cop Make Everyone Safer? Taser Thinks So*, BLOOMBERG BUSINESSWEEK (July 12, 2016).

32. Matt Stroud, *The Company That's Livestreaming Police Body Camera Footage Right Now*, VICE MOTHERBOARD (July 27, 2016), http://motherboard.vice.com.

33. Yaniv Taigman et al., *DeepFace: Closing the Gap to Human-Level Performance in Face Verification*, FACEBOOK RESEARCH (June 24, 2014), *available at* http://research.facebook.com.

34. Monte Reel, *Secret Cameras Record Baltimore's Every Move from Above*, BLOOMBERG BUSINESSWEEK (Aug. 23, 2016).

35. Craig Timberg, *New Surveillance Technology Can Track Everyone in an Area for Several Hours at a Time*, WASH. POST (Feb. 5, 2014).

36. Monte Reel, *Secret Cameras Record Baltimore's Every Move from Above*, BLOOMBERG BUSINESSWEEK (Aug. 23, 2016).

37. Don Babwin, *Chicago Video Surveillance Gets Smarter*, ABC NEWS (Sept. 27, 2007), http://abcnews.go.com; Cara Buckley, *Police Plan Web of Surveillance for Downtown*, N.Y. TIMES (July 9, 2007), Nate Berg, *Predicting Crime, LAPD-Style: Cutting-Edge Data-Driven Analysis Directs Los Angeles Patrol Officers to Likely Future Crime Scenes*, GUARDIAN (June 25, 2014), www.theguardian.com.

38. Sarah Brayne, *Stratified Surveillance: Policing in the Age of Big Data* 9–13 (draft on file with author).

39. *Id.*

40. *Id.* at 23–24.

41. Thom Patterson, *Data Surveillance Centers: Crime Fighters or "Spy Machines"?*, CNN (May 26, 2014), *available at* www.cnn.com.

42. *LAPD Uses Big Data to Target Criminals*, ASSOCIATED PRESS (Nov. 14, 2014).

43. *Id.*

44. Sarah Brayne, *Stratified Surveillance: Policing in the Age of Big Data* 26 (draft on file with author).

45. Chris Hackett & Michael Grosinger, *The Growth of Geofence Tools within the Mapping Technology Sphere*, PDVWIRELESS (Dec. 15, 2014), www.pdvwireless.com.
46. *See* Jenna McLaughlin, *L.A. Activists Want to Bring Surveillance Conversation Down to Earth*, INTERCEPT (Apr. 6, 2016), http://theintercept.com.
47. Laura Moy, *Yet Another Way Baltimore Police Unfairly Target Black People*, SLATE (Aug. 18, 2016), www.slate.com.
48. *In the Face of Danger: Facial Recognition and the Limits of Privacy Law*, 120 HARV. L. REV. 1870, 1870–71 (2007).
49. Stacey Higginbotham, *Facial Recognition Freak Out: What the Technology Can and Can't Do*, FORTUNE (June 23, 2015).
50. P. Jonathon Phillips et al., *An Other-Race Effect for Face Recognition Algorithms*, 8 ACM TRANSACTIONS ON APPLIED PERCEPTION 14:1, 14:5 (2011).
51. Clare Garvie & Jonathan Frankle, *Facial-Recognition Software Might Have a Racial Bias Problem*, ATLANTIC (Apr. 7, 2016).
52. *Id.*
53. *Id.*
54. Eric Tucker, *Comey: FBI Used Aerial Surveillance Above Ferguson*, ASSOCIATED PRESS (Oct. 15, 2015).
55. Ian Duncan, *New Details Released about High-Tech Gear FBI Used on Planes to Monitor Freddie Gray Unrest*, BALT. SUN (Oct. 30, 2015).
56. *Id.*
57. George Joseph, *Feds Regularly Monitored Black Lives Matter since Ferguson*, INTERCEPT (July 24, 2015), http://theintercept.com.
58. Green v. City & Cty. of San Francisco, 751 F.3d 1039, 1044 (9th Cir. 2014).
59. *Id.*
60. *Id.*
61. United States v. Esquivel-Rios, 725 F.3d 1231, 1234 (10th Cir. 2013).
62. *Id.*
63. United States v. Esquivel-Rios, 39 F. Supp. 3d 1175, 1177 (D. Kan. 2014), *aff'd*, 786 F.3d 1299 (10th Cir. 2015), *cert. denied*, 136 S. Ct. 280 (2015).
64. Florence v. Bd. of Chosen Freeholders, 132 S. Ct. 1510 (2012); Herring v. United States, 555 U.S. 135 (2009); Rothgery v. Gillespie Cty., 554 U.S. 191 (2008); Arizona v. Evans, 514 U.S. 1 (1995).
65. General Accounting Office, FACE RECOGNITION TECHNOLOGY: FBI SHOULD BETTER ENSURE PRIVACY AND ACCURACY, GAO-16-267, at 25 (report to the ranking member, Subcommittee on Privacy, Technology, and the Law, Committee on the Judiciary, U.S. Senate, May 2016).
66. *Id.* at 27–30.
67. Clare Garvie, Alvaro Bedoya, & Jonathan Frankle, Georgetown Law Center on Technology & Privacy, THE PERPETUAL LINE-UP: UNREGULATED POLICE FACIAL RECOGNITION IN AMERICA (Oct. 18, 2016), *available at* www.perpetuallineup.org.
68. *Id.*

69. *Id.*

70. Stephen Henderson, *Fourth Amendment Time Machines (and What They Might Say about Police Body Cameras)*, 18 U. PA. J. CONST. L. 933, 933 (2016).

71. Neil Richards, *The Dangers of Surveillance*, 126 HARV. L. REV. 1934, 1953 (2013).

72. Andrew Guthrie Ferguson, *Personal Curtilage: Fourth Amendment Security in Public*, 55 WM. & MARY L. REV. 1283, 1287 (2014).

73. *See generally* Christopher Slobogin, PRIVACY AT RISK: THE NEW GOVERN-MENT SURVEILLANCE AND THE FOURTH AMENDMENT (2007).

74. United States v. Jones, 132 S. Ct. 945 (2012).

75. *Id.* at 948.

76. *Id.*

77. *Id.* at 949.

78. *Id.* at 956 (Sotomayor, J., concurring).

79. *Id.*

80. *Id.* at 963–64 (Alito, J., concurring).

81. Brian Barrett, *New Surveillance System May Let Cops Use All of the Cameras*, WIRED (May 19, 2016).

82. Clifford Atiyeh, *Screen-Plate Club: How License-Plate Scanning Compromises Your Privacy*, CAR & DRIVER (Oct. 2014).

83. Sarah Brayne, Stratified Surveillance: Policing in the Age of Big Data 17 (2015) (on file with author).

84. *Id.* at 55 (fig. 3).

85. *Id.* at 56 (fig. 4).

86. Craig D. Uchida et al., Smart Policing Initiative, LOS ANGELES, CALIFORNIA SMART POLICING INITIATIVE: REDUCING GUN-RELATED VIOLENCE THROUGH OPERATION LASER 6 (Oct. 2012).

87. *Id.* at 3, 10; Anthony A. Braga et al., Smart Policing Initiative, *SMART* AP-PROACHES TO REDUCING GUN VIOLENCE: SMART POLICING INITIATIVE SPOTLIGHT ON EVIDENCE-BASED STRATEGIES AND IMPACTS (Mar. 2014).

88. Amy Feldman, *How Mark43's Scott Crouch, 25, Built Software to Help Police De-partments Keep Cops on the Street*, FORBES (Oct. 19, 2016).

89. Terry v. Ohio, 392 U.S. 1, 8–9 (1968).

CHAPTER 6. HOW WE POLICE

1. James B. Comey, Director, Federal Bureau of Investigation, Press Briefing on Orlando Mass Shooting, Update on Orlando Terrorism Investigation, FBI Head-quarters (June 13, 2016), *available at* www.fbi.gov.

2. Stephen E. Henderson, *Real-Time and Historic Location Surveillance after United States v. Jones: An Administrable, Mildly Mosaic Approach*, 103 J. CRIM. L. & CRIMINOL. 803, 804–05 (2013); Larry Hendricks, *18 Years in Prison for High Country Bandit*, ARIZ. DAILY SUN (June 6, 2012).

3. Press Release, FBI, Wanted: "The High Country Bandits" (Feb. 18, 2010), *available at* http://archives.fbi.gov.

4. Nate Anderson, *How "Cell Tower Dumps" Caught the High Country Bandits—and Why It Matters*, ARS TECHNICA (Aug. 29, 2013), http://arstechnica.com.

5. *Id.*

6. *Id.*

7. *Id.*

8. *Id.*

9. Evan Ratliff, *Lifted*, ATAVIST ch. 5–9 (2011), https://magazine.atavist.com.

10. *Id.*

11. *Id.*

12. *Id.*

13. *Id.*

14. Stephanie K. Pell & Christopher Soghoian, *Your Secret Stingray's No Secret Anymore: The Vanishing Government Monopoly over Cell Phone Surveillance and Its Impact on National Security and Consumer Privacy*, 28 HARV. J. L. & TECH. 1, 36–38 (2014).

15. Brian L. Owsley, *The Fourth Amendment Implications of the Government's Use of Cell Tower Dumps in Its Electronic Surveillance*, 16 U. PA. J. CONST. L. 1, 3–6 (2013).

16. Brian L. Owsley, *Spies in the Skies: Dirtboxes and Airplane Electronic Surveillance*, 113 MICH. L. REV. FIRST IMPRESSIONS 75, 76–78 (2015).

17. Casey Williams, *States Crack Down on Police "Stingray" Tech That Can Intercept Your Texts*, HUFFINGTON POST (Jan. 28, 2016), www.huffingtonpost.com.

18. Robert Patrick, *Secret Service Agent's Testimony Shines Light on Use of Shadowy Cellphone Tracker in St. Louis*, ST. LOUIS POST-DISPATCH (Sept. 6, 2016).

19. *Id.*

20. C. Michael Shaw, *Court: Warrantless Use of Cell Site Simulators Illegal*, NEW AMERICAN (Apr. 1, 2016), www.thenewamerican.com.

21. Devin Barrett, *Americans' Cellphones Targeted in Secret U.S. Spy Program*, WALL ST. J. (Nov. 13, 2014).

22. Brad Heath, *Police Secretly Track Cellphones to Solve Routine Crimes*, USA TODAY (Aug. 24, 2015), www.usatoday.com.

23. *Id.*

24. *Id.*

25. Robert Patrick, *Controversial Secret Phone Tracker Figured in Dropped St. Louis Case*, ST. LOUIS POST-DISPATCH (Apr. 19, 2015).

26. Justin Fenton, *Baltimore Police Used Secret Technology to Track Cellphones in Thousands of Cases*, BALT. SUN (Apr. 9, 2015).

27. Brad Heath, *Police Secretly Track Cellphones to Solve Routine Crimes*, USA TODAY (Aug., 24, 2015).

28. Kim Zetter, *U.S. Marshals Seize Cops' Spying Records to Keep Them from the ACLU*, WIRED (June 3, 2014).

29. Justin Fenton, *Judge Threatens Detective with Contempt for Declining to Reveal Cellphone Tracking Methods*, BALT. SUN (Nov. 17, 2014).

30. Committee on Oversight and Government Reform, U.S. House of Representatives, LAW ENFORCEMENT USE OF CELL-SITE SIMULATION TECHNOLOGIES: PRIVACY CONCERNS AND RECOMMENDATIONS 5 (Dec. 19, 2016).

31. Paula H. Kift & Helen Nissenbaum, *Metadata in Context: An Ontological and Normative Analysis of the NSA's Bulk Telephony Metadata Collection Program*, 13 ISJLP __ (2017).

32. Decl. of Prof. Edward Felten at 30–37, Am. Civil Liberties Union v. Clapper, 959 F. Supp. 2d 724 (S.D.N.Y. 2013) (No. 13-cv-03994), *available at* www.aclu.org.

33. *See generally* Jeffrey Pomerantz, METADATA, 3–13 (2015).

34. Paula H. Kift & Helen Nissenbaum, *Metadata in Context: An Ontological and Normative Analysis of the NSA's Bulk Telephony Metadata Collection Program*, 13 ISJLP __ (2017).

35. Dahlia Lithwick & Steve Vladeck, *Taking the "Meh" out of Metadata*, SLATE (Nov. 22, 2013), www.slate.com.

36. Decl. of Prof. Edward Felten at 30–37, Am. Civil Liberties Union v. Clapper, 959 F. Supp. 2d 724 (S.D.N.Y. 2013) (No. 13-cv-03994), *available at* www.aclu.org.

37. *Id.* at 14.

38. *Id.* at 16, 19

39. *Id.* at 17–18.

40. Jonathan Mayer, Patrick Mutchler, & John C. Mitchell, *Evaluating the Privacy Properties of Telephone Metadata*, 113 PNAS 5536 (May 17, 2016).

41. *Id.* at 5536.

42. *Id.* at 5540.

43. *Id.*

44. Klayman v. Obama (*Klayman I*), 957 F. Supp. 2d 1, 41 (D.D.C. 2013); Am. Civil Liberties Union v. Clapper, 959 F. Supp. 2d 724, 752 (S.D.N.Y. 2013).

45. Chris Conley, *Non-Content Is Not Non-Sensitive: Moving Beyond the Content/Non-Content Distinction*, 54 SANTA CLARA L. REV. 821, 824–26 (2014).

46. *In re Directives Pursuant to Section 105B of Foreign Intelligence Surveillance Act*, 551 F.3d 1004, 1006 (Foreign Int. Surv. Ct. Rev. 2008); *see generally* Peter Margulies, *Dynamic Surveillance: Evolving Procedures in Metadata and Foreign Content Collection after Snowden*, 66 HASTINGS L.J. 1, 51–57 (2014); Laura K. Donohue, *Bulk Metadata Collection: Statutory and Constitutional Considerations*, 37 HARV. J. L. & PUB. POL'Y 757, 825 (2014).

47. Spencer Ackerman, *FBI Quietly Changes Its Privacy Rules for Accessing NSA Data on Americans*, GUARDIAN (Mar. 10, 2016); John Shiffman & Kristina Cooke, *U.S. Directs Agents to Cover Up Program Used to Investigate Americans*, REUTERS (Aug. 5, 2013).

48. Kenneth Lipp, *AT&T Is Spying on Americans for Profit, New Documents Reveal*, DAILY BEAST (Oct. 25, 2016), www.thedailybeast.com.

49. Scott Shane & Colin Moynihan, *Drug Agents Use Vast Phone Trove, Eclipsing N.S.A.'s*, N.Y. TIMES (Sept. 1, 2013).

50. *Id.*

51. Dave Maass & Aaron Mackey, *Law Enforcement's Secret "Super Search Engine" Amasses Trillions of Phone Records for Decades*, ELECTRONIC FRONTIER FOUNDATION (Nov. 29, 2016), www.eff.org.

52. Aaron Cantú, *#Followed: How Police across the Country Are Employing Social Media Surveillance*, MUCKROCK (May 18, 2016), www.muckrock.com.

53. Matt Stroud, *#Gunfire: Can Twitter Really Help Cops Find Crime?*, VERGE (Nov. 15, 2013), www.theverge.com.

54. John Knefel, *Activists Use Tech to Fuel Their Movements, and Cops Turn to Geofeedia to Aggregate the Data*, INVERSE (Nov. 20, 2015), www.inverse.com.

55. *Id.*

56. Joseph Goldstein & J. David Goodman, *Seeking Clues to Gangs and Crime, Detectives Monitor Internet Rap Videos*, N.Y. TIMES (Jan. 7, 2014).

57. Nicole Santa Cruz, Kate Mather, & Javier Panzar, *#100days100nights: Gang Threats of Violence on Social Media Draw Fear*, L.A. TIMES (July 27, 2015).

58. Ben Austen, *Public Enemies: Social Media Is Fueling Gang Wars in Chicago*, WIRED (Sept. 17, 2013).

59. *Id.*

60. *Id.*

61. Cheryl Corley, *When Social Media Fuels Gang Violence*, ALL TECH CONSIDERED (NPR radio broadcast, Oct. 7, 2015), *available at* www.npr.org.

62. Russell Brandom, *Facebook, Twitter, and Instagram Surveillance Tool Was Used to Arrest Baltimore Protestors*, VERGE (Oct. 11, 2016), www.theverge.com; Elizabeth Dwoskin, *Police Are Spending Millions of Dollars to Monitor the Social Media of Protesters and Suspects*, WASH. POST (Nov. 18, 2016).

63. Jan Ransom, *Boston Police Set to Buy Social Media Monitoring Software*, BOST. GLOBE (Nov. 26, 2016).

64. Liane Colonna, *A Taxonomy and Classification of Data Mining*, 16 SMU SCI. & TECH. L. REV. 309, 314 (2013).

65. *See generally Data Mining, Dog Sniffs, and the Fourth Amendment*, 128 HARV. L. REV. 691, 693–94 (2014); Tal Z. Zarsky, *Governmental Data Mining and Its Alternatives*, 116 PENN ST. L. REV. 285, 287 (2011).

66. Erin Murphy, *The New Forensics: Criminal Justice, False Certainty, and the Second Generation of Scientific Evidence*, 95 CAL. L. REV. 721, 728–30 (2007).

67. Laura K. Donohue, *Technological Leap, Statutory Gap, and Constitutional Abyss: Remote Biometric Identification Comes of Age*, 97 MINN. L. REV. 407, 413 (2012).

68. Press Release, FBI, FBI Announces Full Operational Capability of the Next Generation Identification System (Sept. 15, 2014), *available at* www.fbi.gov.

69. Michael L. Rich, *Machine Learning, Automated Suspicion Algorithms, and the Fourth Amendment*, 164 U. PA. L. REV. 871, 876 (2016).

70. Colleen McCue, *Connecting the Dots: Data Mining and Predictive Analytics in Law Enforcement and Intelligence Analysis*, POLICE CHIEF (May 2016), www.policechiefmagazine.org.

71. *Id.*

72. Tierney Sneed, *How Big Data Battles Human Trafficking*, U.S. NEWS (Jan. 14, 2015).

73. *Id.*

74. Bernhard Warner, *Google Turns to Big Data to Unmask Human Traffickers*, BUSINESSWEEK (Apr. 10, 2013).

75. Tierney Sneed, *How Big Data Battles Human Trafficking*, U.S. NEWS (Jan. 14, 2015).

76. Elizabeth Nolan Brown, *Super Bowl "Sex Trafficking Stings" Net Hundreds of Prostitution Arrests*, REASON (Feb. 13, 2016).

77. Tierney Sneed, *How Big Data Battles Human Trafficking*, U.S. NEWS (Jan. 14, 2015).

78. *Id.*

79. Joseph Goldstein, *Police Take on Family Violence to Avert Death*, N.Y. TIMES (July 25, 2013).

80. *Id.*

81. *Id.*

82. *Id.*

83. Jeffery Talbert et al., *Pseudoephedrine Sales and Seizures of Clandestine Methamphetamine Laboratories in Kentucky*, 308:15 JAMA 1524 (2012); Jon Bardin, *Kentucky Study Links Pseudoephedrine Sales, Meth Busts*, L.A. TIMES (Oct. 16, 2012).

84. Jon Bardin, *Kentucky Study Links Pseudoephedrine Sales, Meth Busts*, L.A. TIMES (Oct. 16, 2012).

85. Andrew Guthrie Ferguson, *Big Data Distortions: Exploring the Limits of the ABA LEATPR Standards*, 66 OKLA. L. REV. 831, 841 (2014).

86. David C. Vladeck, *Consumer Protection in an Era of Big Data Analytics*, 42 OHIO N.U. L. REV. 493, 495 (2016).

87. Moritz Hardt, *How Big Data Is Unfair*, MEDIUM (Sept. 26, 2014), http://medium.com.

88. *See* PredPol, PREDPOL PREDICTS GUN VIOLENCE 3 (white paper, 2013), *available at* http://cortecs.org.

89. *Id.*

90. *Id.*

91. The size of Chicago, Illinois, is approximately 237 square miles. City of Chicago, *Facts & Statistics* (2017), https://www.cityofchicago.org.

92. Pedro Domingos, THE MASTER ALGORITHM: HOW THE QUEST FOR THE ULTIMATE LEARNING MACHINE WILL REMAKE OUR WORLD (2015).

93. Matt McFarland, *Terrorist or Pedophile? This Start-Up Says It Can Out Secrets by Analyzing Faces*, WASH. POST (May 24, 2016).

94. *Id.*

95. Frank Pasquale, BLACK BOX SOCIETY: THE SECRET ALGORITHMS THAT CONTROL MONEY AND INFORMATION 38 (2015).

96. Solon Barocas & Andrew D. Selbst, *Big Data's Disparate Impact*, 104 CALIF. L. REV. 671, 691 (2016).

97. *Id.*
98. *Id.* at 675–76.
99. *Id.* at 677–78.
100. *Id.* at 680–84.
101. *Id.* at 688–90.
102. *Id.* at 691.
103. Jules Polonetsky, Omer Tene, & Joseph Jerome, *Beyond the Common Rule: Ethical Structures for Data Research in Non-Academic Settings*, 13 COLO. TECH. L.J. 333, 349 (2015).
104. Latanya Sweeney, *Discrimination in Online Ad Delivery*, 56 COMM. ACM 44 (2013).
105. Michael Brennan, *Can Computers Be Racist? Big Data, Inequality, and Discrimination*, FORD FOUNDATION: EQUALS CHANGE BLOG (Nov. 18, 2015), www.fordfoundation.org.
106. Stacey Higginbotham, *Google's Sexist Algorithms Offer an Important Lesson in Diversity*, FORTUNE (July 8, 2015).
107. Jeremy Kun, *Big Data Algorithms Can Discriminate, and It's Not Clear What to Do about It*, CONVERSATION (Aug. 13, 2015), http://theconversation.com.
108. Andrew Guthrie Ferguson, *Predictive Policing and Reasonable Suspicion*, 62 EMORY L.J. 259, 286 (2012); Max Minzner, *Putting Probability Back into Probable Cause*, 87 TEX. L. REV. 913, 958 (2009).
109. United States v. Grubbs, 547 U.S. 90, 95 (2006).
110. Illinois v. Gates, 462 U.S. 213, 238 (1983).
111. *Grubbs*, 547 U.S. at 95.
112. Erica Goldberg, *Getting Beyond Intuition in the Probable Cause Inquiry*, 17 LEWIS & CLARK L. REV. 789, 790–91 (2013).
113. Maryland v. Pringle, 540 U.S. 366, 371 (2003).
114. *Gates*, 462 U.S. at 231.
115. Terry v. Ohio, 392 U.S. 1, 21–22 (1968).
116. Andrea Roth, *Safety in Numbers? Deciding When DNA Alone Is Enough to Convict*, 85 N.Y.U. L. REV. 1130, 1134 (2010); David H. Kaye, *Rounding Up the Usual Suspects: A Legal and Logical Analysis of DNA Trawling Cases*, 87 N.C. L. REV. 425, 439 (2009).
117. Arnold H. Loewy, *Rethinking Search and Seizure in a Post-911 World*, 80 MISS. L.J. 1507, 1518 (2011).
118. *Id.*
119. Maryland v. Pringle, 124 S. Ct. 795, 800 (2003) (*citing* Ybarra v. Illinois, 444 U.S. 85, 91 (1979)).
120. Tracey Maclin, *The* Pringle *Case's New Notion of Probable Cause: An Assault on* Di Re *and the Fourth Amendment*, 2004 CATO SUP. CT. REV. 395, 411.
121. *See* Bernard E. Harcourt & Tracey L. Meares, *Randomization and the Fourth Amendment*, 78 U. CHI. L. REV. 809, 813 (2011).
122. Andrew E. Taslitz, *Stories of Fourth Amendment Disrespect: From Elian to the Internment*, 70 FORDHAM L. REV. 2257, 2355 (2002).

123. *See* Bernard E. Harcourt & Tracey L. Meares, *Randomization and the Fourth Amendment*, 78 U. Chi. L. Rev. 809, 813 (2011).

124. Daniel J. Steinbock, *Data Matching, Data Mining, and Due Process*, 40 Ga. L. Rev. 1, 30 (2005).

125. Erin Murphy, *Databases, Doctrine & Constitutional Criminal Procedure*, 37 Fordham Urb. L.J. 803, 830 (2010).

126. Alene Tchekmedyian, *Police Push Back against Using Crime-Prediction Technology to Deploy Officers*, L.A. Times (Oct. 4, 2016).

CHAPTER 7. BLACK DATA

1. Charles J. Ogletree Jr., The Presumption of Guilt: The Arrest of Henry Louis Gates Jr. and Race, Class, and Crime in America 129–241 (2010).

2. Upturn, Stuck in a Pattern: Early Evidence of "Predictive Policing" and Civil Rights 5 (Aug. 2016).

3. Solon Barocas & Andrew D. Selbst, *Big Data's Disparate Impact*, 104 Calif. L. Rev. 671, 721 (2016).

4. Christopher Moraff, *The Problem with Some of the Most Powerful Numbers in Modern Policing*, Next City (Dec. 15, 2014), http://nextcity.org.

5. Joshua D. Wright, *The Constitutional Failure of Gang Databases*, 2 Stan. J. C.R. & C.L. 115, 120–21 (2005).

6. Sandra Bass, *Policing Space, Policing Race: Social Control Imperatives and Police Discretionary Decisions*, 28 Soc. Just. 156, 156 (2001); *see also* David S. Cohen, *Official Oppression: A Historical Analysis of Low-Level Police Abuse and a Modern Attempt at Reform*, 28 Colum. Hum. Rts. L. Rev. 165, 180 (1996).

7. Jonathan M. Smith, *Closing the Gap between What Is Lawful and What Is Right in Police Use of Force Jurisprudence by Making Police Departments More Democratic Institutions*, 21 Mich. J. Race & L. 315, 333 (2016); Karla Mari McKanders, *Sustaining Tiered Personhood: Jim Crow and Anti-Immigrant Laws*, 26 Harv. J. on Racial & Ethnic Just. 163, 190–207 (2010).

8. Justin S. Conroy, *"Show Me Your Papers": Race and Street Encounters*, 19 Nat'l Black L.J. 149, 151–61 (2007).

9. Christina Swarns, *"I Can't Breathe!": A Century Old Call for Justice*, 46 Seton Hall L. Rev. 1021, 1024–25 (2016); Andrew P. Cohen, *The Lynching of James Scales: How the FBI, the DOJ, and State Authorities "Whitewashed" Racial Violence in Blesdoe County, Tennessee*, 19 Tex. J. C.L. & C.R. 285, 287–88 (2014).

10. Clarence Page, *Forgotten Lessons of '6os Urban Riots*, Chi. Trib. (Aug. 27, 2014); Rick Perlstein, *From Watts to Ferguson*, In These Times (Sept. 22, 2014), http://inthesetimes.com.

11. Terry v. Ohio, 392 U.S. 1, 14 n.11 (1968) (quoting Lawrence P. Tiffany et al., Detection of Crime: Stopping and Questioning, Search and Seizure, Encouragement and Entrapment 47–48 (1967)).

12. Alvaro M. Bedoya, *The Color of Surveillance*, Slate (Jan. 18, 2016), www.slate.com.

13. James Forman Jr., *A Little Rebellion Now and Then Is a Good Thing*, 100 MICH. L. REV. 1408, 1416 (2002); David Johnston & Don Van Natta Jr., *Ashcroft Weighs Easing F.B.I. Limits for Surveillance*, N.Y. TIMES (Dec. 1, 2001).

14. Alvaro M. Bedoya, *The Color of Surveillance*, SLATE (Jan. 18, 2016), www.slate.com.

15. Alvaro Bedoya, Executive Director, Center on Privacy & Technology, Georgetown University Law Center, email to author (Aug. 12, 2016).

16. Paul Butler, Professor of Law, Georgetown University Law Center, email to author (Aug. 14, 2016).

17. U.S. Dep't of Justice, Civil Rights Div., INVESTIGATION OF THE FERGUSON POLICE DEPARTMENT 72–73 (2015), *available at* www.justice.gov.

18. *Id.* at 2.

19. Michael Feldman et al., *Certifying and Removing Disparate Impact*, KDD '15: PROCEEDINGS OF THE 21ST ACM SIGKDD INTERNATIONAL CONFERENCE ON KNOWLEDGE DISCOVERY AND DATA MINING 259 (2015).

20. Ifeoma Ajunwa et al., Hiring by Algorithm: Predicting and Preventing Disparate Impact (Feb. 28, 2016) (unpublished manuscript, on file with author).

21. Michael Feldman et al., *Certifying and Removing Disparate Impact*, KDD '15: PROCEEDINGS OF THE 21ST ACM SIGKDD INTERNATIONAL CONFERENCE ON KNOWLEDGE DISCOVERY AND DATA MINING 259 (2015).

22. Frank Pasquale, THE BLACK BOX SOCIETY: THE SECRET ALGORITHMS THAT CONTROL MONEY AND INFORMATION (2015).

23. Andrew Guthrie Ferguson, *Predictive Policing and Reasonable Suspicion*, 62 EMORY L.J. 259, 319 (2012).

24. Cathy O'Neil, WEAPONS OF MATH DESTRUCTION: HOW BIG DATA INCREASES INEQUALITY AND THREATENS DEMOCRACY (2016).

25. Frank Pasquale, THE BLACK BOX SOCIETY: THE SECRET ALGORITHMS THAT CONTROL MONEY AND INFORMATION (2015).

26. Mara Hvistendahl, *Can "Predictive Policing" Prevent Crime before It Happens?*, SCIENCE (Sept. 28, 2016); Ellen Huet, *Server and Protect: Predictive Policing Firm PredPol Promises to Map Crime before It Happens*, FORBES (Mar. 2, 2015).

27. Joshua A. Kroll et al., *Accountable Algorithms*, 165 U. PA. L. REV. 633 (2017).

28. Harry Surden, *Machine Learning and Law*, 89 WASH. L. REV. 87, 89 (2014).

29. Joshua A. Kroll et al., *Accountable Algorithms*, 165 U. PA. L. REV. 633 (2017).

30. *Id.*

31. *Id.*

32. *Id.*

33. Stephen Rushin, *The Judicial Response to Mass Police Surveillance*, 2011 U. ILL. J. L. TECH. & POL'Y 281, 282.

34. Monu Bedi, *Social Networks, Government Surveillance, and the Fourth Amendment Mosaic Theory*, 94 B.U. L. REV. 1809, 1841 (2014).

35. Andrew Guthrie Ferguson, *Big Data and Predictive Reasonable Suspicion*, 163 U. PA. L. REV. 327, 387–88 (2015).

36. Andrew Guthrie Ferguson, *Predictive Policing and Reasonable Suspicion*, 62 EMORY L.J. 259 304–10 (2012).

37. Andrew Guthrie Ferguson & Damien Bernache, *The "High-Crime Area" Question: Requiring Verifiable and Quantifiable Evidence for Fourth Amendment Reasonable Suspicion Analysis*, 57 AM. U. L. REV. 1587, 1588–90 (2008).

38. *See generally* Orin S. Kerr, *The Fourth Amendment and New Technologies: Constitutional Myths and the Case for Caution*, 102 MICH. L. REV. 801 (2004).

CHAPTER 8. BLUE DATA

1. Jon Swaine, *Eric Holder Calls Failure to Collect Reliable Data on Police Killings Unacceptable*, GUARDIAN (Jan. 15, 2015).

2. Kimbriell Kelly, *Can Big Data Stop Bad Cops?*, WASH. POST (Aug. 21, 2016).

3. *Id.*

4. Death in Custody Reporting Act of 2013, Pub. L. No. 113–242, 128 Stat. 2860 (2014) (to be codified at 42 U.S.C. §13727).

5. Press Release, White House, Launching the Police Data Initiative (May 18, 2015), *available at* www.whitehouse.gov.

6. *Id.*

7. Sari Horwitz & Mark Berman, *Justice Department Takes Steps to Create National Use-of-Force Database*, WASH. POST (Oct. 13, 2016).

8. Place-based predictive technologies are the subject of chapter 4.

9. Bernard E. Harcourt & Tracey L. Meares, *Randomization and the Fourth Amendment*, 78 U. CHI. L. REV. 809, 862 n.210 (2011).

10. Andrew Guthrie Ferguson, *Policing "Stop and Frisk" with "Stop and Track" Policing*, HUFFINGTON POST (Aug. 17, 2014), www.huffingtonpost.com.

11. Frank Pasquale, *The Other Big Brother*, ATLANTIC (Sept. 21, 2015).

12. Ben Horwitz, *Sneak Preview: NOPD Replacing Current Compstat Process with New, Interactive Open Data Website*, NEW ORLEANS POLICE DEPARTMENT (Aug. 10, 2016), www.nola.gov.

13. ACLU of Illinois, *Newly-Released Data Shows City Continues to Deny Equitable Police Services to South and West Side Neighborhoods* (Mar. 31, 2014), www.aclu-il.org.

14. Judi Komaki, *6 Ways Good Data Could Prevent Tragedies like Freddie Gray's Death*, NATION (May 23, 2016).

15. Person-based predictive technologies are the subject of chapter 3.

16. David J. Krajicek, *What's the Best Way to Weed Out Potential Killer Cops?*, ALTERNET (May 16, 2016), www.alternet.org.

17. Angela Caputo & Jeremy Gorner, *Small Group of Chicago Police Costs City Millions in Settlements*, CHI. TRIB. (Jan. 30, 2016).

18. Rob Arthur, *How to Predict Bad Cops in Chicago*, FIVETHIRTYEIGHT (Dec. 15, 2015), http://fivethirtyeight.com.

19. Rene Stutzman & Charles Minshew, *Focus on Force*, ORLANDO SENTINEL (Nov. 6, 2015), *available at* http://interactive.orlandosentinel.com.

20. Rayid Ghani, *Developing Predictive Early Interventions/Warning Systems to Prevent Adverse Interactions with Police*, CENTER FOR DATA SCIENCE AND PUBLIC POLICY (Feb. 21, 2016), http://dsapp.uchicago.edu.

21. Jaeah Lee, *Can Data Predict Which Cops Are Most Likely to Misbehave in the Future?*, MOTHER JONES (May/June 2016).

22. Michael Gordon, *CMPD's Goal: To Predict Misconduct before It Can Happen*, CHARLOTTE OBSERVER (Feb. 26, 2016).

23. Jaeah Lee, *Can Data Predict Which Cops Are Most Likely to Misbehave in the Future?*, MOTHER JONES (May/June 2016).

24. Rayid Ghani, interview by Audie Cornish, *Can Big Data Help Head Off Police Misconduct?*, ALL TECH CONSIDERED (NPR radio broadcast, July 19, 2016), *available at* www.npr.org.

25. Ted Gregory, *U of C Researchers Use Data to Predict Police Misconduct*, CHI. TRIB. (Aug. 18, 2016).

26. Rob Arthur, *How to Predict Bad Cops in Chicago*, FIVETHIRTYEIGHT (Dec. 15, 2015), http://fivethirtyeight.com.

27. Michael Gordon, *CMPD's Goal: To Predict Misconduct before It Can Happen*, CHARLOTTE OBSERVER (Feb. 26, 2016).

28. Jaeah Lee, *Can Data Predict Which Cops Are Most Likely to Misbehave in the Future?*, MOTHER JONES (May/June 2016).

29. Rayid Ghani, interview by Audie Cornish, *Can Big Data Help Head Off Police Misconduct?*, ALL TECH CONSIDERED (NPR radio broadcast, July 19, 2016), *available at* www.npr.org.

30. *Id.*

31. Rob Arthur, *How to Predict Bad Cops in Chicago*, FIVETHIRTYEIGHT (Dec. 15, 2015), http://fivethirtyeight.com.

32. *Id.*

33. U.S. Dep't of Justice, Civil Rights Div., INVESTIGATION OF THE CITY OF CHICAGO POLICE DEPARTMENT 111 (2017), *available at* www.justice.gov.

34. Jonah Newman, *Program That Flags Chicago Cops at Risk of Misconduct Misses Most Officers*, CHI. REPORTER (Dec. 18, 2015), http://chicagoreporter.com.

35. U.S. Dep't of Justice, Civil Rights Div., INVESTIGATION OF THE CITY OF CHICAGO POLICE DEPARTMENT 111 (2017), *available at* www.justice.gov.

36. Frank Pasquale, *The Other Big Brother*, ATLANTIC (Sept. 21, 2015).

37. U.S. Dep't of Justice, Civil Rights Div., INVESTIGATION OF THE CITY OF CHICAGO POLICE DEPARTMENT 147 (2017), *available at* www.justice.gov.

38. David J. Krajicek, *What's the Best Way to Weed Out Potential Killer Cops?*, ALTERNET (May 16, 2016), www.alternet.org.

39. Consumer data mining is the subject of chapter 1.

40. Floyd v. City of New York, 959 F. Supp. 2d 540, 558 (S.D.N.Y. 2013).

41. Jeffrey Bellin, *The Inverse Relationship between the Constitutionality and Effectiveness of New York City "Stop and Frisk,"* 94 B.U. L. REV. 1495, 1514 (2014).

42. Sharad Goel et al., *Combatting Police Discrimination in the Age of Big Data*, NEW CRIM. L. REV. (forthcoming 2017) (draft on file with author), *available at* http://5harad.com.

43. *Id.* at 6.

44. *Id.*

45. *Id.* at 27.

46. *Id.*

47. *Id.* at 29.

48. *Id.* at 29–30; *see also generally* Sharad Goel, Justin M. Rao, & Ravi Shroff, *Precinct or Prejudice? Understanding Racial Disparities in New York City's Stop-and-Frisk Policy*, 10 ANN. APP. STATS. 365 (2016).

49. Ric Simmons, *Quantifying Criminal Procedure: How to Unlock the Potential of Big Data in Our Criminal Justice System*, 2016 MICH. ST. L. REV. 947, 999–1005 (2016).

50. Max Minzner, *Putting Probability Back into Probable Cause*, 87 TEX. L. REV. 913, 920 (2009).

51. *Id.*

52. *Id.* at 920–21.

53. Rebecca C. Hetey et al., *Data for Change: A Statistical Analysis of Police Stops, Searches, Handcuffings, and Arrests in Oakland, Calif., 2013–2014*, STANFORD SPARQ (SOCIAL PSYCHOLOGICAL ANSWERS TO REAL-WORLD QUESTIONS) (June 23, 2016), *available at* https://sparq.stanford.edu.

54. *Id.* at 9.

55. *Id.*

56. *Id.*

57. *Id.* at 27.

58. *Id.* at 10.

59. *Id.* at 90–97.

60. Jennifer Eberhardt, *Strategies for Change: Research Initiatives and Recommendations to Improve Police-Community Relations in Oakland, Calif.*, STANFORD SPARQ (SOCIAL PSYCHOLOGICAL ANSWERS TO REAL-WORLD QUESTIONS) (June 20, 2016), *available at* https://sparq.stanford.edu.

61. *Id.* at 12.

62. *Id.* at 13.

63. *Id.* at 14.

64. *Id.* at 15.

65. Andrew Manuel Crespo, *Systemic Facts: Toward Institutional Awareness in Criminal Courts*, 129 HARV. L. REV. 2049, 2052 (2016).

66. *Id.* at 2069.

67. Jeffrey Fagan & Amanda Geller, *Following the Script: Narratives of Suspicion in Terry Stops in Street Policing*, 82 U. CHI. L. REV. 51, 55 (2015).

68. Andrew Manuel Crespo, *Systemic Facts: Toward Institutional Awareness in Criminal Courts*, 129 HARV. L. REV. 2049, 2075–76 (2016).

69. *Id.* at 2076.

70. *Id.*

71. *Id.* 2078–80.

72. *Id.* at 2079.

73. The surveillance technologies available in New York City are discussed in chapter 5.

74. Paul Butler, *Stop and Frisk and Torture-Lite: Police Terror of Minority Communities*, 12 OHIO ST. J. CRIM. L. 57, 64–66 (2014).

75. Ray Rivera, Al Baker, & Janet Roberts, *A Few Blocks, 4 Years, 52,000 Police Stops*, N.Y. TIMES (July 11, 2010).

76. *Id.*

77. *Id.*

78. *Id.*

79. The Domain Awareness System was not available in Brownsville at the time of the *New York Times* report.

80. Eli B. Silverman, *With a Hunch and a Punch*, 4 J. L. ECON. & POL'Y 133, 145 (2007).

81. David Rudovsky & Lawrence Rosenthal, *The Constitutionality of Stop-and-Frisk in New York City*, 162 U. PA. L. REV. ONLINE 117, 123–24 (2013).

82. Press Release, Dep't of Justice, Office of Public Affairs, Justice Department Reaches Agreement with City of Newark, New Jersey, to Address Unconstitutional Policing in Newark Police Department (July 22, 2014), *available at* www.justice.gov.

83. U.S. Dep't of Justice, Civil Rights Div., INVESTIGATION OF THE ALBUQUERQUE POLICE DEPARTMENT, FINDINGS LETTER 2–3 (2014), *available at* www.justice.gov.

84. Utah v. Strieff, 136 S. Ct. 2056, 2059 (2016).

85. U.S. Dep't of Justice, Civil Rights Div., INVESTIGATION OF THE FERGUSON POLICE DEPARTMENT 8 (2015), *available at* www.justice.gov.

86. Center for Policing Equity, *About Us*, http://policingequity.org (last visited Feb. 15, 2017).

87. Phillip Atiba Goff et al., Center for Policing Equity, THE SCIENCE OF JUSTICE: RACE, ARRESTS, AND THE POLICE USE OF FORCE 10 (July 2016), *available at* http://policingequity.org.

88. *Id.* at 26.

89. Project on Law, Order, and Algorithms, Stanford University, www.knightfoundation.org (last visited Feb. 15, 2017).

90. Edmund L. Andrews, *How Can We Improve the Criminal Justice System?*, STANFORD ENGINEERING BLOG (Feb. 10, 2016), http://engineering.stanford.edu.

91. *The Counted: People Killed by Police in the U.S.*, GUARDIAN (2016), www.theguardian.com.

92. Wesley Lowery, *How Many Police Shootings a Year? No One Knows*, WASH. POST (Sept. 8, 2014).

93. *Police Data: A Curated Collection of Links*, MARSHALL PROJECT (2017), www.themarshallproject.org; Julia Angwin et al., *Machine Bias*, PROPUBLICA (May 23, 2016), www.propublica.org; Rob Arthur, *We Now Have Algorithms to Predict Police Misconduct*, FIVETHIRTYEIGHT (Mar. 9, 2016), http://fivethirtyeight.com.

94. *See* Joshua Kopstein, *NYCLU's Stop & Frisk Watch App Lets You Rapidly Report Police Misconduct*, VERGE (June 6, 2012), www.theverge.com.

95. Christopher Moraff, *Will New "Respect" Strategy Improve Police-Community Relations?*, NEXT CITY (Aug. 28, 2015), http://nextcity.org.

96. *Id.*

97. Atul Gawande, THE CHECKLIST MANIFESTO 49 (2009); James Reason, HUMAN ERROR 1 (1990).

98. Pamela Metzger & Andrew Guthrie Ferguson, *Defending Data*, 88 S. CAL. L. REV. 1057, 1082–89 (2015).

99. Atul Gawande, THE CHECKLIST MANIFESTO 49 (2009).

100. Steven H. Woolf et al., *A String of Mistakes: The Importance of Cascade Analysis in Describing, Counting, and Preventing Medical Errors*, 2:4 ANN. FAM. MED. 317 (2004).

101. *See generally* Michael D. Ferguson & Sean Nelson, AVIATION SAFETY: A BALANCED INDUSTRY APPROACH (2014); John Davies, Alastair Ross, & Brendan Wallace, SAFETY MANAGEMENT: A QUALITATIVE SYSTEMS APPROACH (2003); ERROR REDUCTION IN HEALTH CARE: A SYSTEMS APPROACH TO IMPROVING PATIENT SAFETY (Patrice L. Spath ed., 2000).

102. Atul Gawande, THE CHECKLIST MANIFESTO 49 (2009).

103. James Doyle, Nat'l Inst. of Justice, NCJ 247141, MENDING JUSTICE: SENTINEL EVENT REVIEWS 3–5 (2014), www.nij.gov.

104. *Id.* at 9.

105. *Id.* at 6.

106. *Id.* at 12.

107. John Hollway, Quattrone Ctr. for Fair Admin. Just., A SYSTEMS APPROACH TO ERROR REDUCTION IN CRIMINAL JUSTICE 4 (Feb. 2014), *available at* http://scholarship.law.upenn.edu.

108. Quattrone Ctr. for Fair Admin. Just., USING ROOT CAUSE ANALYSIS TO INSTILL A CULTURE OF SELF-IMPROVEMENT: PROGRAM REPLICATION MATERIALS INNOVATIONS IN CRIMINAL JUSTICE SUMMIT III 1–3 (white paper, Apr. 20–21, 2015), *available at* www.law.upenn.edu.

109. Ligon v. City of New York, No. 12 Civ. 2274, 2012 WL 3597066, at *36–39 (S.D.N.Y. Aug. 21, 2012).

110. *Id.*

111. Paul Butler, *Stop and Frisk and Torture-Lite: Police Terror of Minority Communities*, 12 OHIO ST. J. CRIM. L. 57, 64–66 (2014); David A. Harris, *Frisking Every Suspect: The Withering of* Terry, 28 U.C. DAVIS L. REV. 1, 45–46 (1994).

112. Brandon Garrett, *Remedying Racial Profiling*, 33 COLUM. HUM. RTS. L. REV. 41, 118 (2001).

113. Kami Chavis Simmons, *The Politics of Policing: Ensuring Stakeholder Collaboration in the Federal Reform of Local Law Enforcement Agencies*, 98 J. CRIM. L. & CRIMINOL. 489, 490 (2008); Samuel Walker, *The New Paradigm of Police Accountability: The U.S. Justice Department "Pattern or Practice" Suits in Context*, 22 ST. LOUIS U. PUB. L. REV. 3, 8 (2003).

114. 42 U.S.C. § 14141 (1994).

115. U.S. Dep't of Justice, Civil Rights Div., THE CIVIL RIGHTS DIVISION'S PATTERN AND PRACTICE POLICE REFORM WORK: 1994–PRESENT 3 (Jan. 2017).

116. Mary D. Fan, *Panopticism for Police: Structural Reform Bargaining and Police Regulation by Data-Driven Surveillance*, 87 WASH. L. REV. 93, 115 (2012).

117. White House, Office of the Press Secretary, FACT SHEET: WHITE HOUSE POLICE DATA INITIATIVE HIGHLIGHTS NEW COMMITMENTS (Apr. 21, 2016), *available at* www.whitehouse.gov.

118. *Id.*

119. *Id.*

CHAPTER 9. BRIGHT DATA

1. Andrew Guthrie Ferguson, *The Big Data Jury*, 91 NOTRE DAME L. REV. 935, 959 (2016).

2. Consumer big data is discussed in chapter 1.

3. Beware technology is discussed in chapter 5.

4. Robert D. Behn, THE PERFORMANCESTAT POTENTIAL: A LEADERSHIP STRATEGY FOR PRODUCING RESULTS (2014).

5. Information in the following paragraphs comes from conversations with Rafael Sa'adah, Assistant Chief, District of Columbia Fire and Emergency Medical Services Department (Dec. 2016).

6. Rafael Sa'adah, Acting Deputy Fire Chief, District of Columbia Fire and Emergency Medical Services Department, & Jessica Bress, Policy Advisor at DC Department of Behavioral Health, Presentation, Final Analysis of SBIRT Pilot Program 05/30/2015–08/02/2015 (Aug. 28, 2015) (on file with author).

7. *Id.*

8. *Id.*

9. Rafael Sa'adah, Acting Deputy Fire Chief, District of Columbia Fire and Emergency Medical Services Department, Presentation, Impact of Synthetic Cannabinoid Use on the DC EMS System (Sept. 16, 2015) (on file with author).

10. The NYPD's Domain Awareness System is discussed in chapter 5.

11. The Chicago Police Department's heat list is discussed in chapter 3.

12. Palantir's tracking software with the LAPD is discussed in chapter 5.

13. Intelligence-driven prosecution is discussed in chapter 3.

CHAPTER 10. NO DATA

1. The characters referenced in this chapter are fictional composites of individuals the author has known.

2. Jonas Lerman, *Big Data and Its Exclusions*, 66 STAN. L. REV. ONLINE 55, 56 (2013).

3. Kate Crawford, *Think Again: Big Data*, FP (May 9, 2013), www.foreignpolicy.com.

4. Jonas Lerman, *Big Data and Its Exclusions*, 66 STAN. L. REV. ONLINE 55, 56 (2013).

5. Joseph W. Jerome, *Buying and Selling Privacy: Big Data's Different Burdens and Benefits*, 66 STAN. L. REV. ONLINE 47, 50 (2013).

6. *Id.*

7. William J. Stuntz, *The Distribution of Fourth Amendment Privacy*, 67 GEO. WASH. L. REV. 1265, 1270–72 (1999).

8. *See generally* Bonnie S. Fisher et al., *Making Campuses Safer for Students: The Clery Act as a Symbolic Legal Reform*, 32 STETSON L. REV. 61, 63 (2002); Corey Rayburn Yung, *Concealing Campus Sexual Assault: An Empirical Examination*, 21 PSYCHOL. PUB. POL'Y & L. 1, 2 (2015).

9. Christopher Slobogin, *The Poverty Exception to the Fourth Amendment*, 55 FLA. L. REV. 391, 401 (2003).

10. Jonathan Oberman & Kendea Johnson, *Broken Windows: Restoring Social Order or Damaging and Depleting New York's Poor Communities of Color?*, 37 CARDOZO L. REV. 931, 949 (2016).

11. Ronald F. Wright, *Fragmented Users of Crime Predictions*, 52 ARIZ. L. REV. 91, 94 (2010).

12. Thomas E. Feucht & William J. Sabol, *Comment on a "Modest Proposal" for a Crime Prediction Market*, 52 ARIZ. L. REV. 81, 84 (2010).

13. Press Release, Bureau of Justice Statistics, U.S. Dep't of Justice, Office of Justice Programs, Nearly 3.4 Million Violent Crimes per Year Went Unreported to Police from 2006 to 2010 (Aug. 9, 2012), *available at* www.bjs.gov.

14. Camille Carey & Robert A. Solomon, *Impossible Choices: Balancing Safety and Security in Domestic Violence Representation*, 21 CLINICAL L. REV. 201, 225 (2014); Jeannie Suk, *Criminal Law Comes Home*, 116 YALE L.J. 2, 15–16 (2006).

15. Myka Held & Juliana McLaughlin, *Rape & Sexual Assault*, 15 GEO. J. GENDER & L. 155, 157 (2014).

16. Press Release, Bureau of Justice Statistics, U.S. Dep't of Justice, Office of Justice Programs, Nearly 3.4 Million Violent Crimes per Year Went Unreported to Police from 2006 to 2010 (Aug. 9, 2012), *available at* www.bjs.gov.

17. *Id.*

18. *Id.*

19. Solon Barocas & Andrew D. Selbst, *Big Data's Disparate Impact*, 104 CALIF. L. REV. 671, 688 (2016).

20. Jeremy Kun, *Big Data Algorithms Can Discriminate, and It's Not Clear What to Do about It*, CONVERSATION (Aug. 13, 2015), http://theconversation.com.

21. Andrew Guthrie Ferguson, *Predictive Policing and Reasonable Suspicion*, 62 EMORY L.J. 259, 317 (2012).

22. Tod Newcombe, *What Predictive Policing Can, and Can't, Do to Prevent Crime*, GOVERNING (Sept. 22, 2014), www.governing.com.

23. *Id.*

24. David J. Roberts & Meghann Casanova, Int'l Ass'n of Chiefs of Police, AUTOMATED LICENSE PLATE RECOGNITION SYSTEMS: POLICY AND OPERATIONAL GUIDANCE FOR LAW ENFORCEMENT 9 (2012), *available at* www.ncjrs.gov.

25. Josh Sanburn, *Storing Body Cam Data Is the Next Big Challenge for Police*, TIME (Jan. 25, 2016).

26. Mike LaBella, *Massachusetts Police Turn to Software to Battle Crime*, OFFICER.COM (Mar. 24, 2014).

27. Andrea Castillo, *ACLU Criticizes Fresno, Calif., PD for Social Media Surveillance System*, GOVERNMENT TECHNOLOGY (Jan. 4, 2014), www.govtech.com.

28. Ryan Gallagher, *Meet the Machines That Steal Your Phone's Data*, ARS TECHNICA (Sept. 25, 2013), http://arstechnica.com.

29. News Release, LAPD Media Relations, Grand Opening of New Facility for Real-Time Analysis and Critical Response Division (Sept. 15, 2009), *available at* www.lapdonline.org; Chris Dolmetsch & Henry Goldman, *New York, Microsoft Unveil Join Crime-Tracking System*, BLOOMBERG (Aug. 8, 2012), www.bloomberg.com.

30. Elizabeth E. Joh, *Privacy Protests: Surveillance Evasion and Fourth Amendment Suspicion*, 55 ARIZ. L. REV. 997, 1002 (2013).

31. *Id.*

32. Jimmy Stamp, *The Privacy Wars: Goggles That Block Facial Recognition Technology*, SMITHSONIAN MAG. BLOG (Feb. 6, 2013), http://blogs.smithsonianmag.com.

33. Nick Bilton, *Shields for Privacy in a Smartphone World*, N.Y. TIMES (June 24, 2012); *Drivers Try an Anti-Photo Finish*, WASH. POST (July 21, 2004), www.washingtonpost.com.

34. Tim Maly, *Anti-Drone Camouflage: What to Wear in Total Surveillance*, WIRED (Jan. 17, 2013), www.wired.com.

35. Catherine New, *Domestic Drone Countermeasures, Oregon Company, to Sell Defense Systems Direct to Consumers*, HUFFINGTON POST (Mar. 20, 2013), www.huffingtonpost.com.

36. Christine Clarridge, *Protesters Steal the Show at Seattle Police Gathering to Explain Intended Use of Drones*, SEATTLE TIMES (Oct. 25, 2012).

37. Brian Wheeler, *Police Surveillance: The US City That Beat Big Brother*, BBC NEWS MAG. (Sept. 29, 2016), www.bbc.com.

38. Kevin Rector & Luke Broadwater, *Secret Aerial Surveillance by Baltimore Police Stirs Outrage*, L.A. TIMES (Aug. 25, 2016).

39. Monte Reel, *Secret Cameras Record Baltimore's Every Move from Above*, BLOOMBERG BUSINESSWEEK (Aug. 23, 2016).

CONCLUSION

1. Jon Schuppe, *New Baltimore Aerial Surveillance Program Raises Trust Issues*, NBC NEWS (Aug. 29, 2016), www.nbcnews.com; Joseph Serna, *Keep the LAPD Drone-Free, Downtown Protesters Demand*, L.A. TIMES (Sept. 15, 2014); Manuel Valdes, *Seattle PD Grounds Drones after Protests*, POLICEONE.COM (Feb. 8, 2013).

2. The Beware alert system is discussed in chapter 5.

3. Wayne A. Logan & Andrew G. Ferguson, *Policing Criminal Justice Data*, 101 MINN. L. REV. 541, 541–42 (2016).

4. Andrew Guthrie Ferguson, *Predictive Prosecution*, 51 WAKE FOREST L. REV. 705, 736 (2016).

5. Fred H. Cate, *Government Data Mining: The Need for a Legal Framework*, 43 HARV. C.R.-C.L. L. REV. 435, 475 (2008).

6. Kate Crawford & Jason Schultz, *Big Data and Due Process: Toward a Framework to Redress Predictive Privacy Harms*, 55 B.C. L. REV. 93, 123 (2014).

7. *See generally* John B. Meixner & Shari Seidman Diamond, *The Hidden Daubert Factor: How Judges Use Error Rates in Assessing Scientific Evidence*, 2014 WIS. L. REV. 1063, 1131 (2014).

8. Viktor Mayer-Schonberger & Kenneth Cukier, BIG DATA: A REVOLUTION THAT WILL TRANSFORM HOW WE LIVE, WORK, AND THINK 61 (2013).

9. Melissa Hamilton, *Public Safety, Individual Liberty, and Suspect Science: Future Dangerousness Assessments and Sex Offender Laws*, 83 TEMP. L. REV. 697, 730 (2011).

10. Kate J. Bowers & Shane D. Johnson, *Who Commits Near Repeats? A Test of the Boost Explanation*, W. CRIMINOL. REV. (Nov. 2004), at 13.

11. Many police departments include mission statements that include actual "Vision" sections.

12. Police department budget limitations are discussed in chapter 1.

13. Field interview cards are discussed in chapter 5.

14. The DOJ investigations into the Ferguson and Baltimore Police Departments are discussed in chapter 2.

15. Libor Jany, *Minneapolis Police to Try Buddy System on Mental Health Calls*, STAR TRIBUNE (Sept. 6, 2016); Jaeah Lee, *What the Hell Happened to the Chicago Police's "Crisis Intervention" Training?*, MOTHER JONES (Jan. 15, 2016); Wesley Lowery et al., *Distraught People, Deadly Results: Officers Often Lack the Training to Approach the Mentally Unstable, Experts Say*, WASH. POST (June 30, 2015).

16. David M. Perry & Lawrence Carter-Long, *The Ruderman White Paper on Media Coverage of Law Enforcement Use of Force and Disability*, RUDERMAN FAMILY FOUNDATION (Mar. 2016), *available at* www.rudermanfoundation.org.

17. Aamer Madhani, *Chicago Mayor Fires Police Chief amid Protests over Police Shooting*, USA TODAY (Dec. 1, 2015).

18. U.S. v. Jones, 132 S. Ct. 945 (2012).

19. Nissa Rhee, *Study Casts Doubt on Chicago Police's Secretive Heat List*, CHI. MAG. (Aug. 17, 2016).

20. Tal Z. Zarsky, *Transparent Predictions*, 2013 U. ILL. L. REV. 1503, 1533–34 (2013).

21. Barbara D. Underwood, *Law and the Crystal Ball: Predicting Behavior with Statistical Inference and Individualized Judgment*, 88 YALE L.J. 1408, 1414 (1979).

22. *Id.* at 1436.

23. *Id.* at 1437–38.

24. United States v. Martinez-Fuerte, 428 U.S. 543, 560 (1976).

25. Christopher Slobogin, *Dangerousness and Expertise Redux*, 56 EMORY L.J. 275, 289 (2006).

26. Albert R. Roberts & Kimberly Bender, *Overcoming Sisyphus: Effective Prediction of Mental Health Disorders and Recidivism among Delinquents*, 70:2 FED. PROBATION 19, 19 (2006).

INDEX

ABOUT THE AUTHOR

Andrew Guthrie Ferguson is a national expert on predictive policing, big data surveillance, and the Fourth Amendment. He teaches Criminal Law, Criminal Procedure, and Evidence at the University of the District of Columbia, David A. Clarke School of Law. He is quoted widely in the media, and his articles have been published in many top law reviews.

CPSIA information can be obtained
at www.ICGtesting.com
Printed in the USA
JSHW041947161221
21315JS00002B/267